Did They Mention the Music?

Did They Mention the Music?

HENRY MANCINI

with Gene Lees

CONTEMPORARY
BOOKS

CHICAGO · NEW YORK

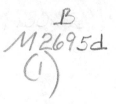

To Ginny

*The journey could not have been made
without our love for each other.*

Contents

Preface
by Gene Lees

November 12, 1987
The great scar of the Grand Canyon passes slowly under the jet's wings as it courses eastward at 35,000 feet. Henry Mancini doesn't even look out the window. He's seen it all before. He flies far too much, has been doing it for years now, to record his movie scores or conduct symphony orchestras, to perform in big cities and small or at the White House for three different presidents, or in London for members of the royal family. Now he is going home. Not to the big house in Holmby Hills, or the other one he owns in Malibu, or the third in Vail, Colorado, which he visits mostly in the winter, to ski. But to his original home in Pennsylvania.

I first met Henry Mancini in Chicago in 1959, when he was on a promotion tour for the *"Peter Gunn"* album and I was the editor of *down beat* magazine. This was shortly before the success of *Breakfast at Tiffany's*, and the song that has ever since been identified with it, "Moon River." It was still possible for songs with tunes as melodic as that and lyrics as literate as those Johnny Mercer attached to it to be hits in America; the great American song tradition had not yet been effaced by rock and roll.

The mood of the man during our first encounter has stayed with me all these years, though I am not sure what to call it. He seemed wary. Or perhaps he was merely baffled by his sudden fame. If he was suspicious, no doubt it was because he had been under assault from elements of the East Coast jazz critical establishment because of "Peter Gunn."

His detractors were so busy deploring what Mancini had done *with* jazz that they overlooked what he was doing *for* it. Up until that time, film scoring was almost entirely derived from European symphonic composition. Mancini changed that. More than any other person, he Americanized film scoring, and in time even European film composers followed in his path.

Although others had used elements of jazz in film under-score before him, it was Mancini who opened the way for the full use of this music in drama. Until then, the extent of jazz use in film was pretty much limited to an alto saxophone's moaning a heavy-handed depiction of a woman's hip-swinging walk. Mancini proved that the vocabulary of jazz could be used to express tenderness, romance, fear, laughter, pensiveness. He established before a broad American public, and before the executives of the communications industry, the extraordinarily expressive range of this music. But his purpose was not to write jazz, any more than it was to write symphonies; it was to underscore drama. "Everything I have ever written comes from the picture," he has repeatedly asserted. Mancini was the principal figure in developing what could be called the song score. Whereas earlier composers in the field had tended to use "classical," i.e., formal, techniques of thematic development and non-melodic orchestral writing (with exceptions, of course), Mancini began writing scores—such as that of *Breakfast at Tiffany's* and those for the Pink Panther series—that contained almost as many fully developed song melodies as a Broadway musical. And he used all sorts of devices of the dance bands to set these melodies off, from jazz walking bass to Caribbean dance rhythms. That he was capable of a quite different kind of writing is evident in the score for the suspense mystery *Arabesque,* which is comparatively abstract, or that for *The White Dawn,* or the stripped and austere score for the Paul Newman version of *The Glass Menagerie.*

The gift of writing melody is a somewhat mysterious one. Even some of the most trained and skillful composers lack it. Conversely, the melodic gift is not the only criterion of musical worth: Tchaikovsky had a torrential melodic talent far beyond anything Beethoven possessed, but no one would argue that Tchaikovsky was the greater composer. Yet the melodic gift is not to be undervalued. It is the gift of Kern, Gershwin, Arlen, Youmans.

In *Breakfast at Tiffany's* Mancini was revealed as an inventive and original writer who enormously expanded the vocabulary of modern orchestration. An awareness of classical orchestration was wedded to a fluency in American big band writing, to sometimes startling effect. This combination made Mancini the first film composer to emerge from the anonymity of that profession and become a public figure, a man known worldwide, with record sales in the millions and a roomful of Grammys, Oscars, and other awards, and a conductor of concerts everywhere.

"What did being an only child do to you?" I asked him just before our plane landed.

"I had to make do, learn to do things myself. I can still make it alone. It's just having to do for yourself."

There was no welcoming committee when we landed at the Pittsburgh airport; he hadn't asked for it. Mancini never has an entourage with him. He requires only his road manager, Jerry Grollnek, and a key group of musicians with him—the rhythm section, the lead trumpet, and a saxophonist. They are a close-knit group who have been with him for years. But they don't always travel with him. They meet him at the job. We were driven to the newly built Vista Hotel, where we checked into our rooms. The first rehearsal was set for the following day.

The four nights of concerts Mancini was about to conduct with the Pittsburgh Symphony Orchestra were already sold out. The program included his *Overture to a Pops Concert*, commissioned by the Boston Pops Orchestra for its one-hundredth anniversary; a slapstick Stan-and-Ollie theme from *A Fine Mess*; three of his television themes ("Hotel," "Newhart," and "Remington Steele"); three movie songs ("Life in a Looking Glass" from *That's Life*, "Crazy World" from *Victor/Victoria*, and "It's Easy to Say" from *"10"*); music from *The Thorn Birds* and *Charade*; themes from *Lifeforce*, *The Great Mouse Detective*, and *The Glass Menagerie*; and part of his *Beaver Valley '37 Suite*, a memoir of his childhood originally written for the Philadelphia Orchestra; and finally, of course, the requisite themes from *The Pink Panther*, "Peter Gunn," and *Two for the Road*, "Mr. Lucky," "Dear Heart," "Days of Wine and Roses," and "Moon River." The last-named song has been recorded more than one thousand times.

The next morning a driver took us to Heinz Hall, a magnificent old theater refurbished a few years ago with a huge grant from the famous food family of that name and made into the home of the Pittsburgh Symphony. The band and Hank's road manager were already there: guitarist Royce Campbell, saxophonist Al Cobine, bassist Steve Dokken, drummer Jack Gilfoy, and trumpeter Cecil Welch. Cecil is a tall southern gentleman from Atlanta, Georgia. The others live in the Indianapolis area. For Hank's West Coast engagements, Jack and Cecil fly in and are joined by Don Menza on sax, Jim Johnson on bass, and Michael Clinco on guitar.

The concert was to last two hours. And the rehearsal was scheduled for two-and-a-half hours. Hank is one of the few conductors who can prepare a two-hour concert in two-and-a-half hours. One of the reasons is that his musicians communicate with the orchestra and lead its phrasing. Hank says that a good many film composers who in recent years have done pops concerts with symphony orchestras present them with extremely difficult scores. The composer who does that chews up rehearsal time on hard passages, leaving an orchestra to scramble. But Hank is deliberately easy on orchestras, which is one reason they like him.

They also like the music. A woodwind player in the Pittsburgh Symphony told Mancini's guys, "You wouldn't believe all the crap we have to play in the pops concerts. This orchestra feels this is pops at its best, that's the reason they like to see Hank come in. It's an easy gig, but this is music, and we recognize it and like it."

As a result of all this, Hank will complete a rehearsal with a good orchestra in ten minutes under two hours and with a less professional regional orchestra in ten minutes over two hours.

And this one came in almost exactly ten minutes under the two hours. "See?" Al Cobine said, as if he'd won a bet.

The orchestra's players were making their way down a crowded corridor to the dressing rooms. A tall violinist said to a petite woman walking beside him, "The thing I like about him is that he doesn't throw his fame at you." The backstage mood was good.

"He has a great deal of reserve about him," Al Cobine said, "at least until you get past it. He's a storehouse of knowledge if you can get him to talk. We've all observed for years how complex he can be. For example, he always seems to know who wrote the lyrics to the old songs. We started talking about some very early characters in jazz, and he knew all about them and what they did. And he remembers faces and names in all the orchestras. He'll ask about them. He has a deep memory.

"Another thing is that he is very patient with people. He can be cutting at times, but he'll say it, and then it's over and forgotten."

Ginny, Hank's wife, says that he always tells her, "When something goes wrong, lay out four bars before you do anything."

"How did all you guys out of Indiana get to work with him?" I asked.

Al said, "I formed a band in '56 or something like that. Struggling, starving. That's when I was in graduate school in political science at Indiana University, moonlighting in the music department. There was a really bad Mickey Mouse band that played on campus and got lots of work. This New York cat who played trumpet, Freddie de Francesco, and I went to a rehearsal the same evening. He eventually would play a very important part in Hank's life.

"Freddie and I played on that band from September through New Year's Eve. And we really hated that band. Freddie was a business major at Indiana U. He said, 'Al, we've got to get off this turkey.' So we formed a quintet, and I wrote a bunch of George Shearing–type stuff. What I didn't know was that Freddie was a genius at getting jobs. He picked up a stack of contracts and wiped the whole place out. He had all the gigs. He formed an octet, with all the best guys in the area. I advised him on the musicians and the band, and helped get the charts together. Whenever he had personnel problems, he'd call me. And we became pretty good friends. Now he wasn't the easiest Italian to get along with. He was aggressive, tough. And funny. He got his degree and in ten years he was in one of the new agencies that took on people like Mancini and Mathis. He changed his name to Freddie Dale. His father was one of the early writers of movie scores. Freddie's ambition was to become a big producer.

"Hank had tried two other times, out of Seattle and out of

Kansas City, to put a band together, and it didn't work out. He didn't like the results. Freddie called me from California and said, 'Do you know who Henry Mancini is?' I said, 'Yeah,' and he asked, 'Do you think you could put an orchestra together?' And I said, 'Yeah.' I'd already been doing a little of that around the area. Jack—" he nodded to Jack Gilfoy "—was there at the very first gig. So was Dick Dennis, who to me is the best on-the-road concertmaster in the whole world because he can take a diverse group of string players, including young kids, and make a section out of it."

Royce Campbell said, "Speaking of Dick, this'll tell you something about Henry. We were in Ottawa, Canada, on tour, and Dick came down with an illness where he was losing the feeling in his fingers. It turned out to be a rare virus and was physically and psychologically traumatic. Henry lined up the best doctors in Ottawa and took care of Dick totally, paid for it all.

"I gotta tell you this story. Remember in Akron?" They all started to laugh. "We were in Akron, playing at the Blossom Music Center with the Cleveland Orchestra. Between the rehearsal and the concert, there was no time to go to a fancy restaurant, so we went up to a restaurant that's part of the park there. There were all these people who were going to go to the concert. One guy with stars in his eyes, we figured he must be a fan of Henry's, was looking over at us. Now at that point, and for at least ten years, Al had had a lot of arrangements published for the music education movement. This guy went right to Al and didn't recognize Henry, and he shook Al's hand and said, 'I've enjoyed your writing so much.' Henry was eating his salad, not even looking up. And the guy raved over Al and walked away and never even noticed that Henry was there at all. And finally Henry looked over to Al and said, 'Okay, I'll give you Akron.'"

They laughed some more at this memory, and as the amusement subsided, Jack Gilfoy said, "There are guys standing in line for our jobs, if any of us quits, because the word is out that it's a good gig."

One of the reasons it is a good gig is that Mancini is a restaurant lover, and the group eats superbly. He asked about the best restaurants in town, and that night we went to Franco's, across the street from Heinz Hall. He prefers Italian food. And he usually eats before concerts, not afterward, as so many musicians do; he says late meals interfere with his sleep.

At the concert's intermission, Mancini's dressing room was crowded. His expression would light up when he recognized faces from long ago, and he would ask after this old friend or that, after someone's brother, or a musician he had worked with in the early days when the Sons of Italy Band played on a bandstand in a vacant lot in West Aliquippa.

I noticed a tiny but vigorous woman among the well-wishers. She was less than five feet tall, and I was astonished to learn that she was eighty-two—she looked about sixty-five. Grinning and with a solicitously loving air, Hank brought her to meet me. This, he said, is Madeleine Paoline. She was his godmother and friend of the family, and she had been his teacher in fifth grade. She sat down on a sofa in the dressing room, formally erect and a little prim in manner.

"What was Henry like in the fifth grade?" I asked her.

"He wasn't a candidate for a Rhodes scholarship," she said. "But he was an alert boy, an average student. He was impish and with a subtle humor. He liked sports, which he was allowed to play until the time his mother or father would yell, 'Henry, time to practice.' He loved to eat. He doesn't look a bit different now than he did then.

"His father was so proud of Henry, it's a wonder he had any buttons left on his shirt. He would send clippings about Henry home to us from California."

This image of his father was at sharp variance with the one I was to get from Hank.

Six months earlier, Hank and I had begun discussing working on a book about his life. The question was whether it should be a biography or an autobiography. There were advantages and disadvantages to both. In the end we decided on the latter, and we evolved a way to work on it. I researched his life among his friends and family, then used the accumulated information to ask him the questions to which I, and others, wanted to know the answers.

But an autobiography by its very nature restrains its subject from stating his or her virtues—except of course in the cases of the most raving egomaniacs. And Hank is anything but that. Indeed, in our early conversations about this book, he asked me almost shyly if I thought it would be of any interest. It would be of interest, I told him, if only because it would be the first book to take the reader into the personal world of the film composer.

But let me state some things about Mancini that he won't. He is, as you may already have gathered, an enormously decent man, and a generous one. His music has made him many times a millionaire, but he donates heavily to charities and endows music scholarships at major universities.

Hank is tall. I once asked him how tall. "Six-one," he said, and added with a grin: "Six-two when I've got a hit." His humor is like that, quick, soft, and sardonic. He is also handsome and elegantly urbane. His tailoring is impeccable. There is to this day a diffident, reticent quality about him, and sometimes in the big home he and Ginny share in Los Angeles he still gives the impression that he isn't quite sure how he got there. He is a connoisseur of wine and a gourmet. No one ever looked more as if he were to the manor born. He speaks beautifully. In the first years I knew him, we never talked of books, and I was surprised later to discover how much he read, indeed how much he knew about many things. He simply doesn't parade it.

Small wonder, then, that I had trouble reconciling the

sophisticated and enormously successful man I have known for thirty years with the little Italian ragamuffin he says he was as a boy growing up in West Aliquippa. On Sunday afternoon, we were going to drive out there to look at it.

Or what was left of it.

—Gene Lees
Ojai, California

Preface
by Henry Mancini

When Gene Lees and I first met to discuss my writing *Did They Mention the Music?*, I was duly concerned about the fact that I am not a writer. He assured me that the burden would be somewhat relieved by the use of a tape recorder. We proceeded.

His questions probed into events long dormant in my mind. A process such as this, I can now testify, is akin to self-analysis. Gene was extremely helpful in organizing my disparate thoughts, gathered on many hours of tape.

I warmly thank my family—Ginny, Chris, Monica, and Felice—for their comments and thoughts on the manuscript. My associate, Lisa Edmondson, pinned down detail after detail throughout the process. I thank her. And to Gene Lees, who is finely tuned into the musical mentality, I offer my warmest thanks.

> —Henry Mancini
> Los Angeles, California

1
Beaver Valley

O n a winter day in 1935, my father, an immigrant steel-
worker, drove twenty miles southeast down the Beaver
Valley to Pittsburgh. He was taking me to town to see a
movie. I was eleven.

Though the Depression was at its depths, the open hearths
of the steel mills of Pittsburgh and its suburbs poured
streams of smoke into the air all day. At night they stained
the sky orange. The soot and fly ash murdered the air that
we breathed.

If you don't know Pittsburgh, let me describe it a little.
Its industries lie along the banks of its rivers, in the valleys
formed by the Monongahela, flowing up from the south,
and the Allegheny, coming in from the northeast to join it in
forming the Ohio. The Ohio flows northwest past Aliquippa
and West Aliquippa, where we lived. It swings west a few
miles farther on and finally south, at last joining the Missouri to become the Mississippi. The city came into being
because of the confluence of its two rivers, which gave it
upstream access to forests and farmlands, downstream exit
to the Gulf of Mexico, and even access to the western
prairies and Montana, where the Missouri rose.

Pittsburgh would have been an important city in any
event, because of those rivers, but the discovery nearby of
coal and iron ore—and also petroleum and natural gas—

determined its character. The opening of the railways assured a further supply of iron ore from the huge deposits of
the Great Lakes region as well: Presque Isle Bay, on Lake
Erie, one of the finest harbors in the St. Lawrence wa-
tershed, is only 135 miles to the north. But it was not just
geography that determined the character of the city. The
Mellon family with its banks; Andrew Carnegie, who arrived in the area in 1848 at the age of thirteen and became
one of the major builders of its steel industry; and Henry
Clay Frick, a native Pennsylvanian who bought up huge
coal deposits and built twelve thousand coke ovens to supply
the steel mills of Andrew Carnegie and of the Jones and
Laughlin partnership; and later on the famous Heinz food
family all left imprints on the city and their names on its
buildings. Pittsburgh has changed since then, but when I
was growing up it was one of the dirtiest cities in America.
Yet because of those families and their endowments for the
arts, it had an active and rich cultural life. Along with all
that steel, it produced some marvelously talented people,
such as the singer Billy Eckstine, the great jazz drummer
Art Blakey, the pianist Erroll Garner, and a dancer I would
meet many years later in California, Gene Kelly.

The steep slopes of the river valleys were thick with trees.
I remember the soft green they became in the spring and the
bright reds and yellows in autumn. Pittsburgh was a striking city, with its own special character and even beauty. I
was in awe of it as we crossed one of the bridges into town.

My father parked the car in a lot near Penn and Seventh.
As we walked away from it, I tripped over my feet. He
cuffed me and called me, in the dialect of Abruzzi, where he
was born, a little *cafone*, a little hick, a rube, and told me I
knew nothing. He was right enough about that. Sometimes
he would call me *animalo*, an animal. Other times he used
the expression *porco Madonna*, a particularly harsh exple-
tive. I don't understand Italian very well, but *porco* means

pig, and *Madonna* of course refers to the Virgin Mary. I guess it loses a bit in the translation.

We walked under the marquee of Loew's Penn Theater. My father paid for our tickets, and we entered a luxurious cavern with a gold-and-white ornate ceiling that seemed as far away as the sky. We settled into red velvet seats, the lights went down, and the big screen lit up with the name of the movie. It was Cecil B. De Mille's *The Crusades*. I still remember the huge black-and-white images of knights in armor, Arab warriors in flowing robes, horses and tents and sand and gigantic faces that opened their mouths and talked. I had never seen a talking picture, only the silent comedies of Charlie Chase, Buster Keaton, Laurel and Hardy, Charlie Chaplin, and the Keystone Cops. But what I remember most of all from that day is the music, the sound of a big orchestra. I had never heard anything like it. I'd never heard anything much but the concert music of the Sons of Italy Band, in which I played flute and piccolo. My father had started me on piccolo when I was eight years old. I was too small to handle the larger flute. It was raining one day, and he was ill with a very bad case of mumps, which is especially painful for an adult, and I could not go outside for my usual games with the boys. We were both quite bored. He told me to go to the closet and take down two instrument cases from the top shelf. He opened the smaller case, put his piccolo together, handed it to me, and said, "Blow." I blew, but no sound came out, just air. Under his tutelage from then on, I blew and blew until I did get a sound, first on the piccolo and then later on the flute. He was determined that I would learn them. Very determined. He would take the wooden perch out of the birdcage, and if I played a wrong note when I was practicing, he would whack me with it.

When *The Crusades* was over, I followed my father to the car. I was still fascinated by the movie and the music in it, music which, I learned many years later, was composed by

Rudolph Kopp. I had thought that there was a big orchestra behind the screen, but he said this just showed what an ignorant little *cafone* I was. He told me the sound of that orchestra was actually *in* the movie. We headed north in the valley along the riverbank toward home. My dad told me I would study hard, go to university, get a degree, become a teacher, and escape the steel mills. But I had already made up my mind I was never going to be a teacher. I didn't tell him then or for a long time afterward, but I knew what I was going to do when I grew up.

I was going to write music for the movies.

My father was a maverick. He was born in Scanno, a little town in Abruzzi, which is northeast of Rome, up in the mountains. From his name, Quinto, which means *fifth* in Italian, we know he was the fifth child in the family. Some of his brothers became professional people in Italy, lawyers and such, although I have never met any of them. From what I can gather, he was sent for a time to live with an uncle. When he was twelve or thirteen, he made up his mind to emigrate. I puzzled for years over why he made that decision and how he got from the mountains—and we're talking about heavy-weight mountains—to Rome and then Naples to board the boat, and then made his way to Detroit and then to Boston, where he worked for a time in a shoe factory. He was all alone. This was 1910 or 1911. It is hard to believe today that children of twelve and thirteen made their way alone from Russia, Poland, and Italy and arrived in the United States without money and somehow survived. But it happened. And my father was one of those children.

He was always independent and in some ways not in the mold of the Italian. While other parents were fighting to get their kids into the steel mills, he wanted me to stay out of them. The other Italian fathers in West Aliquippa were content with their jobs and their lot in life, and they would put him on about giving me music lessons. He'd say, "All right, you'll see. You do what you wanna do, I'll do what I wanna do." That was his attitude.

There were so many blanks in my father's life. He never talked much. How did this kid start playing flute? How did he go from playing flute—and I know that for a while he played professionally—to working in the steel mills?

He was about five foot ten and powerfully built. He *had* to be, working in the steel mills most of his life. Although she always spoke fluent Italian, my mother spoke English perfectly, having been brought here as an infant. But my father had a slight accent. I think he probably taught himself to read and write after he arrived here, just as he learned the flute. He had an old silver frosted Conn flute with a black mouthpiece with two mother of pearl dots on either side of it. He must have had a wild gene in him somewhere, to give him that artistic determination. None of his brothers apparently had it. My father had a sister named Maria, and I have been able to find out that she married a man named Eustacio Silla. She died in Rome in 1969. One of my father's brothers was Enrico, which is Henry in English, and I can only surmise that my father had some feeling for him since he named me after him. Enrico was killed in Yugoslavia in World War I. Another brother, Luigi, also came to America. He was killed in an industrial accident in Steubenville, Ohio. But my father never had any contact with his family, and never spoke to me of them, not even of that earlier Enrico Mancini who died in Yugoslavia.

All this was part of the mystery about my father. How did he learn that flute, and where? I try to picture him sitting in a room somewhere and practicing. That must have been right after World War I, when Enrico was killed.

He was a loner not only in his personal life but in his politics as well. In the mid-1930s the Democratic party had its base in a coalition of groups, including the unions, particularly the steel, automotive, and mine workers, and its various ethnic minorities. My father was atypical for an

Italian in that he was antiunion and a Republican. He voted for Hoover and for every other Republican presidential candidate in his lifetime. I don't understand it, since he was a worker and in the same boat with everybody else.

Wherever there were communities of Italians in the small towns of America, and especially in western Pennsylvania, they were like modules, cocoons, of the old country. It was as if they had taken bubbles of the Italian culture and floated them across the ocean and put them in the little towns in Pennsylvania, but nothing had changed. This was true of all the different immigrant groups, of course, but especially of the Italians.

West Aliquippa had a few Slovak and Croatian families and two or three Jewish families—a boy from one of those families, Jesse Steinfeld, one of my contemporaries, became surgeon general of the United States. But the community was at least 90 percent Italian. In conversation, people slipped back and forth between Italian and English. Except for the fact that I didn't speak Italian, I could have been brought up in the mountains of Abruzzi. I even put olive oil on my hair. My mother said it would make it strong and healthy when I grew up. Even Italian mothers can be mistaken.

Mom had a great buddy in Minnie Shaffalo, whom she visited almost daily regardless of weather. They would sit and have their coffee. Minnie was a somewhat heavy-set lady who supplemented the family income by selling corsets. She was never without a stick of Beech-Nut gum in her mouth. She had a large family, and since I was an only child I frequently found myself playing with the Shaffalo boys. In the parlor of their home, which was on Erie Avenue about fifty yards from the railroad tracks, was an upright player piano. I would put roll after roll of the hits of the day into the piano and be fascinated by the music coming out. Supporting my father's opinion that I was a bit thick, I thought this was the only way the piano could be played. It was entirely by accident that I sat down one day and started fooling around and discovered that one could play this piano alone, without any help from the piano rolls. This was my first encounter with the piano. I must have been ten or eleven years old.

On Sunday morning, all the young lions who'd spent the night before in the Sons of Italy hall smoking their El Ropo cigars and getting drunk on boilermakers (rye whiskey with beer chasers) would come to St. Joseph's ten o'clock mass after all the pews had been filled. They would stand, hung over and nodding off on their feet, backs against the wall, which was painted a very light color. They all wore hair dressings, either Lucky Tiger or olive oil. After months of this, there would be a row of marks on the wall, as if someone had been throwing a dirty tennis ball against it, and it would have to be washed.

Many of the Italian immigrants were staunch supporters of Mussolini, who about that time, 1935, was invading Ethiopia. In little beer gardens with jukeboxes, the men would light up their cigars and sit around tables puffing out clouds of smoke and drinking their wine or their beer while arguing for hours over whether or not Mussolini was doing good for the country.

My dad would get into heated arguments. He'd tell them, "Mussolini's going to run Italy into the ground. He might look like he's doing good now, but you'll see. People are getting hurt over there. And now he's in Africa. You're living here now. Why do you want to bother now about what's going on over there in Italy?"

The union was making its big move in the steel mills at the time. My father wouldn't help.

I remember the bloody strike of the fall of 1937. After school, I went with some of the other kids to stand by the fence at the Jones and Laughlin mill and watch the strikers standing around. And then the company goons were brought in to break some heads. They swung their clubs, and men went down under the blows.

My mother's maiden name was Anna Pece. In Italian, the name is pronounced "pay-chay," although everyone here pronounces it "peace" and the family has grown used to it (as I have grown used to "man-see-nee," although the Italian pronunciation is "man-chee-nee"). My mother's father was a lithographer who apparently had money even when he came from Italy on a visit. He was from a little town called Forlì del Sannio, in the province of Campobasso. It has since then become the province of Isernia. It is adjacent to Abruzzi, where my father was born. My Grandfather Pece decided not to go back and settled in Cleveland. His first wife had died of cancer and he had remarried. My mother had a half-sister from his first marriage, Ismalia. She married a Cleveland man named Ferdinando Melaragno. They lived in New York, and when I was about two years old my mother and father visited them there. They had two children, Ada and Hugo, and here another musical gene turns up, if that's what it is. Of course a passion for melody is part of the Italian character, and the cliché of the cop directing traffic while singing something from *Il Travatore* has more than a little basis in fact. Whatever the reason, my cousin Ada Malaragno was a singer. I am told she would set me on the piano in their house in the Bronx and have me sing "Pony Boy" and traditional Italian songs like "Siciliana Bruna" and "O Bambino," but I really don't remember it.

In the late 1920s my father had learned they were hiring men at the Jones and Laughlin Steel Company in Pennsylvania, and he drove from Cleveland, applied, and was hired. That is how we came to live in West Aliquippa. Although people think of me as being from Pennsylvania—and I consider West Aliquippa my hometown—I was actually born in Cleveland on April 16, 1924.

We used to go back to Cleveland every Christmas to visit my mother's relatives. My mother's people were warm and loving. They were all "uppers," in contrast to my dad. My cousin Helen, who has always been and still is like a sister to me, had a sister, Irma, who was close to my mother. Grandfather Pece died in Cleveland at the age of sixty.

I remember when I was nine or ten, hearing my Uncle Fred and his wife, my Aunt Teresa, talking about when my father played flute in a burlesque house in Detroit. According to them, he played well enough to read, he knew the fingering, and he had a good sound—or at least a loud sound, obviously loud enough to be heard in a burlesque house.

My mother was a little under five feet tall, not exactly stout but a little roly-poly. She was forever humming around the house. She had no formal musical training. She had suffered a rheumatic heart condition when she was young, and, although she didn't really look it, she was frail. I remember her hair. She had the strongest, thickest hair I have ever seen. She had a little fine-tooth comb, popular in those days, as much to clean the hair as comb it. Bathing was not as frequent back then because hot water was at a premium. Like many families on the lower end of the economic scale, she would take a complete bath only once a week. Afterward I would get into the water, which, in the dead of winter, would by then be barely tepid.

My mother was what they used to call a live wire: active and gregarious, she never sat still. When she was among the rest of the Italian ladies in the town, she was always the one laughing and joking. Everybody called her Annie. In her subservience to my father, she was typically Italian for that era. Rarely did she raise her voice to him, though she did once in defense of me and once, on another occasion, over a bottle of pills.

He used to say, "Annie, you're a good cook but a lousy housekeeper." And I have to admit he was right. She disliked housekeeping, and I used to do the dusting for her.

I never saw my father display a trace of affection for her, or for me either, for that matter. I never saw him kiss her, not even on the cheek; or give her a gift, not even at Christmas or on her birthday. Yet she really loved him. He was the classic breadwinner. That was his mission in life, and he was never unemployed. When he would fly off the handle with her, it was mercurial, quick, and incendiary, but then it would subside.

Some years later, when I was in military service, they came to visit me at Scott Field, outside St. Louis. I got a pass and they picked me up in his '37 Chevy, an ox of a car—the car I learned to drive in—that had been repainted an off-white. I noticed immediately that my mother was all dressed up. I think she had only two dresses, and that day she was wearing a nice one, some lipstick, and a little eyebrow pencil. She had apple cheeks anyway, but that day she wore a little rouge.

As I got in the car, I said, "Ma, you look really nice."

And my father said scornfully, "Why do you wear that stuff?"

I said, "Dad, gee, she looks nice." It was one of the few times I ever stood up to him on her behalf.

In our kitchen was a mercury thermometer with a brass back. I was curious about it. One day when I was about thirteen, I took it off the wall and held the bulb with my fingers, and the temperature went up. I said to myself, "I wonder what would happen if I lit a match under it?" What happened, of course, was that it went right through the top. The glass shattered and the mercury scattered on the floor. My father came home. As we were having dinner he looked over at the wall and said, "Where's the thermometer?" I showed him the remains of it. He said, "What did you do?" I told him. He grabbed the brass back of the thermometer, came around to my side of the table, and started beating me with it. I was trying to get out of the kitchen. And all the time he was beating me. My mother was on his back, saying, "Stop, stop!" And then she began to gasp, crying and clutching at her heart. She fell down on the couch, breathing desperately and hyperventilating. Only then did he relent and let me go.

One day I came out of my bedroom to find my father struggling to get a little bottle of pills out of her hand. To this day I don't know what they were, but apparently she was going to take them, and he was determined to get them away from her. At last he did, and he took the bottle out to the back porch and threw it into the neighbor's yard.

Because of her frailty, my mother had had several miscarriages before I was conceived. She had to be hospitalized for the confinement, and she almost died giving birth to me. Her doctor told her she must never have any more children, which may have been one reason for my father's discontent: he had wanted a large family. He was very good with kids—*other* kids. He liked to be around them. But I wasn't a kid; I was his son.

They began to talk about adoption, which again was unusual in those days, particularly in Italian families. I was fully in favor of it. I looked forward to having my little brother or sister come running up the walk into the house. I would have welcomed someone to talk with. My mother and father made out the papers, but somehow nothing ever came of it.

The Ohio River is a substantial stream as it flows past West Aliquippa, and it affects the temperature so that summers along the Ohio were very hot. In winter, the river kept it from getting extremely cold, except in January and February, when the weather was vicious. (In 1970 I wrote a piece describing my boyhood impressions of the area. It is called *Beaver Valley '37 Suite*, and I recorded it with the Philadelphia Orchestra.)

The Pennsylvania school system was on a quarterly basis.

You started school the quarter after you turned five. And I turned five in April, which meant that my vacation came not in summer but in January, February, and March, the worst time of the year. It was always cold and snowy, and since there was maybe only one other kid out of school at that time, vacation was three months of boredom.

You entered West Aliquippa through a tunnel. The community made "Ripley's Believe It or Not" as the only town in the world that had only one way in and one way out. Above the town was the railway line, always busy with freight and passenger trains. Above that was the highway, now part of the Pennsylvania Turnpike. And then above that were the wooded riverbluffs. They looked very high, and they were foreboding.

Our house was adjacent to the Jones and Laughlin open-hearth Bessemer furnace. You cannot shut such furnaces down. If you do, the process of stoking and starting them is arduous. So they are always burning, and at night the furnace near our home spouted flames and huge streams of sparks, making the streets glow bright orange. In daylight you couldn't see the sparks, but they were still shooting into the air so that night and day they came back down as soot. We lived with the smell of it in our noses. In addition to that, we got our heat in the winter from soft coal burning in a pot-bellied stove in the kitchen. My mother made me get down on my hands and knees and clean our old-fashioned furniture, even though it would be dirty again the next day. When I wore a clean white shirt to church on Sunday, by the time I came out of the service the collar looked as if someone had run charcoal around it.

I was a very sickly child. I had all the standard ailments— mumps, measles, chicken pox, tonsillitis, and diphtheria when I was a baby. When I was thirteen or fourteen, I had rheumatic fever, which crippled me, and for a long time I had to drag myself around the house with my hands. That disease is said to leave you with a rheumatic heart—it certainly did my mother—and this has always concerned me, although nothing has manifested itself. Still, it's a somber thing to carry in your mind, when the prognosis for that ailment is so bad and when my father, my mother, and my mother's brother all died of heart disease. Eventually I could walk again, but the disease left my ankles very weak, and all those illnesses left me in fragile health.

Sometimes in the spring, summer, and fall, I walked the three or four miles to Aliquippa High School. The last part of the trip was up that very high bluff, from the brow of which the high school overlooked the Ohio Valley. Sometimes I would take the bus, which cost a nickel each way. I'd walk, too, when I wanted to save the money for ice cream.

The first snowfall always seemed magical. It was lovely when it first came down, putting caps on roofs and clinging to the branches of the trees, clean and white, but it soon became what is called black snow as the soot and fly ash settled on it. Then it would turn to slush in the streets, and your feet were continually wet. If you were fortunate enough to have gloves, they too were always wet. Yet no one ever mentioned the weather; it was something you lived with.

When the borough of Aliquippa was laid out, the districts were called Plan Seven, Plan Eleven, Plan Twelve, and so forth. (West Aliquippa was one of those districts.) The main street, Franklin Avenue, extended back from the river up a wooded ravine. The town was sharply segregated. Plan Eleven, which was off Franklin, was populated by blacks and Italians. Plan Seven was almost entirely black. Plan Twelve was populated by the Cake Eaters, as we members of the minorities called them. The nicer houses were up there. The white-collar workers lived there, away from the mill hands, along with some supervisors and others of the upper echelon of Jones and Laughlin.

I wanted to make friends at that school, and I did make a few. But usually I was reminded very quickly that I was an

Italian, and from West Aliquippa, which was literally on the other side of the tracks—the Pennsylvania and Lake Erie railroad tracks.

I was one of the few flute players in the whole valley, and I played very well, with good technique and good sound. In 1937, when I was thirteen, I was first flutist in the Pennsylvania All-State High School Band.

I also played in the Sons of Italy Band under Carlo d'Atri. The band was made up entirely of immigrants and their sons, all from West Aliquippa. We rehearsed every Sunday morning in the Sons of Italy hall after ten o'clock mass. We rehearsed year-round for the only "jobs" we had—providing the music for the two religious festivals that our church had each summer: the St. Anthony Festa and the Santa Magno Festa. All the music we played had been printed in Italy and was brought to this country when Carlo emigrated to America. By the time I began playing with the band, some of the parts had been Scotch-taped so many times that I could hardly read the notes. The repertoire included many Italian marches, the *Zampa* overture, "Morning, Noon and Night," and my big feature number, the *William Tell* overture.

Carlo was not the greatest conductor in the world, but the fact that we all finished playing a piece at the same time was somewhat of a tribute to him. He had a short fuse and constantly engaged in shouting matches with various members of the band. But in true Italian style, no one was ever injured at a rehearsal. During the festas, in addition to several concerts on a makeshift bandstand in a vacant lot, the big event occurred on Sunday mornings. After high mass, the designated saint was hoisted on the shoulders of six of the strongest men in town. The statue was paraded through town, being lowered so that the townspeople could pin money on the saint's sash. The parade would form with the band first, followed by the saint, and then children and parish members, all in appropriate costumes.

An Italian marching band is awesome to behold. No matter what the tempo of the music, each player just strolls to his own drummer. Most marching bands are highly disciplined units in which everyone is in step in the same tempo and the lines across and forward are straight as an arrow. With the Sons of Italy marching band, anarchy reigned.

My reputation spread. Carlo was friends with Arthur D. Davenport, head of the band and the music department of Aliquippa High School. Davenport had played sousaphone in the John Philip Sousa Band. He was a virtuoso tuba player and a published composer of several marches. He was a short, stocky fellow with thinning black hair combed straight back from a round face. When I was in seventh grade, he heard about me from Carlo and asked me to play for him. He liked what I did and asked, "When are you coming to high school?"

I told him, "Not for two years yet."

He said, "We really need a good flute player. Why you don't come into the band now?"

So my school let me leave early on rehearsal days. At three o'clock, I'd take the bus to the high school, carrying my dad's flute and arriving for band practice at four o'clock. So I played in the high school band two years before I actually went there.

That's when I began to get some heat from the Other People, the people from Plan Twelve. Socially, I felt the exclusion. When they *did* let me participate in things, I was always a tagalong. Had I not been tenacious about wanting new experiences, I would have stayed back in my room in West Aliquippa.

Later, when I did go to that high school, my mother would pack me a lunch—invariably a salami sandwich on white bread, a piece of fruit, and a cupcake. In those days before anybody knew anything about cholesterol, salami was really greasy. It almost dripped. By the time noon came and I'd open the top of my desk and get out that bag, the grease had saturated the brown paper. I would pick it up by two fingers, so as not to get my hands greasy. I would be careful not to put it on my desk, or anybody else's desk, because it would leave a big grease mark. I was very sensitive about this. By the end of the school year, the bottom of my desk had a culture—it was beginning to come to life.

So never for a moment did I forget I was an Italian. Even if I'd wanted to, the Cake Eaters made it impossible. And so, given that my health wasn't the best, and that I was plagued by a sense of exclusion and my embarrassment at living on the wrong side of the tracks, I never dated a girl in high school. I never ate in a restaurant until I left home, except for the ice cream parlor we used to hang around and sometimes a White Castle hamburger place in Pittsburgh.

Sometimes in the summer we would see crosses burning on the top of the hills late at night, two or three of them a night. We weren't close enough to see who was burning them, but we knew it was of course the Ku Klux Klan. Though there was a substantial black population in Aliquippa, there were very few black students in that high school of three thousand. I used to think about it and wonder why they weren't coming to school. And if the burning of crosses on the hills in the night gave *me* a chill, I couldn't begin to imagine what it did to them.

Race relations were never discussed. The subject just didn't come up. Radio said nothing about it. The newspapers had not yet begun to take up causes. The attitude at that time was "Let them get along as best they can."

The first black acquaintance I ever had was a good-looking trumpet player whose name I can't remember. He and I played in a little Beaver Valley territory band led by Mel Koehler, with three trumpets, four saxes, drums, bass, and me on piano.

We used to rehearse at the drummer's house, a rather nice

home in the town of Rochester. He wasn't a very good player, but he wanted very much to play. We used to kowtow to him because he had a house where we could rehearse and his father had a big car we could borrow to get to jobs.

I don't know where this black fellow came from. He was subbing for one of the trumpets. I was about fourteen, and he must have been about sixteen. One day before rehearsal, I sat down and started to play. I knew all the tunes. He came up behind me and started to play his trumpet. He had a lovely approach to playing jazz. He showed me a chord, called a nine-six chord, which was prominent in the piano music of Bix Beiderbecke. The chord produced what was for that period a very modern sound. Duke Ellington was using it. I was obsessed with it. I spent all night exploring that chord, playing it chromatically up and down.

That was one of those important moments in your life. That boy set me off in an entirely different direction. It opened a door for me, that one single chord.

Our house was about a hundred yards from the riverbank, and it was pleasant to walk there in the evening among the fireflies, particularly when, now and then, the wind carried the smell of the steel mill in the opposite direction. The embankment was very steep, which protected us during the periodic floods. In the great flood of 1937, the steel mill was inundated. The water came almost to our door, and we could see entire houses coming down the river with chickens and other animals perched on the rooftops.

Just offshore were Hog Island and Crow Island, both owned by Jones and Laughlin and connected to the mainland by two barges moored side by side to function as a pontoon bridge. The company allowed its employees to grow vegetable gardens there. Our family, like every other family, had a plot, and I would help tend that garden. We grew tomatoes that my mother would make into tomato paste in the Italian way, by letting it dry in the sun. That sounds charmingly traditional, but my memory is of the flies buzzing around it.

The river was always busy with traffic. At least once a day, a big excursion boat would come by, one of those great shallow-draft paddle-wheel steamers with the twin smokestacks. You could hear calliope music coming from them. Sometimes they would pull in at Crow Island, and we would go on all-day excursions on them. There would be a small group playing nondescript music, polkas and that sort of thing. Once a year our church, St. Joseph's, took us kids on an excursion up the river to a place called Rock Springs Park, an amusement park in West Virginia. Carrying our picnic baskets, we would leave before sunrise, going down to the riverbank, across those two barges to Crow Island, and across the island to the sandy shore at the far side, where we got onto this paddle-wheel steamer. I went on these excursions two or three years in a row, but one in particular really affected me.

I must have been fourteen. By then I was trying to teach myself to arrange by listening to records and reading whatever I could find on the subject. When we got on the boat that day, I heard a band, a band I found miraculous. It was a big band with a rhythm section, three trumpets, two trombones, and five saxes, including baritone sax, which was unusual in those days. The leader played piano. There was no guitar. All the musicians were black. And their playing was *tight*. They weren't playing the wide voicings heard in the Duke Ellington band. They were more of the Count Basie–Fletcher Henderson style. And they used no music. Either they had memorized all the written arrangements or they were playing what jazz musicians call head charts, arrangements initially made up as a collective improvisation by the musicians and then fixed in memory and played that way repeatedly. Maybe they were doing both.

I was spellbound by them. Since they obviously had played this music often, it had an effortless quality about it.

It came at you like an extension of the whole collective intelligence of that band. That day was one of the few times I have felt a complete and absolute oneness in a band, as if everyone in it were plugged into the same outlet. I heard that sometimes with the Benny Goodman and Artie Shaw bands.

We shoved off about eight o'clock that morning and got back about eight that night. I spent about ten hours of that day close to that band, listening to everything they did. I would stand by the saxes, then stand near the brass. I talked with them, my mind racing with questions.

To this day, I do not know who they were. They may have been a name band, or they could have been one of those excellent territorial bands, as they called them, that were all over the country in those years. They may have come from St. Louis, possibly even from New Orleans. Whoever they were, that was the first time I had been in the presence of a live band playing that kind of music, what we would now call swing or jazz, rather than polkas or Greek wedding music or Italian songs. The ensemble playing was superb, and they had several great soloists. I do not think my memory is coloring the impression.

I got from them an almost extraterrestrial, a metaphysical, feeling that I still get sometimes when something is so good that the blood drains from your head all the way down into your boots. At such times you know you're in the presence of something extraordinary.

2
Max

I had taken formal flute and piano lessons, but I started arranging on my own. In 1936, the year after I saw *The Crusades*, the Benny Goodman Band became a huge success, launching the so-called Swing Era. It goes without saying that I had no idea that I would ever meet Benny Goodman, and in my wildest fantasies I could not have imagined that I would one day write the score for *The Benny Goodman Story*. I listened to the bands on the radio. I vividly remember the Goodman record of "Flat Foot Floogie." I started to be very interested in how that music was written.

We had a windup phonograph with a variable-speed mechanism. When you slowed a record down, of course, it lowered the pitch. The Artie Shaw Band hit a couple of years later, and I began to study its arrangements. All I knew about music paper was that it had notes written on it for you to play. I didn't know that you could buy blank music paper, so I made my own, laboriously drawing five-line staves with a pencil and ruler. Then I would write out, note by note, all the Artie Shaw sax choruses in four parts. I would spend days winding that machine up. Since I could hear all the lines in the sax and brass sections, I must have had a pretty good ear. Also, I knew all the standard songs with the right chords. I was fourteen or fifteen.

Observing my growing interest in music, my father sent me to Pittsburgh for piano lessons, since I had already worn out a couple of teachers in Aliquippa. My new piano teacher was named Homer Ochsenhardt. He was as German as you could imagine. A strict taskmaster who put me through all the piano books, he was very good for me.

His studio was behind a music store. Across the street from it was another music store with a studio, where a friend of his named Max Adkins sometimes taught. Max Adkins was to be the most important influence of my life.

Max was the conductor of the pit band at the Stanley Theatre in Pittsburgh. He was a great saxophonist and clarinetist who'd had many offers to go on the road with the name bands but preferred to stay in Pittsburgh.

All the theaters that presented stage shows had to have pit bands. The band Max led at the Stanley had twenty or twenty-five pieces and was quite good. They'd play the overture and they'd play for the vaudeville acts that followed. The pit band would descend on its platform and disappear as the traveling name band began to perform onstage. By now, because of the precedent set by Benny Goodman's success, there were dozens of famous bands traveling the country.

The only arranging text available at that time was Frank Skinner's book, and it was already somewhat dated. In any case, I had already gone through it. On Homer Ochsenhardt's recommendation, my father took me to see Max Adkins.

Max was about five-ten and in his thirties. He was married but did not yet have any children. A good-looking man with dark eyebrows and an oval face, he was very personable. He seemed to know everybody, and everybody liked him. He was nicely built, though slight, an elegant man who had as much pride in his looks, his clothes, and his demeanor as Duke Ellington did. He always dressed beautifully. I was a slob. I didn't have long pants—I wore a sweater and corduroy knickers; two pairs would last me through the school year.

My father told Max about me: "He listens to the radio all the time. He's always writing notes on paper. He needs someone to teach him." Max had me play the piano for him. And the next week I went for my first lesson.

I would catch the green bus in Aliquippa, take an hour's ride down the river valley looking at the houses and trees, get off in downtown Pittsburgh, and enter the stage door of the Stanley. That was a thrill, going backstage. Max's little office, where I took my lesson on those days when he was conducting shows, was below the stage. I used to look forward to those days, because I could be with him and see the show free—twice. The first show was at ten o'clock in the morning, the second at two in the afternoon. All the name bands of the time came through, and I saw them all.

The measure of Max as a teacher is this: while I was studying with him, he was also teaching Jerry Feldman (who would later change his name to Jerry Fielding), Bud Estes, and Billy Strayhorn. I knew Strayhorn then; soon after, he went with Ellington.

I think Max was one of the reasons we all made it. He was unusual for that period of history in that he had a system for teaching arranging.

The music publishers used to put out stock arrangements ("stocks") by people like Jack Mason and Spud Murphy. In those days people used to go out a lot to dance. There were thousands of bands all over the country, with anywhere from four or five to fifteen or so members. And there were many music stores that sold sheet music, with entire departments devoted to stocks. These arrangements were designed to be played by fifteen, thirteen, or ten, or even four or five players. It was the arranger's job to create flexibility in these charts, to make them playable by any number; the stocks were written in such a manner that parts could be omitted.

Studying how those stock arrangers put all this together was an invaluable experience. Max gave me the parts of a stock arrangement for the individual instruments and had me reconstruct the full score from them. This way I learned what could be taken out of an ensemble while retaining its skeleton. By reconstructing each arrangement line by line, I came to see what was important and what was expendable.

I began to write for Max's stage band and for a few of the bands around Beaver Valley. I did record takeoffs for them. One was Erskine Hawkins's "Gin Mill Special."

I used to do the copy work on my arrangements during the daily study period at Aliquippa High, sitting at the back of the room. Whenever the teacher would get up from her desk, I'd slip the arrangement away and get out a book. Several times she said to me, "Henry, I just want to say how well you've been doing your homework in this study hall. I see you so involved in your schoolwork, writing away, and you're to be commended." She'd go back to her desk and I'd start working on my arrangement again.

There was an unfortunate side to that, of course: I had tunnel vision. I think that any artist at some time in his or her life has to have that kind of narrow dedication. Writing music was my burning passion. I knew the classical repertoire from the high school orchestra, and I knew everything about popular music and the swing bands. I knew everything about the things that fascinated me but little about anything else. That compulsion prevented me from being a really good student. I think my preoccupation with music in some ways impaired my learning processes. I've always had trouble with languages. When people ask me whether I speak Italian, I cop out by saying my parents never spoke it at home. But just about everybody in West Aliquippa spoke Italian, and the real reason I didn't learn it is that I wasn't interested in anything but music.

I have some regrets about that tunnel vision. Although it made for great success later, making me good at what I do, there are areas I'd like to know much more about. I shut out everything but music. Probably because of this, I have become an avid reader. I usually manage to read most of the better monthly and weekly magazines. I am a news freak with an affinity for sports. Bookwise, I favor biographies of musicians and composers from Bach to the present. On my many trips I am never without something to read.

I learned more than music from Max Adkins. In a way he was like Professor Henry Higgins in *My Fair Lady,* and I was like Eliza Doolittle. The things I learned from Max I carry to this day. We used to go around the corner to Walgreen's and have a sandwich at the counter. Most of the time he would pay. And each time I would see him leave a quarter by his plate. This puzzled me until, after several weeks, I said, "Max, why do you leave money on the counter?"

He explained tipping to me.

His shoes were always perfect; mine were always scruffy. I got a new pair of shoes only when my feet had become too big for the old ones. I asked Max, "How do you get your shoes so shiny? You must spend a lot of time."

"No," he said. "There's a guy around the corner. You go to him and tell him I sent you."

I went. I watched this man, who was black, doing my shoes, which had six months of grime on them. And they started to gleam. I said, "But how do you get them as shiny as Max's?"

"Wait," he said, laughing, "I'm not finished, son." I thought he was going to do a magic trick. He sprinkled some water on his hands from a bottle and went flick-flick on each toe. He started again with that rag. When it came off for the final time, the light was glistening off my shoes and the man was chuckling at me. It was almost a religious experience. And he sent me back to Max with my shoeshine.

Max sent me to my first tailor. Suits with peg-bottom pants and wide shoulders were coming in, and Max already had one. My dad said to him, "The boy needs a suit."

Max said, "I know a wholesale place on the east side." And he sent us there.

My father had one suit, and it had a very straight cut, small shoulders, and narrow lapels. When we entered the wholesaler's shop, I saw a suit like Max's. I said, "I want a gray one, like that." My father did not approve. I said, "I don't want to look like an old man, I want something hep." Hep was the word in those days. I said, "Max wears clothes like that." And that finally convinced him. He paid $14, and I had my first hep suit.

All the while, I was still playing in the Aliquippa High band under Arthur Davenport. A smart alec with a crazy sense of humor, I was irreverent toward authority, always trying to see how much I could get away with. Pretension got my hackles up. To this day, when people come on strong, trying to be other than what they are, I find some way to leave them with a zinger.

Davie, as we called Davenport, overlooked my irreverence most of the time. But one day, possibly because I was talking when I was supposed to be listening to him, I must have gotten to him. He turned red in the face and said, "Get out of here, and don't ever come back." Even as I left the room I was smiling and making a show for the rest of the band.

Through the intervention of my father, I got back into the band near the end of the school year. But it was never the same between Davie and me. I've always been sorry I never made my peace with him.

In spite of my poor study habits, I graduated from high school at seventeen. I continued studying with Max and listening to the bands that came through to the Stanley Theatre.

When the Benny Goodman Band arrived for a week's engagement, Max took me into Benny's dressing room. I was quite shaken—just out of high school and going in to talk with Benny Goodman. Max said, "I'd like this kid to do an arrangement for you." So Benny, in his most enthusiastic way—he was not, as every musician knows, a very warm person—said, "Yeah." He had the sheet music of several songs. He said, "Here, do this one." It was a swing tune and had to be done in that style, moderate tempo. I wrote the arrangement and sent it on to Benny in New York. The band ran it down, and he liked it very much.

At the time, 1942, I was also applying for admission to the Juilliard School of Music. Benny was very encouraging, saying, "Come on to New York." I went. And that was the end of my studies with Max Adkins.

The personal interest Max took in me made the difference between becoming a laborer in the steel mill and understanding there was something to work for out there that I could achieve. He taught me the social amenities, about which I knew nothing. He opened doors to me professionally, including the introduction to Benny Goodman. He was a born leader. And for me, in a very real sense, Max was a lifesaver.

3
What Did You Do in the War, Daddy?

I took a room at the Piccadilly Hotel. The Goodman band was playing two or three weeks at the Paramount. Mel Powell was the pianist and Eddie Sauter the arranger. It was my first time in New York, and I had all those famous and exciting people around me. Benny assigned me to write an arrangement on a tune called "Idaho."

I wasn't making any money, but I had an assignment! And I was in way over my head.

I spent a week with a piano up in a little room that was almost in the attic of the Paramount, writing my arrangement on "Idaho," thinking of all the great brass players in that band, and making the mistake that all but the most experienced arrangers do: when you get a great brass section, you write too high. My arrangement was about a fourth higher than it should have been. But hard! Terribly hard! This doesn't win you any friends in the brass section. I thought the trumpet players in that band were supermen, but they were human, and they had lips like everybody else. They played the arrangement. It was a disaster. It just wouldn't play. Benny called me aside and said, "Well, kid, I don't think you're ready."

I was crestfallen. And I still had to face my audition for Juilliard. I had prepared a Beethoven sonata but nothing else. I played it for a panel of teachers and the dean, George

Wedge. They said, "That's very nice, can you play something else?" I thought for a minute and said, "Yes. I've
written a fantasy on Cole Porter's 'Night and Day.'" I had
written no such thing, but I winged it, embellishing the
tune with every scale, every flourish, every run I could think
of—five minutes of improvisation on "Night and Day."
They said, "Oh, that's marvelous." And I was accepted at
Juilliard.

As I waited for the school year to start, I played piano in
various groups. I was pianist for the Bob Allen Band at the
Pelham Health Inn in the Bronx, and I played with Johnny
Long at the Roseland Ballroom.

The funniest job I had was with Vincent Lopez, whose
band was playing the Taft Hotel with a daily noon radio
show. Unbeknownst to most people, he had a second piano
on the stage, more or less hidden, which I was hired to play.
When we got to the piano solos, I made a big mistake: I
played too loud and too much. I overshadowed him on the
broadcast, and he fired me on the spot.

In the fall term, prior to my eighteenth birthday, I entered Juilliard on a scholarship. Juilliard was then at Broadway and 121st Street. Grant's tomb was around the corner
in the park adjacent to Riverside Drive.

It was not an easy time for me, emotionally or financially.
During the first year, the school's curriculum prevented me
from taking the courses I really wanted—composition and
orchestration. It required that I major in piano, which even
then I knew was not my main love. My piano teacher,
Gordon Stanley, was a pleasant man with great patience. He
needed it with me. After a few lessons I think he came to
understand that, because of my aspirations to write, I was
not putting a supreme effort into the instrument. But he
never got on my back about it. I often have warm thoughts
about that man.

My financial condition would go from fair at the beginning of the month, when my dad sent my allowance, to

destitute at the end of the month, when I had a Hershey bar for breakfast, a Hershey bar for lunch, and a Hershey bar for dinner.

The informal student meeting place at Juilliard was a large stairwell where we sat on the stairs and the inner windowsills talking about all sorts of musical subjects. As students we had access to reduced-rate tickets—two dollars each at that time—to all the major musical events in Manhattan. On the mornings after these concerts, we would gather in that stairwell and discuss what we had seen and heard the night before. Horowitz, Rubinstein, Heifetz, Koussevitzky, and Bruno Walter were among those who endured the criticism of us know-it-all students. It amuses me that we dared to find so much to criticize in their performances. I guess that's why students are students.

During my days at Juilliard I discovered a room in which I was to spend a great deal of time. It was part of the library. There were desks, and on each desk was a 78-rpm turntable with a set of earphones. We had a vast selection of music from which to choose. Back home in West Aliquippa I had my own record player, a Silvertone as I recall. In addition to my large collection of jazz and swing records I had become interested in classical music. Ravel and Debussy had a special impact and influenced me a great deal. I would spend countless hours with their recordings following the scores.

With this treasure chest of records available, I opened up to the new music that was now available to me. I started then a listening discipline that has served me well. I would select a composer, be it Bartók or Mozart, and listen to his music to the virtual exclusion of all others. The scores were always at hand.

I have applied this regimen to the present day with modern composers. In a less pedantic way, I have followed the evolution of popular, jazz, and rock music. I have found that as a film composer all of this listening has proved to be a good investment. I never know what the next film is going to ask of me.

When I turned eighteen in April, I registered for the draft and was soon called up. Had I been drafted in my hometown, I'd have been sent to the 66th Division, whose patch was a black panther's head on an orange circle. They were the grunts of that era, and I would have been in the 66th's band. But because I was called up from New York I was assigned to the Army Air Corps. For basic training I spent six weeks in Atlantic City, in the winter. I was supposed to go to the TTC, the Technical Training Command.

All the old hotels along the Beach—the Traymore and the Marlborough-Blenheim among them—were full of servicemen. We were at the Traymore. At the Knights of Columbus Hotel on a little side street, Glenn Miller was forming his band, putting all the elements together in preparation for going to Yale, where they would be stationed before going overseas. Arnold Ross was the pianist; Mel Powell hadn't come in yet. Trigger Alpert was on bass and Ray McKinley was on drums.

I used to hang around with them after dinner, and despite being in awe of them I came to know them pretty well. They knew what I did and asked, "What are you going to do after basic training?"

I said, "I'll probably be a tail gunner or something."

They said, "You'll be finished basic training in two weeks, why don't you talk with Glenn?"

I said, "Gee, I don't know him." I was embarrassed and frightened. Miller had gone into service at the peak of his career. Many people today don't realize how big these bandleaders were then, as big as Elvis Presley or the Beatles were later on. I knew everything the Miller band had ever recorded. Anyway, my new friends got me an appointment with him and pushed me through the door.

The office was quite small and sparsely furnished with a

desk, a chair, and a coatrack. The man I knew so well from photographs was sitting there in his captain's uniform, very trim. He was thirty-seven. I didn't even sit down. I stood there and saluted.

Most of the great bandleaders of that era were severe disciplinarians because musicians in groups can behave like children, and if you don't control them they'll control you. And Miller had a reputation for discipline. But then, the only other big bandleader I'd met was Benny Goodman. Each of them had a kind of chill about him, but to me Miller seemed very straightforward. His men liked him, and he was cordial.

He looked at me through those rimless glasses and said, "I hear you're an arranger. Do you write well? Are you a good writer?"

I said, "Well enough, for what I've done. I also play flute and piccolo and piano." He said, "Okay," and took down my name and serial number. He dismissed me, I saluted again, and I left. That was the only conversation I ever had with Glenn Miller, and I thought that was the end of it.

I finished basic training. To my surprise, I was assigned not to gunnery school but to the 28th Air Force Band, later designated the 528th. I have read that the life expectancy of a tail gunner in combat was measured not even in minutes but in seconds. Without Glenn Miller I might have been firehosed out of a ball turret or the tail of a *B-17*. I surely wouldn't have been assigned to a band. Glenn Miller, for all the brevity of that conversation, was very nice to me. He didn't have to do that.

The band I was in was being gathered in New Haven, Connecticut, where all the members were from. It was sent to Atlantic City in toto with the 528th Technical Training Command.

The master sergeant of the band, an excellent arranger and conductor with a degree in music from Yale, was Norman Leyden. He would prove to be another significant figure in my life. Norman is now the associate conductor of the Oregon Symphony Orchestra.

We were in Atlantic City less than a year before we were sent to Seymour Johnson Air Force Base in North Carolina, which was hell. The barracks were threadbare and the weather was horrible.

One day the bandleader, Warrant Officer Max Sittenfeld, excitedly called me to his office. He said, "Hank, I just got a call from Special Services. They've assigned the movie star Tony Martin to sing with our band." I was told to arrange a meeting with Tony to talk over the songs he would be singing.

The service bands of that era had twenty-eight musicians. In addition to their marching and concert duties, they were subdivided into smaller units, including a dance band and various small combos. I was pianist and arranger for the dance band, which was quite good.

I was duly impressed upon meeting Tony Martin. Until then, the only two "stars" I had met were Benny Goodman and Glenn Miller. Tony was at the peak of his career, both as a movie star and as a recording artist. He had come out of Oakland as a baritone player in the saxophone section of the Tom Gerun Band, along with his friend, fellow saxophonist, and traveling companion Woody Herman. With surprising ease, Tony made the transition from sideman to international singing star.

We met and ran over the songs. He was in great voice. Over the next several months he and the band performed at several war bond rallies in North Carolina. He also starred in a minstrel show that I arranged and conducted. Tony was reassigned to overseas duty, and the 528th band was sent to Scott Field, Illinois, just outside St. Louis, where my parents visited me.

The shock waves of the Battle of the Bulge were being felt. The high command of the services, in their infinite wisdom, decided that the Air Force musicians would make great infantry soldiers. Therefore, most of the bands were broken up and I was sent to Camp Howze in Brownsville, Texas, for six weeks of basic infantry training. I went from there to Fort Meade, our port of embarkation, and shipped out in 1944. The troopship landed in Le Havre. I heard about Roosevelt's death while I was on a railway siding in France.

In Le Havre I was assigned to the 1306th Engineers Brigade. They assigned engineer companies by height. That's not as silly as it sounds; it was partly a matter of strength. When workers are doing tough physical work together, carrying heavy objects and that sort of thing, it's helpful if they are more or less the same height. Company A was made up of men up to six feet tall. I was taller, so I was assigned to Company B.

We were passing down through Luxembourg, on our way to the front lines, when somebody pulled out my MO number. Each profession had a number, and mine identified me as a musician. The company chaplain needed an organist, so he sent for me. He said, "There's the organ, over there." It was a box, one of the GI pump field organs that they issued to the chaplains. My duties included driving his jeep, behind which we towed a trailer that he'd had the engineers build for him and in which he slept and organized his services. When we'd arrive at an encampment, I'd get an orange crate or something like that from the mess hall, set it up as an altar, then pass out the hymnbooks and play—out in the middle of a field somewhere on this silly pump organ.

The chaplain was a soft-spoken southerner. For all his piety of manner and the cross on the lapels of his officer's tunic, he was an absolutely dreadful human being. I talked to the driver I was replacing, just before he left. He told me the chaplain would have him drive down to Epernay in the champagne country. There the chaplain would load up the trailer with champagne, for which he paid almost nothing, then bring it close to the front and park the trailer and sell it at vastly inflated prices to the GIs on the line. He insisted on their drinking it then and there because he had to return the bottles. He'd made many such trips and had already put away a great deal of money.

There were abandoned churches in many of the villages we passed through. The chaplain would remove their stained-glass windows, some of which no doubt had been there for centuries, take them to the engineers, and order them to crate and ship them home, to be sold after the war. I drove a lot of those beautiful windows to the engineers; I suppose they're all in the United States somewhere now.

The guys in the outfit disliked that man intensely, and for them the expression "Tell it to the chaplain" took on a special irony; they wouldn't tell him anything.

Following elements of Patton's Third Army, the 1306th made its way on a southeast course through Germany. We passed many bombed-out places—Mainz, Würzburg, Bamberg, Passau. It was early May 1945 when we came into Linz, Austria.

One morning, our company was sent out on assignment. We weren't told where we were going. I was with the chaplain, driving the jeep. We proceeded east for about fifteen miles and went through a small village. Making a final turn leaving the town, we came upon an expansive meadow of lovely green grass reaching to the top of a nearby hill. Perched on it was a huge graystone structure. It was the Mauthausen concentration camp. We went in.

The scene inside was unreal, dreamlike. Under American supervision, surviving prisoners wearing striped uniforms and carrying rifles were escorting squads of SS troopers who were in full uniform. The SS men were carrying shovels and, with the rifles of the prisoners trained on them, were using the shovels to give decent burial to the dead, many of whom had been simply lying there naked in the dirt. The smell of quicklime was everywhere. The cremation ovens were still warm, with traces of smoke rising from the chimneys.

At the end of the day we left, and as we drove back to our camp I saw the villagers through different eyes than I had a few hours before. Within a mile of them, unspeakable horror had occurred; here life went on as usual. Some of them must have known. No one could convince me otherwise.

The war in Europe was over on May 8. Japan was still in the war, and we were to be reassigned to the Pacific Theater. The division headed by truck convoy for the south of France. I was driving a jeep. We trailed all the way down the Rhone Valley through beautiful countryside, timeless stone villages with red-tile roofs; dropped down through Lyons; and arrived at last at a marshaling area at Arles, just outside Marseilles. I made friends with some bandmen stationed there. They were in search of a flute player and, as luck had it, anything I could do they needed. I went to the warrant officer of the band and asked if he could get me transferred. He did, and I joined that band. Next thing I knew I was in another service and another convoy. Now I'd been in the Air Corps, the engineering corps, and the infantry.

The band was assigned to Nice. We ended up at the Ruhl Hotel, right on the Promenade des Anglais. Nice was the enlisted men's rehabilitation center; Cannes was the officers' R and R. It was one of the best periods of my life, ever, in Nice at that time. Paradise. It was a beautiful city.

My cousin Helen had married a young man named Ralph Musengo, who served in the Army's Counter Intelligence Corps, the CIC, working with the Italian partisans, mostly Communists, behind German lines in the north of Italy. One reason for his assignment was that, unlike me, he spoke fluent Italian.

After the war ended, Ralph was stationed as a special agent at the crossing point at Ponte San Luigi in the south of France, near the Italian frontier. My mother wrote to him asking that he find me. Of course, she had nothing to worry about: I was having a perfectly good time, and I was writing for the band.

Ralph was headquartered in a villa near Nice in the Italian town of Ventimiglia. Toward the end of the summer of 1945, he called on my commanding officer and asked if I and a couple of my friends could visit him for a few days. Ralph picked up my two friends, both Italian-Americans, and me in an Alfa Romeo! It had been owned by Mussolini's mistress, Clara Petacci, who had been executed with him and hung by her heels in a Milan filling station. No doubt everybody who lived through that period remembers a horrible and widely published photo of them strung up in the air.

An insight into Ralph's character is that, when the political situation stabilized, he turned the car over to the newly installed Italian government. He wasn't anything like my chaplain.

The villa he took us to was owned by a Swiss millionaire named Enrico Wild (pronounced "Vild") whom Ralph had helped to locate and rejoin his wife, Magda Brard, a French concert pianist who had toured the United States as a child prodigy.

Wild dabbled in hypnosis, to which I turned out to be susceptible. He put me into a trance, regressed me, and announced that I was a reincarnation of Verdi. He found that in lives previous to that one I had been an engineer for the building of the Great Pyramid and also an officer in Montezuma's court.

One of the heaviest mistrals of the century hit Nice that winter. The wind came in off the Mediterranean and buckled the boardwalk on the Promenade des Anglais.

The quota system by which the military authorities repatriated troops was based on points assigned for months in service, months overseas, months in combat, and other criteria. Gradually I accumulated enough points to go home, although I wasn't all that eager to leave Nice. My number came up, and I watched the low, dry mountains of the Cote d'Azur receding as we sailed from Marseilles to New York.

4
Ginny

Immediately after getting my discharge on March 30, 1946, at Fort Dix, New Jersey, I went to New York and sought out my old master sergeant, Norman Leyden, who had been mustered out earlier. He was now chief arranger of the Glenn Miller–Tex Beneke Band.

Glenn Miller's plane disappeared over the English Channel on a flight to France on December 15, 1944. I have read that it may have been hit by bombs jettisoned from a British aircraft above it, but it's still not known for certain what happened. Jerry Gray, who had written one of Miller's biggest hits, "A String of Pearls," led the Air Force band until the war ended, then stayed on as an arranger with its civilian edition.

The band was now the property of Glenn's widow, Helen. She and Glenn's manager, Don Haynes, decided to assemble a new band around the nucleus of musicians who had been in the Air Force band. The logical one to lead it was Tex Beneke. He hadn't been in the Air Force band; he'd led a band of his own in the Navy. But he was by far the best-known Miller sideman, not only because he was a fine player—Tex is, as a matter of fact, one of the most proficient saxophone players I have ever encountered—but because of his vocals on "Chattanooga Choo-Choo" and so many of the big Miller hits.

The Miller Air Force band had a good-sized string section, patterned after the Artie Shaw and Tommy Dorsey orchestras, and Don Haynes and Helen decided to retain the pattern. The postwar band had thirteen strings—ten violins, two violas, and a cello. Its personnel included some incredible players, among them Conrad Gozzo, one of the greatest lead trumpet players who ever lived. Also on trumpets were Pete Candoli and Graham Young, with Paul Tanner, Jimmy Priddy, and Bob Pring on the trombones. Rolly Bundock was the bass player, Bobby Gibbons the guitarist, and Jack Sperling the drummer. One of my best friends, Sal Libero, who had been in the Air Force band with me, joined the sax section. I used some of these players later in the "Peter Gunn" score. It was a band I really wanted to write for, and when Norman said there was a possibility that I could join it on piano, I was, needless to say, excited.

But first I went home. I took the train from Penn Station to Pittsburgh, where my father picked me up in his Chevy.

We'd heard in Europe that the 66th Division, which contained a lot of kids from western Pennsylvania, had been badly mauled in Belgium. But in Aliquippa, as I talked with some friends who had survived the 66th and like me had just come home, I learned something more. They told me how the weather had closed in when the Germans counterattacked and surrounded them near Bastogne. They fought for days without air support, and the Germans chewed them up. Everybody who could hold a gun—cooks, clerks, musicians—went on the line. The band was wiped out. It dawned on me that had I been drafted in Aliquippa instead of New York, I might now be dead. I realized that without the training and encouragement of Max Adkins, I would never have gone to New York. I wouldn't have been equipped to be admitted to Juilliard, and I certainly would never have met Benny Goodman who, although he didn't really hire me, had tilted me toward making the move.

So now I owed Max something besides music and a modicum of the social graces: my life.

My father was harping on me, like a stuck record, to go back to school, to get a degree in music, and to teach. I told him I was not going back to school, that I had a job with Tex Beneke—although I didn't really have it yet—and it was an opportunity I couldn't pass up. He was not reconciled to it.

In Pittsburgh, still in my uniform, I dropped by the Stanley to see Max. He smiled and was glad to see me. By now some of his students had made or were making names for themselves, including Billy Strayhorn, Duke Ellington's right-hand man, almost his alter ego, and Jerry Fielding, who was writing for Alvino Rey. Later Jerry became a fine film composer. I imagine Max was pretty proud of his boys.

I told Max too that I didn't want to go back to school. I had gained valuable arranging experience in the service and thought I might be better off getting into the business immediately, particularly when there was a very real chance that I could join Tex Beneke. Max was warm and support-ive, as always.

After that I took the train back to New York. These were the days before the diesel and electric locomotives, and those old puffers were dirty with soot, particularly at the end of the war.

The copyist for the Beneke band was Jimmy Jackson. When you write an arrangement or a composition, the score is turned over to a copyist, who painstakingly copies out each part by hand for the individual musicians, the first trumpet part, the second trumpet part, and so forth. Today, there are electronic devices that will notate music, but by and large the copying is still done in pen by hand. A good copyist is valued highly. The writing must be legible and accurate; otherwise you spend time in rehearsals correcting copying errors. Jimmy was a fine copyist and a very good jazz arranger. Like Norman Leyden, he had befriended me.

Jimmy had an apartment in the West Fifties in New York.

During the war, the luxury liner *Normandy*, pressed into service as a troopship, had been torched—by whom is debatable to this day. It still lay on its side in its pier at the end of Jimmy's street. Later it was cut up for scrap, but it was still there when I made the move to New York and stayed with Jimmy until I was able to get a basement apartment in an old brownstone with another musician, one I'd known when we were students at Juilliard.

Norman told me the Beneke band's pianist was leaving shortly and that he had recommended me to Tex. Tex didn't even audition me: he took Norman's word for my ability and hired me at $125 a week. The band was just completing an engagement at the Capitol Theatre. I sat in once to familiarize myself with its book, although I really knew the older Miller arrangements from my days of analyzing records, and we went on the road.

We played the Glen Island Casino, the Meadowbrook, Coney Island in Cincinnati, and all the theaters. Sometimes we would stay in a location for a week or two at a time. In theaters we would play up to six shows a day. It was an exciting time. Nobody had even a remote idea that the age of the big bands was ending. The public still idolized bandleaders like Benny Goodman, Artie Shaw, Duke Ellington, Count Basie, Woody Herman.

When you were on the road with a band, you lived in a capsule, a cocoon. There was no other world but the band, because you were always leaving behind the people you met along the way. The only continuity you had was with the band itself. You breathed and talked the life of the band. You could almost complete everybody else's sentences. You knew everything about each other. You were always on that bus, and you settled into a groove. Everything came down to two things: where do we eat, and what time does the job start? I was by now more than slightly interested in girls, but even they didn't enter into it that much; you were always waving good-bye to them through the bus window.

I cannot remember ever finding a restaurant that was any good, nor can I figure out how we got our pressing done. We did our socks and underwear ourselves in the hotel room sink, but how we did our pressing is still a big mystery to me.

We had two uniforms with Tex, a brown and a blue. It was very important that you didn't turn up in the wrong uniform, so we would ask John O'Leary, who had been Glenn Miller's road manager and paymaster for years. A classic Irishman from Boston, he looked like Pat O'Brien, except that he was a little shorter. He was always smiling, always happy, and he never had a bad word to say about anyone. Miller had loved him, and Tex couldn't have done without him.

We all had nicknames in that band. I roomed for a while with Sal Libero and gave him the nickname Lard, and he gave me mine, which was Weirdo. I did crazy things because of that irreverence I had for authority and, I suppose, just because they were fun. My sense of humor was, to say the least, strange.

On the road with a band, living in that confined world, traveling together, eating together, the exposure is intense. Everyone's character comes to the fore. You can't hide anything. Jokes start to happen, poking fun—and sometimes very vicious fun—at the quirks of each person. Yet it's all done in good spirit.

Before Sal came into the band, I had roomed with Conrad Gozzo. Gozzo had hardly any neck, and when he played trumpet what little neck he *did* have disappeared into his body cage. He had a great high range, and he was utterly dependable. He defined the term *lead trumpet*, and the musicians still talk about him. He really drove that band, and any other band he was in. He'd yell at the guys, "Come on, you bastards, blow!" Because of the way his neck disappeared when he played, his head seeming to come right out of his shoulders, he looked like a little Gopher, particularly when wearing the brown uniform. So of course his nickname was Gopher. Until he died, Gozzo was on all my albums, starting with *The Music from "Peter Gunn."* Tenor saxist Stan Aronson, who was in the very first Miller band, was known as Moose; his nose had a life of its own.

One of the practical jokes that earned me my nickname went slightly astray at the Earle Theater in Philadelphia. The stage was, as usual, tiered; the sax section on the lowest riser, the trombones behind them on the next riser, and the trumpets behind the trombones still higher. I sat at the piano up at the back, next to the drums and close to the strings. One of my good friends in the band was a fellow Clevelander, a viola player named Stan Harris. Stan was a flaming liberal, always onto some cause, making a speech defending the downtrodden, decrying this injustice or that in our society. It wasn't that I disagreed with him on some of these matters, but I just couldn't help pulling his leg about it. I'd say, "Stan, you're losing your marbles." This had been going on for about six months.

We played five shows a day, and one day I got an idea. Between shows I went out to a toy store and bought a bag of marbles. During the next show, there was a pause as Tex stood at the front of the stage at the microphone, introducing the next singer or soloist. It was very quiet. I took the bag out of my pocket and poked Stan. I said, "Hey, Stan, here are the marbles you lost." And as I handed the bag to him, it broke and all the marbles spilled. It was so quiet. I can still hear the sound of those marbles, rolling across the tier I was sitting on, then falling down the next tier and rolling, and then the next tier. You could really hear them: roll-roll-roll, pock! roll-roll-roll, pock! It seemed like it was going to go on forever. Tex could hear them coming. Finally all these marbles rolled across the stage. Had he stepped on them, he might have fallen flat.

Tex—who got his own nickname from Glenn Miller when he joined the band in 1938—is not a reactor. He is one of the calmest men I've ever met. An atomic bomb could go off in the next room and Tex wouldn't turn a hair. When one or two of the marbles touched his foot, he looked down and went straight ahead with his announcement. Finally he kicked some of the marbles into the footlights, never giving a thought to where they had come from.

I was not called on to write arrangements, but if I had an idea for an original instrumental, I'd go to Norman and Tex, and Tex would say, "Go ahead." I did some backgrounds for the singers, and I got my first experience writing for strings. I was most adept at ballads, although I did some up-tempo arrangements. I didn't, and to this day still don't, consider myself a jazz arranger on the level of Bill Holman, Neal Hefti, or Gil Evans.

The vocal group was the Crew Chiefs, who had been with Miller in the wartime band. They left, and in Los Angeles Tex hired a group called the Mello-Larks to replace them. But no sooner had they come with the band than the lead girl left. Tex replaced her with Ginny O'Connor, who had been with Mel Tormé's group, the Mel-Tones.

I was not blind to her attractions, but still, lightning did not strike when we met, nor did an invisible string section take up a theme softly in the background. We musicians were leery of Hollywood people. When we played the Palladium, the movie stars would come in to dance and be seen, and we were very skeptical of them. When I met Ginny I looked down my nose at her as a Hollywood type.

I first began to be aware of her at the Million Dollar Theater, when I started coaching the group. It was not a job I relished, and I was doing it for the extra money. Don Haynes said, "I want you to rehearse this group, teach them the Crew Chiefs' material. Keep track of your hours and we'll pay you." None of the boys in the Mello-Larks read well, but Ginny did. She was singing lead, although she has always preferred to sing second. She was also assigned some solo spots.

I made note of my hours in a little book. When the group knew all their material, I gave Don Haynes the bill, which came to more than $500. He said, "Well, this is a lot of money." He had a charming way about him. I ended up settling for one hundred.

I was unaware of any attraction Ginny felt toward me, and I didn't want to know about attachments. I was only twenty-three years old, just out of uniform, on the road with a band, with the women of the world out there waiting for me! We'd give the girls the wink from the bandstand and, unless the band was pulling out immediately after, meet them later. That's the way it was in those days. In the meantime, John O'Leary had taken a protective interest in Ginny. He was like a mother hen with her, as you might expect of an O'Leary and an O'Connor on a band bus.

I think Ginny saw something in me as a musician that I didn't see in myself. The guys in the band all knew what was happening. If I got on the bus late, I'd find all the seats taken except the one beside her. They'd left it open for me.

Ginny remembers what happened better than I do, so I'll relate her recollection of events. She says that because of the way she was always looking at me on the bandstand and getting no response, the guys started calling her Dopey. And then, because I remained oblivious to what was happening, they started calling me Dopey as well. We were the two Dopes.

One night after the job—and I do *not* remember this for the obvious reason that I don't want to—I asked her if I could walk her back to the hotel. She says she was delighted that she'd apparently succeeded in waking the dead. She opened her hotel room door. I walked in and flopped on the bed and said, "Just what are you trying to prove?"

She was terribly embarrassed. After a minute or two I left. She burst into tears and called Rolly Bundock, our bass player, who came down to her room in his bathrobe. Still in tears, she told him, "I'm giving Tex my notice in the morning. I'm so humiliated. I just cannot get back on that band bus with him. I can't do it." Rolly sat with her until dawn, letting her talk it all out. She didn't give her notice. But she didn't sit with me on the bus, either. She sat with the Mello-Larks.

I had preserved my freedom. Little did I know that I was about to make a deep and lifelong commitment.

When we arrived in New Orleans, I asked her if she'd like to go to a movie. When she said yes, I suggested that we first have dinner in the hotel restaurant. From that time on it was simply assumed that we would be married. No doubt because of a pattern set by my father, I have never been very good at expressing my feelings for people in words. Apparently I never made a formal proposal. But at least I gave her a ring. Ginny says she remembers flashing it in the spotlight onstage to the guys in the band, as if to say, "See?" This was during the engagement at the Earle Theater when I spilled the marbles; it may even have been the same show.

We both knew the nicknames we had acquired from the guys, and now we used them too. We'd meet and it would be, "Hi, Dope."

"Hello, Dope."

In the dead of winter that year, we played a dreadful theater in Jersey City. Our hotel was in New York, and Ginny and I traveled back and forth on the subway to the job. Ginny had one coat, and she was miserable with the cold—a California girl who had never experienced winter.

We found we had much in common. We were only months apart in age. Her family, like many American families, endured hardship during the Depression. My father was a musician, and so was her mother. Her mother had played piano in department stores, demonstrating sheet music. And, interestingly, despite her name, O'Connor, Ginny was half Mexican and had spoken Spanish before she spoke English. She had a slight Mexican look around the eyes. Her mother's maiden name was Gessenius.

We talked about the things young people falling in love always do: childhood and growing up and our ambitions. At the age of twelve, on Saturdays she had taught younger children to tap-dance, earning two dollars for the day. Her mother in turn played piano in return for Ginny's dancing lessons. Ginny said she lived for Saturday movie matinees, saving her pennies, hoping she would have enough for a couple of hours of escape from reality.

But there was one great difference in our backgrounds: Ginny knew a lot about Hollywood. Her Irish father, Johnny O'Connor—from whom her mother, Josephine, was now divorced—was a teamster, driving trucks at MGM. She had a lot of friends who were in or close to the movie business.

Ginny had been a member of a vocal group called the School Kids, which she joined at Los Angeles City College. Ben Pollack, the drummer and bandleader, had introduced them to Mel Tormé, who, in addition to being an outstanding singer, was an arranger. He'd taken over leadership of the group, writing their arrangements and rehearsing them, and eventually changed the group's name to the Mel-Tones.

One friend in particular whom she talked about was a kid named Sammy Davis, Jr. He, his father, and his uncle made up the Will Mastin Trio. Sammy was a friend of Mel Tormé's, and when the trio came to Los Angeles, he would call Mel, who had appeared in a few movies; in fact, Ginny and the Mel-Tones had been in one of them with him. Mel knew all the Hollywood young crowd, people like Mickey Rooney, Peggy Ryan, Donald O'Connor, Gloria Jean, Judy Garland, and Blake Edwards.

The Mel-Tones were popular at parties because when somebody would ask, "Have you heard these kids sing?" Mel would say, "Okay, kids," sit at the piano, and blow everybody's socks off. Whenever Sammy was in town, he and the Mel-Tones would go partying together. After the Mel-Tones had finished singing, they'd say, "You've got to see this kid dance." So they'd roll back the rug, and Sammy would astound everybody. They didn't know he could also sing.

We'd talk into the night on the band bus and in the bad restaurants we always seemed to find, those bleak coffee shops with Formica countertops and stark fluorescent lights, living that life on the road together. Several movies produced just before the war glamorized the band life. Two of them, *Sun Valley Serenade* and *Orchestra Wives*, featured the Miller band. Others featured the Harry James, Artie Shaw, and Tommy Dorsey bands. In those movies the musicians were always gaily grabbing their horns and blowing tunes on buses and trains, and, in one particularly silly scene in *Sun Valley Serenade*, in open sleighs in winter. The reality was nothing like the movies, and Ginny was learning it quickly. So was I, of course, but that life was much harder on women than on men. Ginny said she found it lonely, and she didn't think we were getting anywhere. By then I was making what for me seemed like pretty good money, $300 a week with the writing. She was making $90.

When spring came, we worked some amusement park ballrooms and pavilions. Ginny said she couldn't face another winter on the road. By then we were talking seriously about getting married. I had told her about seeing *The Crusades* and my dream of writing film scores. She said the place to do that was Hollywood, and the time to do it was now. I told her I just wasn't ready to leave the band yet.

We played Cleveland, and Ginny met my cousins, including Helen and her husband, Ralph Musengo, also home from the war and out of uniform now. Ginny made a side trip to West Aliquippa to meet my parents who, while they didn't exactly disapprove, were surprised at our engagement. Ginny's mother did disapprove. She didn't want Ginny to marry a musician. She said that as a musician's wife Ginny would starve. She wanted her to marry someone in a solid profession.

Ginny gave Tex her notice, and he began auditioning singers to replace her. Ginny remembers a slim little teenage girl waiting backstage to audition at the theater we were playing. She was muttering to herself, "I can't sing with this Mickey band. I just can't sing with this Mickey band." It was jazz singer Jackie Cain, who shortly thereafter would marry pianist and singer Roy Kral and form the marvelous duo known as Jackie and Roy.

In July Ginny left the band, returned to California, and moved in with her mother in Rosemead. She began studio singing then. We wrote letters back and forth—we couldn't afford phone calls—and finally I told Tex I had to leave the band because Ginny and I wanted to get married. Tex had no bandleaderly airs; he was always one of us. He wished us happiness and said if I couldn't play piano in the band, at least I could continue writing for it, which for some time I did. Ginny's mother set up a room for me in her house, and I lived there until we were married and moved into an apartment in Burbank.

5
Two for the Road

Ginny wanted to be married at the Church of the Blessed Sacrament in Hollywood. She had gone to school in that parish and made her first communion there at the age of eight. She made herself a promise that when she was married, it would be in that church. But the rules were sticky about performing the wedding service for people who didn't live in the parish. I don't suppose I was much help because I hadn't been to church in years. But Ginny was very determined and talked to the priest, and no doubt having a nice Irish name like O'Connor helped. Finally he relented, and we were married there on September 13, 1947.

The reception was held in Hollywood at the Brunswick Mansion, an old rented mansion with a rolling lawn, on Adams Boulevard. My mother and father had driven out in their big old '37 Chevy. Ginny's father, Johnny O'Connor, was there with his new wife, Millie, and their two children, Maryann and Bob. He hadn't been too eager to put up money for the reception, so the weight of the expenses fell on Ginny's mother, Jo. Jo wasn't making a lot of money at the time, and neither was her husband, Jim Byrne, the stepfather Ginny grew up with and the father of her half-sister, Maureen. Jim was the son of Jim Byrne of the Irish Republican Army, famous for his money-raising in this country for the IRA. For punch, Jo added 7-Up to some cheap white wine. Ginny's matron of honor was Vera Shea Gordon, a dancer and showgirl married to Alan Gordon, an entrepreneur and important publicist at that time. Jerry Gray was my best man.

Jerry was the only one who knew the mass well enough to know what to do. At the rehearsal the night before, Ginny said to the priest, "Now, Father, most of our attendants are non-Catholics. Would you give them directions on when to sit and when to kneel?"

He said, "Oh, that's very simple. They can just follow you."

Ginny and I gave each other a look, because we didn't know. When it came to the ceremony the next day, we kept glancing at Jerry and doing what he did.

We spent a week in Las Vegas on our honeymoon, then took a new, freshly painted, two-bedroom, $90-a-month apartment on Parrish Place in Burbank. Because the country still faced wartime shortages, we didn't have a telephone at first. We got along well on very little money. We were young and happy and still without serious responsibilities. It was a carefree time. We slept until midday and went to movies and newsreel theaters in the afternoon. I was studying at Westlake School of Music on my GI bill and privately with Ernst Krenek, Dr. Alfred Sendry, and Mario Castelnuovo-Tedesco. I had a bit saved up, and I was writing a little for Tex at $50 a score.

Neither the Ventura nor Hollywood freeways had yet been built. Los Angeles County was made up of small and quiet communities set far apart among the citrus groves and ranches. The smell of orange blossoms in the San Fernando Valley, even up until the late 1950s, was euphoric.

Jerry Gray, who also had settled in Los Angeles, had taken a liking to me. I knew his whole family by then. Jerry was Italian, born Graziano; Artie Shaw gave him the name Gray when he joined Shaw's first band on violin. Jerry was now working as conductor of the orchestra on a network radio program, "The Bob Crosby Show," on the air fifteen minutes a day, five days a week. Conrad Gozzo had also left Tex and was part of that band, which was small, only nine men. But they were all top men, including Willie Schwartz (another Miller alumnus), Ronnie Lang, Ted Nash, Murray McEachern, and Jimmy Rowles. The show was all music, and a lot of it. Jerry helped sustain me in those first days in California.

When you're young, where your next meal is coming from is important. When somebody asked us out for hamburgers, it was an event, but the real thrill was an invitation to Jerry's house for dinner. He had a big family, including his father and mother—the typical Italian mother who loved to cook and did it superbly. Going to Jerry's was like a trip back home.

Through Ginny I met Harry Zimmerman, an arranger, conductor, and composer who had several shows on the Mutual Radio Network, one of which was "The Family Theater," dramatizations of classic books sponsored by the Catholic Archdiocese of Los Angeles. Harry Zimmerman was the first man to let me compose for drama. He assigned me to write a radio score for *A Tale of Two Cities*. And I conducted it, by the skin of my teeth; I didn't know what I was doing.

David Rose was also good to me. David, at that time the king of string writers and one of my idols, was music director on a lot of half-hour radio shows, including one on Mutual called "California Melodies." He too gave me writing assignments. I composed the music for several episodes of "The FBI in Peace and War."

Like Max Adkins, David had more than a musical influence on me. He taught me about some of the amenities of life, the good things. One thing that he taught me—and I was a willing pupil—was the love of wine. David had a good cellar, and he was an avid pursuer of fine French wines.

This was before the California wines had really come into their own. I would watch what he bought. Sometimes, along with our friends Pete Rugolo and Dick Hazard, we would go down to the Central market in Los Angeles to shop. He would scrounge around, and we'd load his car with his latest treasures.

David was at the top of his career at the time. He had been a conductor in radio for many years, as well as an arranger and composer, and he'd had many hits with compositions such as "Holiday for Strings," "Our Waltz," "Manhattan Square Dance," and "The Stripper." He lived in a beautiful home in Sherman Oaks.

David has always been a nut for steam engines. He has a real miniature steam locomotive and train that run around his house. When he went to Europe, which was at least once a year, he would find some steamboat to bring back. And I mean big ones, up to forty feet long. One year he brought back from Hamburg a German police boat covered with armor plating that you couldn't pierce with a howitzer.

David certainly made my life smoother, and we became and remain good friends.

So with assignments from Jerry, Harry, and David, and club dates—I played with Bob Crosby—and with Ginny doing studio jobs, we managed to keep our heads above water in those years from 1947 to 1952.

For a long time we had no furniture in our living room. Billy Barty and his partner, who used to do the Philip Morris commercials as Johnny the bellboy, would come over and do their gymnastics, tumbling, and song-and-dance routine because they had all the space in the world to knock about in—two talented little guys bouncing around that empty living-room floor. I wrote the music for their act.

One of our close friends was Nick Castle, the hoofer and choreographer, who later became godfather of our children. Nick was a New York kind of person, streetwise and funny, with prodigious energy. He was about five-eight, very lean in the manner of dancers, with his hair combed straight back. He was often hyper and on edge, though in a likable way. He smoked constantly. Nick was still another Italian. He'd worked extensively at MGM and Fox with Fred Astaire and Gene Kelly, and he was highly respected.

Soon after Ginny and I were married, I was writing some arrangements for the Skylarks, an excellent vocal group that had been with Harry James. In those days the vocal groups, such as the Modernaires, had nightclub acts. They would do backup for singers, as well as fifteen or twenty minutes of their own material, which entailed more than singing; these acts were choreographed. And Nick was the choreographer most in demand.

The star system in the movie industry was starting to fade. With television on the rise, the studios were making fewer pictures. People who had been on salary at the big studios suddenly didn't have steady incomes. But if you could sing or dance, there was work in the new hotels that were springing up in Lake Tahoe, Reno, and Las Vegas. There was also work in Miami, Chicago, and New Orleans. Most major cities had places that hired major acts, such as the Fairmont Hotel in San Francisco.

And a great many of these people went to Nick Castle for his help in putting their shows together. I fell into being Nick's arranger.

Nick had a little studio next door to a delicatessen on Pico Boulevard, just west of Beverly Glen. It consisted of a bare room with a wooden floor, a coatrack, an upright piano, a mirrored wall, and a ballet barre. Nick worked days in the studios and nights in his own place with these understandably worried stars. Night after night I went there to help him get them ready for appearances in clubs and hotels. An impressive parade of people came through, someone new every night. I wrote act music for Ann Miller, Anna Maria Alberghetti, Jane Powell, Kathryn Grayson, Betty Hutton, and Ginny Sims. Some of that music is still out there, still in use.

One of the people I wrote for was Buddy Rich. Buddy was a dancer and singer as well as a great drummer, having started in vaudeville with his parents when he was four. In 1950 he decided to give up drums, as he was inclined to do from time to time, to go back to song and dance. I wrote his whole act, a half-hour's worth of music, which amounts to a lot of notes, a lot of pages of orchestration, and a lot of hours at the piano. Of all those people Buddy was the only one who stiffed me. He owed me a good amount of money, and we needed it, so I reported him to the musicians' union. He paid me eventually and never held it against me. We were great friends. He mentioned the incident only once, saying, "Sorry you had to wait, babe."

I wrote a song with Nick around that time, specifically to get myself into ASCAP, the American Society of Composers, Authors and Publishers. I had come to understand that you can be the greatest arranger in the world and get paid the highest fees for your work, but only composers get paid residual benefits for their music. Even when I was with Tex Beneke, I had started to write originals.

ASCAP, which was founded in 1914 by a small group of composers, including Victor Herbert, and lyricists, collects money for the use of music in radio, television, concert halls, restaurants, indeed wherever music is played for profit. ASCAP monitors radio and television, and the income is distributed to its members according to the frequency with which their music is used.

Arrangers do not get paid each time their writing is used on radio and television. I saw the situation and realized that to create some kind of long-range security for my family I would have to establish myself as a composer, and the first step was to become a member of ASCAP. I wrote to ASCAP to ask how to go about it. They replied that you had to have radio or television performances of a song or have a song published. There was no way at that point that I could have music performed on radio or TV, but there was a way to join: set up my own company and publish and print the music myself.

Nick Castle was working with a marvelous dancer named Arthur Duncan, later a regular on "The Lawrence Welk Show." Nick came up with an idea for a song for Arthur's act, a song to be called "The Soft-Shoe Boogie." I wrote the music and Nick wrote the lyrics. So here was my big chance to get into ASCAP.

I set up a publishing company and had five hundred copies printed, almost all of which stayed in my garage. And so this dumb song was my first published piece of music, and it was my entree into ASCAP. I didn't get the first check for a long time. It was for $14.73. I kept it and still have it, framed.

After Ginny and the Mello-Larks left Beneke, they put an act together, with Nick's help. Nick was choreographing and I was writing the arrangements for Betty Hutton's act, and the Mello-Larks were hired to go with her to the Golden Gate Theater in San Francisco. Betty was a big star at the time, and she had a sensational act. She was a very good singer as well as a gifted comedienne with a talent for knock-about farce and apparently inexhaustible energy. She was also very pretty. The show in San Francisco went well, so well that she asked the Mello-Larks to go with her for an engagement at the London Palladium.

The Palladium opening, however, was to be September 13, our first wedding anniversary. I could tell that Ginny was torn. She had never been abroad and wanted to accept the offer. I told her, "Take it. Go. There's no telling when you'll get another chance."

She said, "Are you sure it's okay?"

I said, "Absolutely. Go."

I wired two dozen roses to her for her opening night and our wedding anniversary. Later she told me that she had a shabby little dressing room, with the roses piled in a big tub in the middle of it.

They stayed in London a month. While they were at the London Palladium, I got a job at the Hollywood Palladium with the Art Mooney orchestra. I hated it. The band used to sing "I'm Looking Over a Four Leaf Clover," Mooney's big hit record, with me playing the melody on the glockenspiel. I refused to sing it to begin with, and finally I began deliberately playing wrong notes. Art gave me my notice. One of the distinctions of my career is that I was fired by both Vincent Lopez and Art Mooney.

My mother and father came out to visit the summer after Ginny and I were married, driving all the way across the country. They liked it, and then in 1949 they wrapped up everything in Pennsylvania and moved out here. I realized when he arrived that year that my dad had it in his mind that they were going to live with us, as is the custom with families in Italy. We didn't even have a house yet, only our apartment.

I was not working very much, and things were very difficult for Ginny and me. With what little money I did have I helped my parents buy a house in Bell, southeast of Los Angeles. It was a little crackerbox of a place, but comfortable.

My relationship with my father grew more strained and eventually turned a little nasty. He went back to work in a shoe factory, doing I suppose what he had done in that shoe factory in Boston not long after his arrival from Italy.

Then my mother had the first of eight heart attacks. We found her the best around-the-clock nursing care. She had a telephone by her bedside, and the dread of hearing our phone ring at odd hours of the night was a nightmare for us. She was visibly deteriorating.

My dad became even more difficult to deal with. He felt

he was being punished for something, and he blamed everyone. He was even angry at my mother for being sick. He wouldn't give her the time of day, yet she remained sweet and quiet. I don't think his attitude did much to make her want to get well.

I would try to talk with my parents every day. We would drive the two hours there and back at least once a week. He became very sullen and more difficult to communicate with, and I came to feel guilty about the situation. He was always civil to Ginny, but he really took his anger out on me.

He never let me forget that I hadn't gotten a degree in music. He pounded me with it. When I would get an assignment, turn in a piece of work I was proud of, and try to tell him about it, he'd say, "Well, if you had your degree you'd be teaching school." He simply never let up on that, even after the success of *The Music from "Peter Gunn"* and "Moon River."

I have felt an overwhelming sadness, the kind of pain you can't control, emotion that overwhelms you to the point that you break down and sob, once in my life. It was in 1951, after we received the call that my mother was dying. We drove to Bell, and I cried in the car. A priest was there. We were at her bedside when she released the death rattle. It's a sound you don't forget.

At that time Universal Pictures was turning out forty or fifty feature films a year, plus a great many short subjects, twenty-minute two-reel pictures featuring the big bands. Most of the major bands, including Duke Ellington and Count Basie, appeared in these shorts, casual bits of entertainment that have become classics by default, valued historical documentation of the music of that era.

Ginny was, once again, instrumental in the next step in my career. She knew Will Cowan, a wonderful man who produced twenty-minute, two-reel musical shorts at Universal. The band would play an opening number and a closer, with a juggler, singer, or some other act featured in between.

Will Cowan booked Jimmy Dorsey for one of these shorts, then hired the Mello-Larks to appear in it as well. They needed an arrangement for the job. The group had their choice of arrangers, but they chose me since I was their "official" arranger.

I wrote an arrangement on "Skip to My Lou" for Jimmy Dorsey and the Mello-Larks. Milt Rosen, assistant to Joe Gershenson, the head of the music department, heard it in rehearsal. There weren't any wrong notes, which was the best recommendation an arranger could have in those days, and it wasn't too hard to play. Since that brief and disastrous experience with Benny Goodman in New York, I had made it my business to write music that was easy on the players.

Milt Rosen called Joe Gershenson over to listen to it. The studio had a few musicals coming up and needed somebody experienced in modern dance-band writing, as opposed to the European symphonic approach to scoring that predominated in movies at that time.

Frank Skinner, who was under contract to Universal and was a fine composer in the classic style, used to do all their important pictures. Many composers in Hollywood were not comfortable conducting, but Frank Skinner was also an able conductor. The other scores written at Universal were conducted by Joe Gershenson, who, in addition to being a fine musician, knew drama from long experience conducting the scores to silent movies in the orchestra pits of theaters.

And at just this point in Universal's history, although he did not tell me this until later, Joe needed someone to cover that other, nonclassical, base for them. I was a young guy who had a big band experience and knew something about strings. Joe and Milt had been looking for somebody with just my kind of qualifications. So after we finished the short with Jimmy Dorsey, they called me in and tested me by assigning me a composition job—one scene in an Abbott and Costello picture called *Lost in Alaska*.

I see the picture once in a while—all those pictures I did at Universal are still out there somewhere; I can tell by my ASCAP reports. Film is forever.

That film was my baptism of fire. The very first film writing I did was for a sequence in which Lou Costello is bitten on the ass by a crab—high-class stuff. But I took the assignment seriously.

I agonized so over that sequence that I might have been scoring a battle in *War and Peace* or the Atlanta fire in *Gone with the Wind*. That bit of music took me two weeks to write. Now, if pressed, I can write the music for an entire picture in two weeks. But that's how my film-scoring career began, with a crab biting Lou Costello in *Lost in Alaska*.

For that first bit of film writing, I was paid $225 a week. It was good money in 1952, and we were glad to get it, even though the job was supposed to last only two weeks.

It lasted six years. I worked from nine to five in a small office just off one of Universal's soundstages, turning out music for movies both good and bad and learning my trade.

Our son Chris was born July 2, 1950, at Cedars of Lebanon Hospital. I was ecstatic at having a son. I now had insurance that the name would be around for a while. It's funny, sometimes, how images stick in the mind forever. The image I have of that day is of our doctor coming out of the delivery room, still in his surgical gown and cap, his face mask hanging around his neck, congratulating me. As I shook hands with him, all smiles I'm sure, I glanced down at his shoes. They were brown and white saddle shoes. And they were sprinkled with blood.

At this time my dad felt very much alone. I tried to talk with him as much as I could, but every telephone conversation with him left me in a very depressed mood.

As delicately as I could, I bought him a comfortable mobile home. Now that I had a decent income, I put him on the payroll as a music librarian and bought him a new car. In the back of his mind he still couldn't figure out why he wasn't living with us.

6
Universal Studios

U niversal Pictures was an old-line movie company, located on a huge piece of land in North Hollywood, just over Cahuenga Pass from Hollywood itself. It was owned by Decca Records when I went to work there. On the front of that property were street after street of soundstages. The back lot, as it was called, consisted of countless acres of open land and foothills where they used to shoot outdoor action scenes for westerns.

The lot was a very friendly place, homey instead of bustling, as it is now, and very quiet. Except for people moving sets from here to there, there was little discernible activity, although behind the closed doors, in the offices and on the soundstages, everyone was working, turning out our fifty to fifty-five pictures a year. We were like a family, and if someone whom none of us knew came into the commissary at lunch, it was an event.

The young actors under contract included Clint Eastwood, Clint Walker, James Garner, Jeff Chandler, Tony Curtis, Rock Hudson, George Nader, Barbara Rush, Julie Adams, Piper Laurie, and Anita Ekberg. The studio had, in effect, a stock company, a school for actors, a great place for training with a very able woman named Sophie Rosenstein as drama coach. The younger actors had to study dancing, horseback riding, gun toting, and voice. One of my friends at that time was David Janssen. We would always kid each other because I was making more money than he was—and he was one of the star actors in the stable.

The music department consisted of Joe Gershenson; his assistant, Milt Rosen; composers Frank Skinner and Hans Salter, who were given complete pictures to score; and, at my level, composers who were assigned the overflow, several of us working on various parts of the same picture. It also included an excellent orchestrator named David Tamkin, who in working on our scores gave us all lessons in orchestration, and a music librarian named Nick Nuzzi. He was an Italian. Not an Italian-American, like Jerry Gray, Nick Castle, and me, but a real one. From Italy. With an accent. Nick had a curious walk, a kind of shuffle, due to flat feet. He had the proverbial hard exterior with a heart of gold, and he was warm to me because not only was I the youngest composer in the place, but I was also Italian. He took to me. He also took from me, on one occasion, which I'll get to.

The composer I worked with most was Herman Stein, a marvelous musician now semiretired from the profession. He used to sit up in his room, without a piano, and write. This amazed me, this ability to write without a piano, although there are many composers who do. When we were overloaded with work, which happened once in a while, Joe Gershenson and Milt Rosen would call in outsiders. One time Shorty Rogers came in when we needed some arrangements. Shorty is a great jazz trumpeter and an excellent composer whom I had known from the band days. He was to play a critical role at a turning point in my life. Bill Lava, Irving Gertz, and Heinz Roemheld, who wrote "Ruby," also came in and helped out.

A few years ago Herman Stein was interviewed about the old days at Universal by *CinemaScore: The Film Music Journal*. I was fascinated by his memories of that time:

> We'd grind pictures out like a factory in those days. Sometimes two or three of us would work on a picture. One of us would come up with the main theme and the others

would use that theme in the cues we'd do. [In film parlance, cues are simply the various pieces of music in the film.] Sometimes I would do a reel or Hank would do a reel, or Skinner would do a reel, that sort of thing. It was quite a collaborative effort. Sometimes somebody would inherit the main title, and we would have a theme there. Whoever had to use that particular theme would compose it in his own particular way. For example, we had a picture called *It Came from Outer Space* that was a little different. I remember that I did the main title and some other cues, and we also had some library music. Everybody would do different things, but for continuity, somebody would come up with a certain theme for this character or that character.

It Came from Outer Space is one of the films I worked on with Herman. I wrote brief cues with such titles as "Talking Wires," "The Thing Strikes," "Zombie George," and "Rescued," as well as the end title.

The list of Herman's films at Universal surprised me because I realized when I read it that I'd worked with him on at least 116 of them—including such great works of art as *Abbott and Costello Go to Mars, Abbott and Costello Meet Dr. Jekyll and Mr. Hyde, City Beneath the Sea, Veils of Bagdad, Creature from the Black Lagoon, Revenge of the Creature, Ma and Pa Kettle at Home, The Kettles in the Ozarks, Tarantula, Francis in the Haunted House,* and one of the very first rock musicals, *Rock, Pretty Baby.* There were, of course, better pictures as well.

We, the composers, were never invited to the previews, only Joe Gershenson as head of the music department was. The executives would screen the new pictures on weekends. On Monday morning, those of us who had written music for them would wait for Joe's report. He would come into the office, and we would ask anxiously, "Did they mention the music?"

Occasionally one of us would be called on to do something other than write music for films.

Miss Universe contests were held every year at Long

Beach. The top six finalists would be given contracts at Universal. The contest took place in July, so around September we could expect the new crop of lovelies, who would come in and do small jobs here and there. Sometimes one of them would get a decent part, and a few went on to do some good things.

The studio used to put together an annual road show, produced in-house and then sent on tour to promote the company's pictures. The girls would learn little routines and go out and do their stuff. I was rarely involved in it, but one time I was told, "Go up to the rehearsal hall. Some girl's up there who needs help with her act. Go up and work with her." Years before, Paul Whiteman had rehearsed *The King of Jazz* in that rehearsal hall, which was in fact built for that picture. It was huge.

I walked in. There stood a tall Swedish girl in her prime—Anita Ekberg. She was one of the especially attractive girls under contract, and well connected in the studio. I was about thirty-four at the time and not, shall we say, unaware of her endowments. But I was married, and in any case I understood the situation: this was a bar of candy up there on the top shelf, too far away. You don't fool around, not if you are making $300 a week. Careers have been destroyed in Hollywood for that breach of protocol.

I sat down at the piano and said, "This is the song they want you to sing on the tour."

She immediately said, "I don't want to go." They were sending her to Alaska.

I was just doing my job, so I said, "Well, let's try the song." I don't remember what the song was, but it was awful, and she didn't want to do it anyway. I said, "If you work on this, you might be able to make the trip."

She said in her Swedish accent, "I don't want to go to Alaska." We didn't rehearse the song, and that was the last I saw of her. She didn't make the trip. It helps to have connections.

A particularly close friend of mine at Universal was Jeff

Chandler, who was headed for superstardom. He was also an aspiring lyricist with whom I wrote several songs. Jeff was always interested in singing. He had a rich, resonant speaking voice and a good singing voice, though he had a pitch problem. To record him, you'd have to do two or three takes for each section of a song. Still, his voice had a lovely quality. He was one of the people I wrote act music for, and he played engagements in Las Vegas.

Jeff and I just kind of fell in. He would come around to my office between takes. I think the first song we wrote was for a Ross Hunter film called *All I Desire*. I wrote an arrangement of it for Jeff. Then Tony Curtis did a picture called *Six Bridges to Cross*, and we needed a song for it, to be sung over the end credits.

Jeff and I knew Sammy Davis, Jr., and he and Jeff had become very close. Sammy wrote in his first autobiography, *Yes I Can: The Story of Sammy Davis, Jr.*, that Jeff was like an older brother to him.

Sammy's career was just cresting, and he was beginning to find his identity as a singer. The Will Mastin Trio was playing the New Frontier in Las Vegas for $7,500 a week. Jeff called Sammy and told him, "Hank and I want you to do our song at the end of the film." There was a natural tie-in to the situation: Sammy was recording for Decca, and Decca owned Universal.

Sammy said, "Well, man, I'm here for the next month. I'll tell you what, I'll come down for the day and record for you and then come back to Vegas." We sent him a copy of the tune, and I wrote the arrangement.

Sammy was happy not only because of the money the Will Mastin Trio was making. When they'd played Vegas before, they had been forced to reside in the shanty section of town because "colored" were not allowed to stay in the hotel they worked. But Sammy and the trio were hot now, and the New Frontier had surrendered, paying them well and assigning them the best rooms.

He had a hit record going for him, and it seemed the years of humiliation because of his color were over. Even the Vegas police had begun to treat him cordially. And now he was excited—more than Jeff and I realized—that he was going to make his first movie sound track.

In *Yes I Can*, Sammy described what happened that night. He finished his job after midnight, had a hamburger, and had his valet, Charley, bring his new Cadillac convertible to the front door. Sammy told Charley to drive for a while. As they pulled out of town, Sammy looked at the big neon sign that spelled out his name across the desert. Then he slept for a while in the back seat.

After a time, he took over the driving and Charley slept in the back. The sun was coming up over the mountains. Sammy turned on the radio and heard his own recording of "Hey There." A green car driven by a woman passed him. Then it slowed indecisively. Apparently she was going to make a U-turn on an open highway. He tried to maneuver around her, but there were oncoming cars. He hit the brakes and slammed into her rear fender.

He heard Charley moaning in the back seat. Blood gushed from his mouth; his teeth had been knocked out. When the police arrived, Charley couldn't speak for the blood in his throat. He pointed to Sammy's face. Sammy put his hand to his face and found his eye hanging on his cheek by a thread. He tried to stuff it back into its socket. He was on his knees, murmuring, "Don't let me go blind. Please, God, don't take it all away!"

In the ambulance he thought, "I'm never going to be a star. They're going to hate me again."

At 9:00 A.M. the orchestra was assembled at Universal. Jeff Chandler, Joe Gershenson, and I were waiting. The clock moved on to 9:10, and then 9:15. We were all very uneasy. Sammy was too much of a pro to be late like this. And if something had happened, he would certainly have called Jeff. I rehearsed the orchestra. Still no Sam. Noon came, and Joe and I dismissed the orchestra for lunch.

Then Jeff had a hunch. He called the sheriff's department and asked if they'd had a report of an accident involving Sammy Davis, Jr. Jeff found out that Sammy was in a hospital in San Bernardino. He'd lost an eye.

Sam asked Jeff to sub for him. Jeff flew to Vegas with that act music I'd written for him and filled in for Sammy at the New Frontier. First thing out of the hospital, Sammy came in and recorded the song.

Jeff Chandler later died very young of medical bungling—from complications that arose when a doctor left a suture in him after routine surgery. His friends were furious and heartbroken. Sammy of course staged an amazing recovery, becoming a bigger star than ever. Sammy, his wife Altovise, Ginny, and I are still very close.

7
The Salt Mine

I once referred to the music department at Universal as a salt mine. But it was a good salt mine, and younger composers in film today do not have access to that kind of on-the-job training. Being on staff there I was called upon to do everything. I mean, *everything*. Whenever they needed a piece of source music, music that comes from a source in the picture, such as a band, a jukebox, or a radio, they would call me in. I would do an arrangement on something that was in the Universal library, or I would write a new piece for a jazz band or a Latin band or whatever. I guess in every business you have to learn the routine—in film scoring, the clichés—before you can begin to find your own way.

In Yiddish vernacular, my boss, Joe Gershenson, was a *shtarker*, well aware of the ways of the street and the world. He produced several pictures at Universal before he became head of the music department. He was producing a desert epic (a "tits and sand" movie) and was having trouble with the feminine star who insisted that she could not do the film because her astrologer felt that the stars were not in the right place in the heavens at that time. Joe asked the star and her mentor, both well-known names, to come in for a meeting with him. The astrologer proceeded to expound on all of the reasons that the star could not do the picture. Joe let him talk.

He then picked up the script and said to the man, "I don't believe you've seen the new script."

He walked across the room, his back to the lady, and opened the script to a certain page, into which he had slipped a $100 bill. The star did the film.

Because of the nature of the production and distribution systems, Universal's pictures were made for a specific and predetermined price. There were no huge budget overruns as there are today.

All the westerns, Creature pictures, the Francis, Ma and Pa Kettle, and Abbott and Costello films came in at exactly ten reels, an hour and a half. On these cheaper B pictures, very little money was budgeted for music.

Joe Gershenson would call in Herman Stein and me to look at a picture. Herman and I would decide where the music would go and discuss it with Joe—or with the producer, if he came around. Usually, though, the producer was off in another part of the factory making his next picture. Directors rarely showed up at our screenings. They were out in the hills of the back lot, shooting another chase.

Film composers refer to this phase of viewing a film, planning where music should go and what it should be like, as "spotting" the picture.

After we saw the picture, Joe would say, "Hank, you take half and, Herman, you take half." Which half didn't matter. I would get my five reels and Herman his five. If the love theme fell in his half of the picture, he'd write it. And if he used it in the first half of the picture, I would use it in the second half, and vice versa. The theme, whichever of us wrote it, would be just a melody line, which we would then arrange and give to David Tamkin for orchestration.

We certainly didn't produce great music by this process. It was Universal's style, and you didn't try to write Arnold Schonberg for their pictures. We did our best, but we couldn't afford to fool around with lofty aesthetic aspirations, and what we turned—or churned—out deserves to be referred to bluntly as what it was: mostly crap.

For the really low-budget pictures, those at the very bottom of the barrel, an even less creative way of scoring had been developed, a ruthlessly ingenious system of cribbing the music of earlier Universal pictures. Even this contributed to my learning, since it forced me to analyze these older (and often excellent) scores.

Cheap period pictures and westerns usually got this treatment. Anything in the Universal music library was fair game. If Universal owned it, we could steal it. I used a lot of music by Miklos Rozsa from *The Killers*, the Hemingway story. Rozsa had no say in this. The studios, not the composers, owned the scores.

Assigned to one of the Francis the Mule or Kelly the Dog pictures (Kelly was one of the animals that never made it at Universal), you'd go to the library and tell Nick Nuzzi, "Give me the music from so-and-so and so-and-so"— pictures you thought might have some things you could use. You'd get a big stack of music by eight or ten different composers and proceed to create a score out of it.

It was in doing this that I learned that just about anything works, no matter how incongruous it is with the scene. I made good use of this discovery with "Baby Elephant Walk" in *Hatari!* and *The Pink Panther*, among other films. Nothing illustrates this principle better than Disney's use in *Fantasia* of Stravinsky's *The Rite of Spring* with animated scenes of the dawn of the world—music that was written for a ballet about a fertility rite.

Music that is *not* in the mood of the scene can have interesting effects. For example, in a brutal murder scene, cheerful music coming, let's say, from a radio would heighten the horror. In his film *The Victors*, Carl Foreman used Frank Sinatra's recording of "Have Yourself a Merry Little Christmas" behind the scene of the execution in a snowy Belgian field of a GI for desertion. The effect was harrowing. This is known in film music as scoring against the scene, and I learned a lot about it lifting music from those old Universal scores.

I would get a piece of music by, say, Frank Skinner. Then, with a stopwatch, I'd figure out the tempo I wanted and make note of it on the sketch paper: how many bars I would use to get from here to here; then how many from this other piece to get to the next scene. Timings must be figured out before a single note is written.

Sometimes—in westerns particularly—you'd get three-minute action sequences. Three minutes is a long time, especially in a chase sequence, requiring a lot of bars of music. Often I would use fragments from ten or fifteen different pieces of music for three minutes of film.

The trick was to fit these bits together smoothly. Sometimes I'd score a new bar or two as a bridge, perhaps going from a few bars of Frank Skinner to a bit by Miklos Rozsa. It would get pretty hairy here.

And you had to be careful about the instrumentation. Sometimes you were working from scores written for orchestras larger than the one we had available. Therefore, you'd have to alter the instrumentation of the music, cutting it down to the resources of our orchestra. And so, by one means or another, I'd make sure Skinner's music didn't bump into Rozsa's, and by this process we'd assemble a score inexpensively. It was mechanical and uncreative, but I cannot imagine a better apprenticeship in the profession than taking apart and reassembling all that music. By the time I was through, I knew those scores intimately. I'd really studied the work of my elders and predecessors and discovered what they did and why.

David Tamkin was one of the nicest things that happened to me at Universal. A Russian Jew with a blustery way about him, he had a ruddy face and thinning hair and always smoked a cigar. He held forth in his little music castle, a bungalow in back of the music department.

David was our chief and only orchestrator. When we

wrote our sketches, the various sections of the orchestra were condensed, i.e., the trumpets were on one stave, the trombones on another stave, woodwinds, strings, and percussion likewise. David was invaluable in advising which instrument would play what. He would then proceed to assign each individual instrument its own stave on the full score. Full scores can total thirty or forty staves.

David, who was strictly classically oriented, had done a lot of orchestration for Miklos Rozsa, Dimitri Tiomkin, and Franz Waxman. I had to prove to him I knew what I was doing. I was in a new area, doing movie scores, not arrangements for a dance band. I now faced different criteria, and every time I went to David's office I felt I was making up for the orchestration classes I had been unable to take at Juilliard. I learned a lot from David Tamkin, and I'm still grateful to him.

I was writing with six-line sketches in those days. Now I use ten-line paper, which makes it easier. Sketching is, for all purposes, composing. I'm very possessive about what I write and, having started out as an arranger, to me the orchestra is of primary importance. I have a feeling for the top line of a melody, but I think orchestrally. Some composers have been known to give another composer or an orchestrator only the top melody line and timings and say, "Here, fill this in." I have never used a ghostwriter. I just couldn't do that. I would take my six lines to David Tamkin and we'd have a session. He'd orchestrate it, and then we would take it down to Nick Nuzzi, who ran not only the library but the copying department—one of the best copying departments at that time.

Nick was also our bookie. We would place our bets on the morning line, yet I never saw anybody came to collect the money. Nick would take our book and run our bets, which in my case usually were five dollars. I remember well a horse that ran at Santa Anita. Its name was Existentialist, and the jockey was named Skuse.

I had a Volkswagen at the time and on my way home from the studio at five o'clock, I would tune in to a radio station that ran recreations of the races. Existentialist had been a long shot, about a hundred to one, and on the way home I found out he'd come in. I was excited. Ginny and I certainly could use the money. The next day, I went to the library and said, "Hey Nick, I won."

He said, "Yeah, you won."

I said, "At a hundred to one! Five times one hundred, that's five hundred bucks!"

He said, "No, no, no, there's a limit."

So, Italian or not, he never paid me the five hundred. I got thirty bucks out of it.

By now Ginny and I had left the apartment in Burbank. We lived for a short time in a two-bedroom apartment in Toluca Lake before buying a house on Vantage in North Hollywood, near Laurel Canyon and Burbank Boulevard. It had two bedrooms, a den, a kitchen, and a little service porch. My rented upright piano was in the den, with the bathinette and Chris's playpen. Ginny was always amazed that I could write there, but I'd block everything out and go to work.

Chris still remembers that house, and a picture of five generations of Ginny's family taken at a family reunion. The story ran in the *Los Angeles Times* and showed Chris, Ginny, her mother, her grandmother, and her great-grandmother. Chris remembers being kissed by all those grandmothers.

Ginny and I had decided that we wanted four children, and we wanted to have them close together. It seemed the time to start on the next one was now. During a routine checkup when she was seven months pregnant, Ginny was surprised by her doctor and called me from his office. She said, "Henry, you're not going to believe this, but we're going to have twins." Neither Ginny nor I had a history of twins in our families.

The girls, Monica Jo and Felice Ann, were born at St. Joseph's Hospital in Burbank five minutes apart on May 4, 1952; Monica arrived first. After a difficult pregnancy, Ginny had an easy delivery, but her troubles were just starting. She had three babies in diapers: Chris toddling and getting into everything, and two in their cribs. I helped her as much as I could, dunking diapers in the toilet and that sort of thing, but she had the burden of it.

Ginny said she felt as if she had been turned into a robot that somebody wound up in the morning. Then she would keep running with diapers and bottles until she could collapse in the evening. We decided that three were quite enough.

There was no question of her continuing to work. She gave up singing to raise the children.

Meantime, at Universal they were starting to trust me with more important pictures. Now and then I was getting to write an entire score by myself.

One of the first was a picture called *Man Afraid*, in 1957. Later that year I did a full score on *Damn Citizen*. I received screen credit for both. When several of us worked on a score, Joe Gershenson was given the credit as musical director, which was all right with us. But when Joe assigned us a score for a picture of our own, he would always make sure we got full credit.

We had known for some time that Universal was going to do *The Glenn Miller Story*. Film biographies of musicians had not been successful—and not very good, either. They had a success with *The Eddie Duchin Story*, and there were a few other notable exceptions. And now plans for the Miller picture were moving forward.

Since I knew quite a bit about Miller—though I had met him only once, I had heard a lot about him while I was with the band—I wondered what the writers were going to come up with. I remained skeptical about the picture even after I was assigned to the project. At least it was bigger than one of the routine westerns.

Then I found out Jimmy Stewart was going to play the title role. And he really took to it. He got a Dixieland trombone player named Joe Yukl to coach him on the handling of the trombone. Yukl practically lived with Jimmy. Almost every time I see Jimmy, we talk about it. Jimmy truly conveyed an impression that he played the instrument, down to the smallest details of handling it. He knew that little gesture trombone players make when they blow the spit out of the valve, and how the wrist of the right hand moves on the slide. He even captured that curiously stiff smile Miller had.

There was a great deal of dissension on that picture because Tex Beneke wasn't in it. Glenn's widow, Helen, withdrew the band's library from Tex, in effect firing him from the band, not long after I left. Tex wasn't the only one who had played roles of varying degrees of importance in Miller's life but now was cut out of the story by Helen and Don Haynes. Also left out were Billy May, Ray Eberle, and Marion Hutton—Betty Hutton's sister, who'd sung with the band.

All the band's arrangements were in a warehouse in New Jersey. When they were shipped out to me, I had to make sure everything was there because they had been edited. If nothing else, Miller was a first-class editor. Sometimes you would find cuts marked on the score, in ink. But sometimes the musicians hadn't bothered to write down the changes. So one of the first things I had to do was straighten out all those arrangements.

The writer of the screenplay, Oscar Brodney, and the director, Anthony Mann, asked if I could help them dramatize a sequence illustrating the arranging process. They said, "We want to show in a montage how Miller would write an arrangement." In the movie they had the band failing and

Miller accidentally discovering a new sound when the trumpet player, who is supposed to play lead over the sax section, gets hit in the mouth and has to be replaced by Willie Schwartz on clarinet. In real life, Miller did not come up with that sound so serendipitously. The idea of clarinet lead on a sax section did not, as far as I know, originate with him. But he used it extensively on ballads, making it his trademark. The public did indeed love it—and still does.

I gave Brodney and Mann the sequence they wanted. The camera is in close on Miller's hand writing notes on the score page. You hear the bass walking a four-four beat in ballad tempo. Then that sax section comes in, and you hear "Moonlight Serenade" as the camera pulls back to show the full band performing. It was not all that realistic, but it was very effective on film, one of the high points of the picture.

I used several medleys of Miller's hits for montages. But the further I got into the music, the more I realized that there were places the well-known Miller pieces wouldn't fit, especially scenes between Miller and his wife, who was played by June Allyson. I thought we needed an original love theme, something the public did not know. I went to Joe, who said, "Okay, write something." A lyric was added by Don Raye, and it became "Too Little Time," my first film song.

The picture went very well. Everyone was surprised by its success. So Universal decided to do *The Benny Goodman Story*, with Steve Allen playing Benny. Steve tried to give him some personality, but there was only so much you could do to warm up Benny Goodman.

Unlike Miller, Benny was still alive. His band was reassembled, and they rerecorded all the old hits. I had little to do with him. He didn't remember me from my early attempt to write for his band in New York. A few years later, when I had some hit songs, he began to remember me.

After the Goodman picture, I did a film called *The Voice*

in the Mirror, with Richard Egan. And then in 1958, I was assigned to *Touch of Evil*, which Orson Welles was going to direct.

Welles obviously needed the money; he was always running short. He assembled a good cast, including members of his stock company from his Mercury Theater days as well as Akim Tamiroff and Marlene Dietrich. Russ Metty was the cinematographer, and he gave the picture an effective, brooding look. It was an incongruity to have Orson Welles on the same lot that gave you Bonzo, Francis the Mule, Ma and Pa Kettle, countless horrible horse operas, and all those awful Creature pictures that Herman Stein and I scored. I didn't know what he was doing there. But he knew.

As he was shooting the picture, he wrote a letter to Joe Gershenson that I wish I'd kept. It was a three-page description of the music as he would like to have it.

I had studied the script and by now was seeing rushes of the picture, so I read the letter with great interest. Welles's description of the music as he wanted it was exactly what I was already planning to do. He wanted no scoring as such— that is to say, underscore, the disembodied music that comes from nowhere behind a scene to enhance or establish mood. All the music had to be what we call source cues. All art is based on convention. In real life people do not stop in the middle of a sentence and express their deepest emotions by singing, yet we accept such behavior in our Broadway musicals and opera. We all know that in real life when boy meets girl, an invisible string section does not begin to play softly from the sky. Yet we accept this convention on the stage, as in the case of Bizet's incidental music for *L'Arlé-sienne*, and in our movies. Generally speaking, underscoring in film serves to accentuate or bring out emotions in a scene. But by an unspoken convention we accept without thinking about it that the characters in the movie cannot hear this music that is bringing us to tears, or pulling us to the edge of the seat with suspense. Source music, on the other hand, is actually part of the story, music the characters can hear if they want to pay attention to it.

Orson Welles had a perception of everything in the film, including the music. He knew. He truly understood film scoring. And since he was making a grimly realistic film, I think he reasoned that even the music had to be rooted in reality. And that meant it all had to come from the story itself; it would have to be source cues.

There would be a lot of music in the picture, most of it with a big band Latin sound in a Stan Kenton vein. Realizing that the score would exceed the resources of our staff orchestra, I took the matter up with Joe. I said, "If we're going to do this right, we're going to have to go outside and hire a whole band. We just can't get the right sound with our people." Joe gave approval, and I hired Shelly Manne on drums, Jack Costanza on bongos, and a big brass section, including Conrad Gozzo, my old roommate with Tex. It was a tremendous band.

I went down on the set to observe the shooting, which I don't usually do. Watching a movie being made is unbelievably boring. It has been compared to watching paint dry. Since movies are rarely shot in chronological sequence, you get no sense of the story on a set, no sense of forward motion. The actors do the same lines over and over until they and the director are satisfied with the readings. Then the camera angle is changed, which usually takes some time, during which the actors and other crew members talk about the weather, their golf scores, their problems with their kids, or they read the racing form. Then they do the same scene again, and possibly even a third and fourth time. This is to give the director and film editor the various angles of the scene they need later for intercutting. It's interminable, it's mind-numbing, and I try to have as little as possible to do with it.

I was waiting for the film and its timings. But, because of his extensive knowledge of every aspect of his profession,

Welles was very interesting, so I hung around as unobtru-
sively as possible, and he never even noticed I was there.
The exteriors were shot near the ocean at Venice, California,
the interiors on a soundstage at Universal.

At last the film was nearing completion, and as it came
time to score, I told Joe we should have a meeting with
Welles so that we'd all know what we were doing, particularly in view of his strong feelings about the music.

It was a rainy Saturday morning, I remember. Welles
swept into Joe's office in a cape and a dark hat and with a big
cigar, one of those Monte Cristo giants. It seemed as if
doom, the wrath of hell, was invading the music department.

Al Zugsmith was the producer of that picture. I think Al
was a producer by virtue of owning stock in Decca, which
owned Universal. He was a Hollywood guy, streetwise, slick,
and shrewd. I could not imagine a producer as incompatible
with Orson Welles as Al Zugsmith, and they had a standoff-
ish relationship throughout the whole picture.

At last we were all together in Joe Gershenson's office. It
went well enough. Joe introduced me to Welles. Al Zugsmith was sitting on a couch. Welles started to cruise the
room, saying, "Here we'll do this and here we'll do that."

Then Zugsmith made some point that wasn't exactly to
Welles's liking. I can't remember what it was, but I certainly
remember Welles's reaction to it. He let it go by for a couple
of minutes. But he walked a little faster as he talked, obviously getting his offensive up. He continued walking,
faster and faster, getting angrier and angrier, and directing
the stream of his fury at Al Zugsmith.

I was sitting there taking it all in. By now I was used to
movie people, but this, after all, was Orson Welles, and I
was working on his picture. At the height of his rage—he
had just met me a half hour ago—he snapped around,
looked at me, pointed a long finger at me, and said from a
great height, "Who's he?"

That was my only encounter and my only conversation, if you want to call it that, with Orson Welles. After that meeting, I never saw him again.

Possibly the composer in film history most admired by film composers themselves was Hugo Friedhofer, who began scoring pictures almost when talkies were first introduced. I once wrote that a single nod from that man was worth more than all the baubles the industry could bestow. For all the Oscars and Grammys I have been awarded, perhaps nothing has pleased me more than being told by a mutual friend that Hugo respected my music.

Hugo once said, "I've known two geniuses in this industry, Orson Welles and Marlon Brando, and the industry, not knowing what to do with genius, destroys it." Hugo scored the one film Brando directed, *One-Eyed Jacks*. He said that the long version of the film as Brando made it was the "damnedest, differentest western I ever saw." But the studio executives chopped it down in size, removing the opening sequence that established the motive for the later events and even changing the final scenes to give it a happy ending. They took music Hugo had designed for one scene and moved it to another. The film was butchered.

A similar fate befell *Touch of Evil*, which nonetheless withstood the assault.

I don't think Welles ever heard the music I wrote. He didn't stick around for the recording sessions, and I have been told that he refused even to look at the picture because of his anger at what the studio had done to it. He made his final edit, what is called the director's cut, which he had the right to do, and that was it. His job was done, and he was long gone. The powers that be got their hands on the picture, and they cut it up and cut it down, taking some great stuff out of it. Some of it has been restored now and, like *One-Eyed Jacks*, it has become a bit of a cult picture. But the public has never seen the powerful movie that I saw when I scored it. It was a pity, but a pity all too common in Hollywood.

Touch of Evil was previewed at a theater on Sunset Boulevard in Pacific Palisades. It was pretty rough at that time, still fairly close to Welles's cut. It was gritty. It had a course texture, a brooding sense of violence, and a drug scene, almost unheard of in those days.

Joe Gershenson told me the next day that he and Zugsmith and some of the others were having a meeting on the sidewalk when an old lady came up to them and said, "Are you gentlemen the producers of the picture?" Joe said she must have been about seventy years old, wearing a cloth coat and carrying a handbag. They said that they were indeed the producers, expecting a compliment, and all of a sudden she started flailing them with her bag and denouncing them for this work of the devil.

Touch of Evil was one of the best things I did in that period of my life. It's one of the best things I've ever done.

And it was one of the last scores I wrote on staff at Universal.

8
Peter Gunn

The days of the music department at Universal were almost over; indeed the days of Universal itself, as an old-line movie studio, were about finished. Unlike those at Warner Bros., who were deeply involved in television, the executives at Universal lacked foresight. Theaters around the country were closing as more and more television sets went into American homes. By order of the Supreme Court, the studios were no longer allowed to own theaters and had been stripped of guaranteed distribution for their pictures. Staff musicians earned an average of $300 or $400 a week, a lot of money at that time, which made the big studio orchestras difficult to justify and sustain. One by one they were dismissed. Finally, Universal was up for sale, and MCA bought it in 1957 and in time turned it into the biggest television factory in the world. MCA acquired it for a ridiculously low figure, something like $11 million, for its entire catalog of films, its physical plant, and all that back-lot real estate.

The whole studio system, and with it the star system, was coming to an end. The new films were being made by independents. The ax fell, as we knew it would. When the Universal orchestra's contract expired, it was not renewed. Along with Herman Stein, David Tamkin, Frank Skinner, Nick Nuzzi, and the copyists, I was given my notice. Our friendly little family of musicians was broken up.

At the time, I was working on a picture with Jimmy Cagney, *Never Steal Anything Small*, the last film I did there. I was making $350 a week and, with three children to care for and mortgage payments, we counted on it. When I told Ginny I'd lost my job, she was concerned. In later years she has said that the experience taught her never to fear the future. "One door closes, another opens," she says.

I had worked with Blake Edwards on three pictures. One was *This Happy Feeling*, with Debbie Reynolds. Another was *Mister Cory*, with Tony Curtis; it was about a professional gambler and had rumblings of what was to become the TV series "Mr. Lucky." Blake had written the screenplay. I didn't write the score for that picture, but as often happened when they needed music in a pop vein, I had been brought in for some source cues. The third picture I worked on with him was *The Perfect Furlough*, with Tony Curtis and Janet Leigh.

Blake began visiting movie sets as a little boy. His stepfather, Jack McEdward, was a motion-picture production manager, and Blake's father, J. Gordon Edwards, was a silent-film director. Blake started in radio, creating the "Richard Diamond, Private Detective" series as a vehicle for Dick Powell and writing some scripts for it. He also wrote for "The Line-Up" and "Yours Truly, Johnny Dollar." Dick Powell, who by then, along with others, had founded Four Star Productions, helped Blake break into television as a director.

Blake had even done a little acting. There was no aspect of the industry and its crafts he didn't understand, and if Universal was unaware of the impending impact of television, Blake had no such lack of vision. He even foresaw how well detective shows would do in the new medium.

Most of us ate lunch on the lot, because the commissary was so good; the chefs were excellent. The barbershop and a little candy shop were in a building near the commissary. Both buildings are gone. The Black Tower, as they call it—

the big glass MCA-Universal office building—stands there now.

Though I was out of a job, I still had my pass to the studio. I went in one day not to work but to get a haircut and have lunch. After getting the haircut, I went out into the sunlight and encountered Blake, Don Sharpe, who had been the producer of "I Love Lucy," and some other men. They had just ended a meeting at which they'd been planning a thirty-minute television show.

Blake and I are contemporaries; he was then thirty-eight and I was thirty-six. He saw me as one of the younger people, and he was looking for something new for television. It's possible that he would have called on me anyway, but I don't think so. I believe he did what he did that morning purely on impulse, and I have often wondered what would have happened to me if I hadn't needed a haircut.

I said, "Hello, Blake."

He said, "Hello, Hank. How's Ginny?" He'd known her since the days of the Mel-Tones, when he was part of that young Hollywood group. I told him she was well, and he asked me to send his regards.

Blake is about five foot ten. Some Indian blood is apparent in his chiseled features, with strong cheekbones and jawline. He watches his weight, and he has always been lean. He has a back problem and is sometimes in great pain. He is deliberate in his movements and always very direct, not circumspect, always knowing where he is going. He wore his hair on the short side in those days. He has a bizarre sense of black humor. I think because of it his wife, Julie Andrews, calls him Blackie. That style of humor is prevalent in his pictures.

We stood there chatting for a few minutes, then Blake said, "Hey, would you be interested in doing a TV show for me?"

Not exactly overwhelmed with offers, I said, "Yes. What's the name of it?"

He said, "It's called 'Peter Gunn.'"

I asked, "What is it, a western?"

He laughed and said, "You'll see." We made an appointment.

Blake had set up a production company, Spartan Productions, in partnership with Don Sharpe. Don was a golden boy in those days, a master. If he wanted to do something, he got at least to make a pilot. In those days, you didn't have to audition if you had a sponsor. And he already had a sponsor for "Peter Gunn," Procter & Gamble. He had a commitment from them, their ad agency, and NBC for thirteen weeks; as it turned out, we did thirty-three episodes that first year.

Blake had cast Lola Albright for the role of Edie, Peter Gunn's girlfriend. Edie was to be a singer. Blake asked me to go over to Lola's house and set up a song for the pilot. We decided on the Rube Bloom–Johnny Mercer song "Day In—Day Out." She sang nicely, with a beat and good pitch. In the story, the girl was supposed to be a jazz singer, with a soft approach to a song. A belter would have been inappropriate to the part; Lola was perfect. We recorded her doing that song before shooting started.

One of Blake's great assets is his sense of the visual, including such details as how people should look in a part. Blake had picked Craig Stevens for the role of Peter Gunn, but he wasn't satisfied with the way he looked. Craig had a very full head of hair, but Blake had him get the short, neat haircut that became such a part of the character—and part of Craig, who still wears his hair that way. Blake perceived the character of Peter Gunn as being very different from the old style of movie private eye—the Sam Spade or Philip Marlowe type, the ruffled figure with the beat-up fedora. Peter Gunn was always well dressed; you almost never saw him without a jacket and tie.

I remember how Blake used that in one episode. Gunn gets waylaid by a street gang, falls down, and gets mud on his jacket. It struck me forcibly, and if it did that to me, it was certainly going to hit the public. It was the only time Peter Gunn was ever mussed.

Blake and I immediately established a comfortable working relationship, yet we rarely had meetings, even then. In our thirty years together I can remember few actual meetings, and usually they had to do with concepts of songs, planned in advance, as for *Victor/Victoria* and *Darling Lili*. In the pictures I scored for Blake, I would always let him hear the theme, and from then until the recording dates he always left the music entirely to me.

The idea of using jazz in the "Gunn" score was never even discussed. It was implicit in the story. Peter Gunn hangs out in a jazz roadhouse called Mother's—the name was Blake's way of tweaking the noses of the censors— where there is a five-piece jazz group. In the pilot, five or six minutes took place in Mother's. That's a long time, so it was obvious that jazz had to be used.

It was the time of so-called cool West Coast jazz, with Shelly Manne, the Candoli brothers, and Shorty Rogers, among others. And that was the sound that came to me, the walking bass and drums. The "Peter Gunn" title theme actually derives more from rock and roll than from jazz. I used guitar and piano in unison, playing what is known in music as an *ostinato*, which means obstinate. It was sustained throughout the piece, giving it a sinister effect, with some frightened saxophone sounds and some shouting brass.

The piece has one chord throughout and a super-simple top line. It has been played through the years by school marching bands as well as rock bands throughout the world. The synth group The Art of Noise had a major hit with it in 1987. Never has so much been made of so little.

The music budget for each segment of "Peter Gunn" was $2,000. That was for me, copying, and musicians. Musically in situations like that you fall back on your string section. I didn't have any money to buy a string section, so I was happy that a small jazz group could be used. The original orchestra was four woodwinds, four trombones, one trumpet, and five rhythm. At the same time, so small a band made me find different ways of producing tension and suspense.

That's when I started using bass flutes. The instrument was virtually unused at the time, and still isn't used much. The reason is simple: it has little power and doesn't project. You can use it only with microphones; it's impractical for a symphony orchestra. The first time I recall hearing a bass flute in film was in Alex North's score for *Death of a Salesman*. I knew what the sound was, and as a flute player I'd seen a few of the instruments. A man in Los Angeles named Ogilvie made bass flutes. Harry Klee, one of my fine flute players, owned one. Some of the other players acquired them, and I used three at first in the "Peter Gunn" music and four when another one became available. It was probably the first time a section of bass flutes had ever been used. I used them for a dark effect, sometimes writing a fall—a descending figure—at the end of a note, which gave a kind of paranoid effect. That sound, along with the walking bass, became one of the trademarks of the "Peter Gunn" music. Another was the use of free improvisation under dramatic scenes.

Several of the musicians I used had been with me with Tex Beneke, including Rolly Bundock, bass; Jack Sperling, drums; Jimmy Priddy, trombone; and Pete Candoli, trumpet. My favorite trombonist, Dick Nash, joined the band. We used to record once a week, on Wednesday nights. Later, when Rolly and Jack went to work on staff on "The Tonight Show," I replaced them with Shelly Manne on drums and Red Mitchell on bass. John Williams played piano the first year. When he left to pursue a brilliant career as a film composer and conductor, he was replaced by Jimmy Rowles.

It was unusual enough for movie-score albums to be

released. Certainly no one thought of putting the music of a dramatic television show out on record. And "Peter Gunn" hadn't even gone on the air yet. When the pilot was completed, Blake took it to NBC. One of the people who heard it there was Alan Livingston, who had a background in the record business. He called Si Rady at RCA Records and told him he thought the company should consider releasing the score on record. By now we were in production, and we had a lot more music. Si Rady pointed out to me that Shorty Rogers, who was under contract to RCA, had a guaranteed sale of eighty thousand albums, which was big for jazz. If Shorty would record the music, Si said, we might have that kind of sale. I was pleased by the idea, and Si said he'd set up a meeting with Shorty.

Blake was friendly with Ray Anthony, who had just had a hit with the "Dragnet" theme. In keeping with record-company mentality, it seemed logical to the people at Capitol that Ray should do the next detective-show theme that came along, and the "Gunn" theme was taken to him. He liked it. I asked Ray if he wanted me to do an arrangement on it for him, which I did. He had a big hit on that one too.

I had lunch with Shorty, a small, compact man with dark hair and a trim vandyked beard. He is a genuinely sweet man, very pure—pure of body, of heart, and of mind. He had seen the pilot. And immediately he said to me, "Hank, I have no reason to record this. It has no connection with me. *You* wrote it, *you* arranged it, and *you* should record it. This music is *yours*."

I said, "But, Shorty, I'm not a recording artist. I'm just a film writer, nobody knows who I am. You have a name." But he was adamant, and at the end of lunch he repeated, "It's your baby, and you should do it."

So Shorty Rogers became another of the people who represented a turning point in my life. I don't know what would have happened to my career if Shorty had decided that day to make the record.

RCA finally chose to record the "Gunn" music under my

name, though not with what I would describe as burning enthusiasm. The best I can say for their attitude toward the project is that it was perfunctory. They did two things, the first of which no record man in his right mind would ever do. They signed me for one album only, with no options. The second tip-off to their attitude was the number of pressings. Furthermore, they didn't put out a single until long after Ray Anthony had the hit on the main theme.

"Peter Gunn" went on the air in September 1958. RCA had pressed only eight thousand copies of the album and had printed only eight thousand covers. When you had a hot record, the pressing plant could gear up to turn them out immediately. The problem was the covers—they took longer. And suddenly all hell broke loose. Within a week they had sold those eight thousand albums. RCA used to have stock covers, with abstract designs on the front, that could go on any record. And so the second pressing of *The Music from "Peter Gunn"* came out in those stock covers. They were running around like madmen at RCA, trying to keep up with the demand.

The album promptly became number 1 on the *Billboard* chart and held that position for ten weeks. And even when it dropped back a bit, it stayed on the charts for a total of 117 weeks, more than two years. In all, it sold more than a million copies, which was unprecedented for a jazz album. Since it was released under my name instead of Shorty Rogers's, suddenly out of nowhere, I was a successful recording artist. Almost overnight *"Peter Gunn"* put me in the public eye.

We were living in Northridge when the *"Peter Gunn"* album hit. It was a neighborhood where the kids could play on the street and ride their bikes. They all knew each other. "Peter Gunn" aired on Monday evenings, and since it was not a particularly violent show, some kids were allowed to watch it. Many of them in our neighborhood knew the music.

I had several cartons of the albums lying around the house. Aside from an initial few, record companies do not give you copies of your albums. I'd bought these from RCA, probably for something like a dollar each. One day I happened to look out the window and saw our twins, Monica and Felice, not yet eight, doing business on the curb, selling the albums to their little neighborhood friends for a quarter apiece.

Because RCA didn't have a contract with me, I was able to negotiate very good terms on a three-year contract. We went back into the studio and recorded *More Music from "Peter Gunn."*

The television show was itself a huge hit, and I could see at least a couple of years' work ahead of me. Things were swinging. Blake was preparing to move from television into movies. He was already talking of doing *Breakfast at Tiffany's* and told me he wanted me for the score. I was getting other film offers, and my price was going up. Still, all these things were futures; I couldn't be sure about them.

Ginny and I had often talked about taking a trip to Europe. About the time I started working on "Peter Gunn," she said, "I don't want to talk about 'some day' any more. I want to book it, now. Even if we have to book it a long way in advance. I think you're going to get very busy, and we may not have a chance to go later." So we booked the trip, a year in advance. We saved our money carefully and managed to build up our bank account to about $6,000. We planned to blow it all, going first class all the way. We flew to New York and went over on one of the last crossings of the *Liberté*.

We docked at Southampton and went from there to London, which Ginny had loved since the time she had worked there with Betty Hutton at the Palladium. From there we flew to Paris. We traveled for about six weeks through France, Switzerland, Italy, Spain, Denmark, and Sweden.

It was during that trip that I had the first notion of what

the recording artist VIP treatment was like. When we left, the album was number 1 on all the charts. It was out in all the countries we visited and a big success everywhere, and it had achieved this on its own; the show had not yet been seen on European television. So in every city, Ginny and I were met by RCA people. They didn't really know who I was, but they knew something was happening, and we were treated graciously. We went to Rome, where we stayed in a hotel we loved, and then spent a week at the Carlton Hotel in Cannes, where we had—in spite of the week in Las Vegas when we were married—what seemed like our real honeymoon. From there we went to Spain, and then Scandinavia, and flew back on SAS.

When we got home, our bank account contained less than $5.

By then Ginny was very involved with charity work for SHARE, which stands for Share Happily and Reap Endlessly. They were preparing to do a benefit. I was at home one day while she was rehearsing at the Coconut Grove. When the mail arrived, I began to open it, worried as usual about bills and money. I suppose my eyes went wide. I drove immediately to the Coconut Grove to show this thing to her. She tells me she can still see it in her mind.

It was the first royalty check on the *"Peter Gunn"* album—$32,000.

I was pleased to learn that I had been nominated for an Emmy for my work on the "Peter Gunn" show. Among other nominees, I was up against a terrific musical show, the first Fred Astaire special, which was directed by my close friend Bud Yorkin. I had high hopes, but I lost. The winner was David Rose.

Soon after that, I learned that I had been nominated for four Grammys for *The Music from "Peter Gunn,"* including Album of the Year. This was to be the first year of awards presented by the National Academy of Recording Arts and

Sciences (NARAS). The record business had long been a pillar of the American entertainment industry, and many people felt that recognition should be given to worthy artists.

NARAS evolved from an initial meeting of five distinguished recording executives—Paul Weston, Lloyd Dunn, Sunny Burke, Jesse Kaye, and Dennis Farnon. Through their efforts many other people became involved, and the Academy was born in 1957, with Paul Weston as its first president.

That first year the award ceremony was a far cry from the star-filled media event that it has become. There was a dinner at the Beverly Hilton Hotel, akin to a large family gathering. The spirits were high and the atmosphere warm.

I don't think any of us knew what a Grammy looked like, nor could we have guessed what it would come to mean. Ginny and I were having dessert when I heard my name called. It was as winner for Best Arrangement—*The Music from "Peter Gunn."* I accepted. As we were having coffee I heard my name again, this time announced by Peggy Lee. It was for *The Music from "Peter Gunn,"* Album of the Year. And it had won against impressive competition: Ella Fitzgerald's *The Irving Berlin Songbook*, Frank Sinatra's *Come Fly with Me*, Frank Sinatra's *Only the Lonely*, and Van Cliburn's *Piano Concerto in B-flat Minor, Op. 23, by Tchaikovsky*. Call me Mr. Lucky.

NARAS has undergone many changes since that time—sometimes slowly but always with the interests of the membership in mind. Given the many facets of the record industry, NARAS must be complimented on its efforts to keep pace with the changes.

9
Moon River

While doing "Gunn" that season of 1958–59, I had also written the score for *The Great Impostor*, a rather good film with Tony Curtis, directed by Robert Mulligan. Blake had asked me to do *Operation Petticoat*, which starred Cary Grant, but I was just too busy, so our friend David Rose wrote that score. Then Blake directed a picture at Fox called *High Time*, with Bing Crosby. I agreed to do that score and met Bing for the first time.

I had heard that he was very cool and aloof. Johnny Mercer used to talk about looking into Bing's cool blue eyes. But all my dealings with him were cordial.

I was interested in him for a reason other than music. I had never smoked cigarettes, but now I had begun to smoke a pipe. Bing was a pipe smoker. Wherever he went he had a pipe in his mouth, a great pipe with the thinnest stem I'd ever seen. Finally I said, "Bing, that's a very unusual pipe."

He said, "Yeah, Hank, it's called a Merchant's Service pipe. I got it in London. I love it because it's so light that I don't have to take it out of my mouth when I'm making a golf swing."

He gave me one just like it. He also gave me the address of the shop where he'd bought it, and when I went to London I searched up and down little streets and finally found the place. I bought those thin-stemmed pipes by the dozen and gave them to people. Everyone asked about mine, and once at a party the great cellist Gregor Piatagorsky saw it and became intrigued by it. (Those were the days when you could smoke anywhere.) Piatagorsky was an avid pipe smoker, so I sent him one of the pipes.

The pipe became a little crutch for me. When I sat down to work in the morning, I'd light it; something seemed to happen and I'd start writing. I smoked a pipe for a long time and finally quit a couple of years ago.

Meanwhile, I was continuing to record, and for that reason people began to submit songs to me. *High Time* contained a very good song by Sammy Cahn and Jimmy Van Heusen called "The Second Time Around." I was the first to record it. It was nominated for the Academy Award that year.

Blake moved the production of "Peter Gunn" over to MGM. There was a lot of office and studio space available for rent in those days, because of the cutback in film production. As soon as Ginny and I got back from the trip, Blake told me he had acquired the rights to the *Mr. Lucky* title. It had been a movie with Cary Grant which, like *Mister Cory*, was about a gambler. Blake went into production that summer, with John Vivyan in the title role and Ross Martin and Pippa Scott in the key supporting roles.

Now I was working simultaneously on two half-hour shows a week, "Gunn" and "Lucky." On Tuesdays I would look at the next "Peter Gunn" episode in the schedule; that night I would go in to MGM and record the score for the episode before it. On Wednesday I would go in and watch the next "Mr. Lucky," and that night I would record the music for the current episode.

Each show had roughly fifteen minutes of music. I would write the music for both shows between Thursday and Sunday. Jimmy Priddy, whom I had first known when he was in the trombone section of Tex's band and who was a regular member of that little "Peter Gunn" band, was also my copyist, and he would be standing by. I'd turn out my pages and give them to him, and he'd get the music ready to record. Jimmy is still my copyist.

The music for "Mr. Lucky" was designed to have a sound as different from that of "Peter Gunn" as possible. I thought that a string section would immediately take it out of that territory, but strings were hardly unusual in film and television. I needed something else. I'd heard Wild Bill Davis play the Hammond organ. His playing was concise, swinging, and energetic. Another keyboard player, Buddy Cole, was also an expert organist, with a distinctive sound. So I wrote the theme for strings and assigned the punctuations normally given the brass to the Hammond organ, with Buddy playing the part. In the second chorus I had him take a solo on the melody. It was very unusual. We did an album of the show's music, *Music from "Mr. Lucky,"* from which the single went to the Top Ten on the charts. This album too was very successful.

Some time later we did a followup, *Mr. Lucky Goes Latin.* Buddy felt that I had stolen his sound and refused to play on the second album.

"Mr. Lucky," a very stylish story about a suave, hip guy who runs a gambling boat somewhere off the California coast, was an immediate success. But it went on the air shortly after the TV quiz show scandals, started by "The $64,000 Question" and the revelation that its champion contestant, Charles Van Doren, had been given the answers to tough questions in advance. That and other scandals had cast a pall over the industry, and the network executives were frightened of any hint of moral criticism. "Mr. Lucky" became the target, particularly in the South, of that element in the American population that later became known as the moral majority. They took umbrage that the character ran a gambling boat, and around the fourth or fifth show Blake began to get pressure from CBS. The sponsor didn't seem to be concerned, but CBS insisted that Blake change Mr. Lucky's character from that of gambler to restaurateur and turn the ship into a restaurant. Blake fought, telling CBS, "You'll take the balls out of the whole story."

In the end he went along with them, and the minute Mr. Lucky lost his gambling boat, the show's ratings took a nosedive. No longer excellent, they remained good enough to keep the show on the air, but Blake was unhappy. At the end of the year, he said, "I'm not going to lend my name to this," and closed the show down.

In any event, his television days were over because his film career was taking off. He had been very involved in both programs, in the writing and casting and selection of directors; he directed a few of the "Gunn" episodes himself. He gave Boris Sagal his first job as a director. One of Lamont Johnson's first jobs was on "Gunn." Gene Reynolds, who went to "M★A★S★H," and George Stevens, Jr., directed episodes of that show. Blake was bringing in new young people, and the casting on it was excellent—Blake has a marvelous eye for casting, and throughout the industry are character actors who started in "Peter Gunn."

About the time I was doing the score for *High Time*, Blake said, "The next one is at Paramount. We're going ahead on *Breakfast at Tiffany's*. I'd like you to come over and do it." Blake was to direct it; Dick Shepherd and Marty Jurow were the producers, and the screenplay, based on the Truman Capote novella, was by George Axelrod. They had considered a number of actresses for the role of Holly Golightly and finally chose Audrey Hepburn. It was the first time I'd met her.

I went over to Paramount for a meeting with Blake and the producers. Dick and Marty felt that because the story had a New York location they should hire a Broadway composer to write the song that the script called for—a scene where Holly Golightly goes out on the fire escape with her guitar and sings. I would do the score, with someone else doing the song. This was not unusual—we'd used a Cahn–Van Heusen song in *High Time*—but this time

I felt differently about it, and I was not happy when I left that meeting.

My agent at MCA, Henry Alper, said, "You have a hell of a picture here with a great director and a great star—don't rock the boat. Let someone else do the song; you do the score."

But the albums *"Peter Gunn"* and *"Mr. Lucky"* were nothing if not a series of songs without words, and I knew I could write a tune. So I said to Blake, "Give me a shot. Let me at least try something from that scene." Blake took it up with Dick and Marty, who relented and agreed to let me try it.

No decision had been made on who would sing the song. Audrey was not known as a singer. There was a question of whether she could handle it. Then, by chance, I was watching television one night when the movie *Funny Face* came on, with Fred Astaire and Audrey. It contains a scene in which Audrey sings "How Long Has This Been Going On?" I thought, You can't buy that kind of thing, that kind of simplicity. I went to the piano and played the song. It had a range of an octave and one, so I knew she could sing that. I now felt strongly that she should be the one to sing the new song in our picture—the song I hadn't written yet.

That song was one of the toughest I have ever had to write. It took me a month to think it through. What kind of song would this girl sing? What kind of melody was required? Should it be a jazz-flavored ballad? Would it be a blues? One night at home, I was relaxing after dinner. I went out to my studio off the garage, sat down at the piano (still rented), and all of a sudden I played the first three notes of a tune. It sounded attractive. I built the melody in a range of an octave and one. It was simple and completely diatonic: in the key of C, you can play it entirely on the white keys. It came quickly. It had taken me one month and half an hour to write that melody.

I took it in and played it for Blake, who loved it. He

asked, "Who would you like to do the lyrics?"

I went for the best. I knew Johnny Mercer, who was in the habit of writing lyrics for melodies he just happened to hear and like. He would hear some music on his car radio and call the station to ask what it was; that was another of his habits. He heard "Joanna," from the second *"Peter Gunn"* album, and wrote a lyric for it. Nothing came of it, but that was the start of my professional relationship with Johnny. We wanted to write together.

So I called him.

This was the low point of Johnny's artistic life. Illiterate songs were high on the charts, and doo-wop groups were thriving. Johnny came to see me. He talked about the condition of the music business. We were almost ten years into the rock era, and he didn't have much hope for his kind of lyric or my kind of music. After I played him the melody, he asked, "Hank, who's going to record a waltz? We'll do it for the movie, but after that it hasn't any future commercially." I gave him a tape of the melody and he went home.

Had Johnny been a military man he would have been another Patton. He used to attack a song three ways. He could hear a melody and see different angles from which to approach it and then write three different lyrics, each one valid, each one fully worked out, and each one different from the others.

Once Blake and the producers decided they loved the melody, they left it to John and me to decide what the lyric should be—another example of the trust Blake put in me. John called me one morning and said he had three lyrics to show me.

That evening I was conducting the orchestra for a benefit dinner at the Beverly Wilshire Hotel. The rehearsal call was for four o'clock. I told John, "Meet me in the ballroom of the Beverly Wilshire around noon."

I waited in the ballroom, which was deserted and dark but for a couple of bare-bulb work lights. John came in with an envelope full of papers. I sat down at the piano and started to play. The first lyric he sang was a personal one about the girl, with the opening notes covered by the words "I'm Holly." John said, "I don't know about that one."

Then he showed me another, quite different, and finally a third one. He said, "I'm calling this one 'Blue River.' But it may change, because I went through the ASCAP archives and found that several of my friends have already written songs called 'Blue River.'" There was nothing to prevent John's using it: legally, you cannot copyright a title. But John was reluctant to use "Blue River." His kind of honesty has not caught on with many of the young songwriters today.

John said, "I have an optional title. 'Moon River.'"

I said, "You know, John, there used to be a radio show coming out of Cincinnati that had that title."

"It wasn't a song, was it?"

"No, it was just a late-night show where a guy would talk in a deep voice about various things."

"Okay," he said.

Sitting there on the bandstand in that deserted ballroom, I started to play the melody again, and he sang the third lyric. Every once in a while you hear something so right that it gives you chills, and when he sang that "huckleberry friend" line, I got them. I don't know whether he knew what effect those words had or if it was just something that came to him, but it was thrilling. It made you think of Mark Twain and Huckleberry Finn's trip down the Mississippi. It had such echoes of America. It was one of those remarkable lines that gives you a rush. It was the clincher.

A day or two later we played it for Blake, then for Dick Shepherd and Marty Jurow. Everybody loved the song. And everybody was convinced that Audrey should do it. I taught it to her, and we prerecorded.

There have been more than one thousand recordings of "Moon River." Of all of them—and I am not overlooking the recordings by many of my singer friends—Audrey's performance was the definitive version.

But I made a mistake with it.

The quality of sound recording in movie and television scoring was poor. The control board at Universal, where we did *"Gunn,"* was ancient. Although they had good mikes, the technique of placement was primitive—one mike for the whole rhythm section, for example. Sound was never given priority, and the equipment was falling further and further behind. The recording studios around town were always ahead of the movie studios in equipment and technique. While film and television scores were still being recorded in mono, stereo, which for years had been in the experimental stage, was coming into the general marketplace. And one of the reasons I had re-recorded *"Gunn"* was the demand for stereo. *The Music from "Peter Gunn"* was one of the first of the stereo albums, which may have contributed to its success. After that I continued re-recording my scores in stereo for album release.

That started me on a method of operation. I re-recorded *Mr. Lucky* and then the *Breakfast at Tiffany's* music. When it seemed appropriate, I rewrote some of the cues so that they would be complete tracks in the albums rather than tailing off into silence.

One of my bigger goofs was having a chorus, not Audrey, sing that song in the album version of the score.

A problem arose from the re-recording of those scores. The albums were made up of the most melodic material from the films. A lot of the dramatic music—which is what I really loved to do and really thought I had a feeling for—was left out. *Days of Wine and Roses* and *Charade* had a lot of dramatic music that was never released on record. For the albums, I used the source music that was the common denominator for my record-buying audience. And there was pressure from the record company: they didn't want to know about dramatic music. It may have hurt my reputation as a writer of serious film music. To this day, I would love to have an album of some of those scores as they were heard in the film. The albums gave me a reputation, even among producers, as a writer of light comedy and light suspense, and at that time it was not easy for them to think of me for the more dramatic assignments. I did that to myself.

We recorded the song and scored the picture. Everyone was very high on it. Audrey, Mel Ferrer—who was then Audrey's husband—Blake, Ginny, Marty Rackin, who was head of Paramount, Dick Shepherd, Marty Jurow, and I went up to a preview near Stanford. The limousines took us back to our hotel in San Francisco, where Marty Rackin had a suite. The preview had gone very well. We continued to be excited about the song, no one more so than Blake, and we were elated about the picture as a whole, although we realized it was running long and would have to be cut. As is usual in those situations, everybody has different ideas about what should and should not go. It is a subjective process, with everyone trying to protect his or her own interests and involvement in the picture. We were all sitting around, nobody saying anything. Marty Rackin had his arm on the mantelpiece of the fireplace. He was very New York and personable, a tall, trim, and lovely man in his forties, with fine features.

The first thing Marty said was, "Well, the fucking song has to go."

I looked over at Blake. I saw his face. The blood was rising to the top of his head, like that thermometer when I put a match under it. He looked like he was going to burst. Audrey moved in her chair as if she were going to get up and say something. They made a slight move toward Marty, as if they were thinking about lynching him.

The song stayed in the picture.

But I still wish I'd had Audrey sing it on the album.

After "Mr. Lucky" was canceled, I kept remembering one of the main props of the show. The big gambling ship in the story was anchored out to sea, and a big launch was used to shuttle the clientele. Episode after episode, I watched it cutting through the water. I inquired about the boat and was told it was in a slip at San Pedro, the Los Angeles harbor. What was going to happen to it? I was told it would be sold.

I made a deal and got it at a very good price.

I renamed it the *Gunn Boat* and kept it down at Newport Beach. On weekends I would take Ginny and the kids down there and take the *Gunn Boat* out for a run. We still did not have the freeways, which meant we had to drive all the way through the communities of Los Angeles County to get there.

I mentioned earlier that David Rose collected steam engines, including trains and boats. He kept his boats near mine at Newport Beach, a very wealthy and snobbish area, its marina populated by sail purists. David's boats didn't run on gasoline or diesel fuel; they ran on steam, generated by coal. The sailors down there liked David personally—it would be impossible not to like David—but they hated his boats.

On the weekends, Ginny, the kids, and I enjoyed going out for a cruise. I would get up on my flying bridge with my sailor's cap on and have a wonderful time. Usually, toward the end of the trip, we would put the drinking flag up and have one of our afternoon toddies. One Sunday I was sitting there luxuriating in the sea air, my foot up on the flying bridge, leaning back with a drink in one hand and guiding the boat with the other, when I saw smoke coming toward us. It was David, chugging along in one of his steamboats, the black smoke pouring out of it. It reminded me of Little Toot in the cartoons. He drew nearer, and I could see him, his wife, Betty, and their kids. Then I saw that he too had a drink in his hand.

As his boat passed mine, he raised his drink in a kind of salute and called out, "Aren't you glad you practiced, Hank?"

10
Days of Wine and Roses

N o matter how blasé anyone pretends to be about the
Academy Awards, there is a rush when you are nominated. My first nomination had come in 1954, when Joe
Gershenson and I were nominated for Best Score for a
Musical Picture for *The Glenn Miller Story*. I received three
nominations in 1961: one for the *Breakfast at Tiffany's*
score, a joint nomination with Johnny Mercer for "Moon
River," and another for the title song of the film *Bachelor in
Paradise*, which had a lyric by Mack David. Ginny and I
decided to do it right. On Academy Awards night we hired a
limousine and picked up Johnny and his wife, Ginger. They
had a lovely home in Bel Air, not really very large in view of
Johnny's incredible catalog of songs and his ASCAP rating,
but beautifully decorated and charming. It seemed to be
snuggled in a hollow of trees next to the golf course, and at
the back of the property Johnny had a studio where he
wrote. I guess the lyric to "Moon River" was written here.
Johnny had been a champion typist when he was a young
man, and he wrote his lyrics on a typewriter.

We were already feeling a little high on excitement as we
drove that March evening to Santa Monica, where the
award ceremonies were held in those days. We drove down
Pico Boulevard and turned right at the ocean to arrive at the
Santa Monica Civic Auditorium. The limousine was moving

104

slowly because of the traffic, and ours and all the other vehicles were surrounded by teenage girls, screaming when the movies stars arrived. They crowded around the cars and peered in the windows in search of celebrities. Movie composers did not fall into that category, and in the age of rock, Johnny—who had had a solid career as a singer—was not recognized either. I remember one little girl with a squeaky voice who stuck her head in our open window and inquired, "Are you anybody?"

We went in and found our places. Surprisingly, the only seating for all these people in tuxedos and evening gowns was hard folding chairs, set out on the floor of the auditorium. The longer you waited to see if your name would be called, the harder those chairs seemed to get.

As pleased as I was about the nomination for the song, being nominated for the score was much more gratifying, because I didn't—and still don't—think of myself as a songwriter. Most of the songs in my career have been written as instrumental themes for scores and had lyrics added later. I write themes that can be used in different ways, and developed in the course of the scores.

The people in your own branch vote for the nominations, whereas the full membership votes for the actual awards. Thus, to be nominated for a score means your fellow composers have made the selection. I had grown up as an arranger, and to be nominated by my colleagues among such peers as Miklos Rozsa and Dimitri Tiomkin made me feel as if I had suddenly arrived exactly at the end of the rainbow. But I didn't think I could win.

For one thing, my score was up against tough competition: Rozsa's for *El Cid*, Tiomkin's for *The Guns of Navarone*, Morris Stoloff and Harry Sukman's for *Fanny*, and Elmer Bernstein's for *Summer and Smoke*. For another thing, while it was a very successful film, *Breakfast at Tiffany's* was not a true box-office hit. It had such style in the acting and directing; it was as hip as you could get for that time. Nor was it a big picture in scope, just a gentle, softly humorous, introspective picture about a girl named Holly. It was not the kind of score you'd think would win an Academy Award. Even though it served all the purposes required of it, it did not seem to be in the dramatic sense parallel to many of the great Alex North and Al Newman scores. In all honesty, without the enormous success of "Moon River," I don't believe the score would have been nominated. All this was running through my mind as we sat there on those hard, getting harder, chairs.

Nominees are always given aisle seats, so they won't have to climb over a row of knees if they should win, so Johnny was seated on the aisle just in front of me. Johnny and I felt pretty good about "Moon River"'s chances. In a way, though, I was at a disadvantage. It isn't a good thing to have two nominations in one category, because you are competing against yourself, and if you are getting any kind of sympathy ballot, you're splitting it. Still, "Moon River" had had much more exposure than "Bachelor in Paradise" and already seemed to be on its way to being a standard.

As was the custom, all the nominated songs were sung during the course of the ceremony. Ann-Margret sang "Bachelor in Paradise." Virtually unknown, she was then working with a little group down in Newport Beach, and her appearance on television that night was the real launching of her career. And of course Andy Williams, who had the big hit record of it—so much so that for all practical purposes it has become his theme song—sang "Moon River."

They announced the nominations for the best score for a dramatic or comedy picture. Then I heard my name. I felt as if I'd been hit with a cattle prod. I jumped up, gave Ginny a kiss, and ran up to the stage where my old Air Force buddy, Tony Martin, and his wife, Cyd Charisse, handed me an Oscar. It was a long way from Seymour Johnson Field.

The next category was best song. I was still in shock from winning for best score when I heard my name again. Johnny grinned that impish smile of his, and we went up and picked up two Oscars presented by Debbie Reynolds.

After the ceremony, we went to the Academy dinner ball at the Hilton Hotel and, as they say, danced the night away. Talk about highs! The first Grammy awards, for *"Peter Gunn,"* had given me a two-day high. This was a four-day float.

It was in direct contrast to the downer that occurred after the 1970 Oscar awards. I was nominated three times, for best song ("Whistling Away the Dark"), best original song score (for *Darling Lili*), and best original score (for *Sunflower*). Total Oscars: zero.

I have never trusted this thing called success; I have always been skeptical about it. Something had been happening since the excitement started over *"Peter Gunn,"* and with two awards for *Tiffany's,* I felt I had landed on a plateau and that I should allow myself to start enjoying at least a little security.

The award meant I now commanded better money for a score. The fee for a top score was at that time about $15,000. (One of the measures of inflation is that today you can ask $150,000 and up.) I received $12,500 for *Breakfast at Tiffany's,* and I realized I now could ask the going top price. That was the beginning.

But Ginny and I didn't go crazy. We remained cautious with money, thinking of the children's future. We kept the house in Northridge, and I still continued working on that rented piano in the office off the garage, waiting for assignments. A good one was about to arrive.

In 1962 I got a call from Paramount. I was hot over there because *Breakfast at Tiffany's* was their picture. I was asked to come in to look at a picture that already had music by

another composer that they didn't think worked for the
picture. He was actually a recording artist, not experienced
at film, although he was talented.

I went to Paramount and took a look at it. It hadn't yet
been edited down to its final cut, but it looked good, and
there were a lot of very interesting things in it. The film was
Hatari! The star was John Wayne, and the director was the
great Howard Hawks. Hawks, one of the industry's legends,
directed such films as *The Road to Glory, Dawn Patrol,
Scarface, Sergeant York, His Girl Friday, Ball of Fire, To Have
and Have Not, Red River,* and many more. I jumped at the
chance to work on a picture with him.

Further, it offered an opportunity to score a big-scope
film of a kind I hadn't done up to that point. I saw it as a
way to open up and broaden my image, one associated with
romantic strings and flutes and jazz.

I had a meeting with Hawks in his office. I found him to
be a true gentleman. He was a tall man with gray hair cut
short. He was a ramrod, straight as an arrow. We discussed
the picture, and I told him my ideas about the score. I went
to work. Shortly after I started into the score, Howard called
and told me he had a lot of musical instruments he had
brought back from Africa. He asked if I wanted to take a
look at them. Of course I did!

I went over to see him. He dragged out a big box and
opened it, an absolute treasure chest of authentic African
musical instruments, including the thumb piano, shell
gourds, and giant pea pods. These instruments are just what
you'd think they are, huge pea pods, about two feet long,
which African musicians dry in the sun. When you shake
them, the seeds inside set up a rustling rhythm, like maracas
but with a very distinct sound. I was entranced and immediately decided to use them in the score. Howard also had
some tapes of chants of the Masai, and so, with those
instruments and the tapes from which to adapt authentic
material, I was in pretty good shape to score the animal

Henry's parents, Quinto and Anna Mancini, in West Aliquippa in 1940.

Henry in his native Cleveland. The year was 1928, and he was four. A neighbor's dog was called in for the occasion.

A picnic outing with family friends, July 29, 1941. Back row: Dominic Lalama, Frank Lalama, Nofrey Lalama, Jr., Stella Lalama. Front row: Arthur Paoline, Quinto Mancini, Nofrey Lalama.

The Ambridge community band in 1938. Henry is standing, fourth from the right in the second row. His father, Quinto, is seated, far right first row. Vaclav Klimek is the conductor.

Max Adkins, Henry's
arranging teacher and the
most influential figure in
his life, in Pittsburgh,
1939.

The Mel Koehler Orchestra in
Beaver Falls, Pennsylvania, 1938.
The pianist, wearing a slightly
apprehensive expression, is Henry.
He was fourteen.

♪ In the Army Air Corps. The photo was taken in 1943 at Seymour Johnson Field, North Carolina.

The Tex Beneke Orchestra at Eastwood Gardens, Detroit, July 1946, with Henry on piano. The big band era was drawing to a close, but Henry got his experience writing in its idiom with Tex, a well-loved leader.

The Mello-Larks, 1946–47: Ginny O'Connor, Bob Smith, Tommy Hamm and Jack Bierman. Ginny soon learned she had no taste for the big band life on the road.

Life on the road: Ginny during the days with the Mello-Larks and Tex Beneke. Hotel Capitol, New York City, 1946.

Henry and Ginny in the Beneke days, in Cleveland, 1946. They made a side trip to West Aliquippa to tell Hank's family they planned to marry.

On their wedding day, September 13, 1947. The money was slim, the hopes were high.

Henry's mother, Anna, holding newly born Chris Mancini, in North Hollywood in 1950. Ginny looks on. To the right is Quinto Mancini and in the foreground Ginny's great-grandmother, Doña Chona Ruiz.

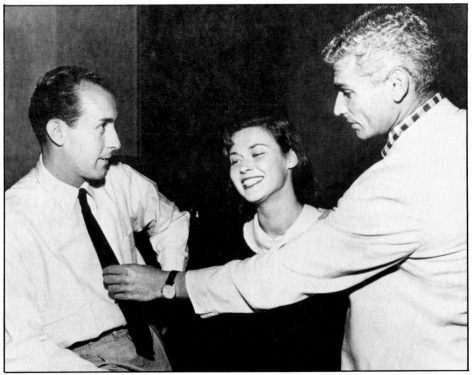

One of Henry's close friends during the Universal days was actor Jeff Chandler, seen here with Hank and Gia Scala in 1955.

The music department at Universal Studios in 1956. From left to right: Ruthie McDonald, secretary; Max Rapp, orchestra contractor; Lillian Russell, secretary to Joe Gershenson; Milt Rosen, assistant to Gershenson; Joe Gershenson, head of the department; David Tamkin, orchestrator; Louis Gershenson (Joe's father); Henry; Nick Nuzzi, head of the music library; Harris Ashford, accountant. Rosen and Joe Gershenson gave Henry his chance to write for movies.

A favorite son's homecoming. Hank and Ginny ride through West Aliquippa in July 1961.

With friends Cyd Charisse and Tony Martin in 1962 on the night Henry received the Academy Award for *Breakfast at Tiffany's*. Henry and Tony met in military service in 1943.

Choreographer Nick Castle in 1962. He styled and shaped the night club acts of many a film star in collaboration with Henry, who wrote the arrangements for these shows.

Saxophonist and arranger Al Cobine with Freddie Dale, Henry's longtime friend and agent. Photo taken at Purdue University in 1967.

Debbie Reynolds presented the Oscar statuettes to Hank and Johnny Mercer for "Moon River" from *Breakfast at Tiffany's*, Best Song category, 1962.

Henry with master director Howard Hawks at a Paramount
Studios recording session of Hank's score for Hawk's *Hatari!*,
1962.

scenes, of which there were many. In fact, the picture opens with an animal scene. The music starts out very softly, gaining momentum as the scene unfolds until finally the rhino charges one of the jeeps and gores one of the characters.

Howard shot a lot of material without knowing exactly where or even if he was going to use it. And he shot one such scene with Elsa Martinelli, a sort of cameo or vignette.

In the story there were three baby elephants who had taken to the girl played by Elsa Martinelli because she was the only one who had been able to figure out how to feed the little creatures. Howard had written this detail into the story because this had happened in real life, during the shooting. Those little elephants were crazy about Elsa. They followed her everywhere.

Elephants like to wallow in cool mud, and they love the water. Elsa took the elephants to a watering hole to bathe them. They filled their trunks and squirted each other and Elsa. It simply happened, and Howard shot it. He had now edited this material into a scene that, while absolutely charming, was not really necessary to the story. Howard said, "I don't know what to do with this. I'm thinking of cutting it out. But before I do, take a look at it and let me know if you have any ideas."

So I looked at the scene several times and still thought it was wonderful. As the little elephants went down to the water, there was a shot of them from behind. Their little backsides were definitely in rhythm with something. I kept thinking about it; it reminded me of something. I thought, Yeah, they're walking eight to the bar, and that brought something to mind, an old Will Bradley boogie-woogie number called "Down the Road a Piece," a hit record in the old days, with Ray McKinley on drums and Freddie Slack on piano. Those little elephants were definitely walking boogie-woogie, eight to the bar. I wrote "Baby Elephant Walk" as a result.

I went in to see Howard. You didn't have demo tapes to give to producers in those days. I played it for him on the piano. He loved it.

I was always looking for unusual instruments and somehow had become aware of an electric calliope made by a man named Mr. Baccigalupi in Long Beach. You didn't get all the spit and whoosh you do with a regular steam calliope. It had a perfect sound, light, airy, and perfect for what I had to put there on the screen, and there was only one like it in the world. On top of that I thought that, because the elephants were little creatures, I would use an E-flat clarinet over the calliope. It created something with a really different sound to it, especially in the middle of Africa. This is another example of how the incongruous in scoring sometimes works best—what we call playing against the scene.

I scored two pictures for Howard. The second was *Man's Favorite Sport*, which followed about two years later. I must repeat that Howard was a great gentleman, and he never raised his voice.

One day, as I worked on *Hatari!*, he came to the office I was using at Paramount. I knew he wanted to say something because I'd seen the same uncomfortable look and attitude in my father when he had something to say but couldn't quite get it out. With my father I would normally just say, "What is it, Pop?" But here was Howard Hawks standing there unable to say something, and I asked, "What can I do for you, Howard?"

He hesitated some more, in acute discomfort, and finally he said, "Hank, would you mind very much if I sat in on the recording sessions?" A lot of things went through my mind at the time. Here was this director of so many great films asking a composer whether he could be present when the score was being recorded. In no way did he *have* to ask me— it was *his* picture, and he was legendary, one of the truly great directors in the history of motion pictures. It was like the old joke, Where does an eight-hundred-pound gorilla sleep? Anywhere he wants to.

Of course the answer was yes.

But that is the kind of man Howard was. A gentle, modest, decent man, and it is no wonder that his memory is revered.

The same year I did *Hatari!* I scored another picture for Blake Edwards, *Days of Wine and Roses*, with Jack Lemmon and Lee Remick.

The film was a departure for Blake, who until now had been associated with private eyes and romantic comedies. This was a deep drama, adapted from a "Playhouse 90" play, about a husband and wife who become alcoholics. Blake decided the score should include a song.

He said, "I think 'Days of Wine and Roses' is a very good title for a song."

I agreed.

Blake said, "Get together with Johnny and see what you can come up with."

The title determined the melody. I went to the piano and started on middle C and went up to A, "The days. . . ." The first phrase fell right into place. That theme was written in about half an hour. It just came, it rolled out. I played it for John on the piano at my house.

By then he had one of the first cassette recorders, and he taped it. Like most lyricists, Johnny liked to hear the tune over and over again.

I had learned something about John from "Moon River"—that he will get back to you with a lyric; there was no point in prompting him. I made the mistake of calling him once and he let me know he wasn't ready. After that, I never made any moves until he called me. And before long he did, saying, "Hank, I've got it, I've got the lyric."

We still had the *Gunn Boat* at that time, and I took the

family down one Sunday to Newport Beach, arriving in the afternoon. John and Ginger had a house there. I sat down at the piano, and John gave the first performance of "Days of Wine and Roses." There were no changes, but for one word. Where he had "the golden face that introduced me to . . . ," he changed "face" to "smile," and it was perfect.

We were all elated with his lyric, which, like "Moon River," was unusual in that it was allegorical. It was simply beautiful, and at that time Ginny and I were the only ones other than Ginger who had heard it. I was a little envious of Ginger because her ears were always the first to hear all that wonderful poetry that Johnny wrote.

I said, "We'd better get this to Blake." I called him that evening, and he made arrangements to hear it the following morning in a soundstage near where he was shooting the picture. Blake asked if Johnny and I minded if Jack Lemmon came along to hear the song. We said it was fine with us.

Johnny and I went over to Warner Bros. next morning. We had an old upright piano in the middle of a huge soundstage. Those old soundstages have a haunted feeling. It wouldn't do to call them barns; many of them were big enough to hold five barns. They were built of wood, and the rafters creaked. They seemed filled with the ghosts of old movies, and they had an aura of the thousands of people who had worked there.

Johnny Mercer was one of the finest demonstrators not only of his songs but anybody's songs. He had a captivating style. I sat down in that huge soundstage and played, and Johnny sang "Days of Wine and Roses" in his best bullfrog voice with a crack in it and the jazz inflection that was always there somewhere.

When I play songs for producers, I don't want to look at them because I have a tendency to get paranoid about halfway through.

I was sitting with my shoulder toward Blake and Jack. Johnny, of course, was facing them. When we were through, there was a long, long, heavy, terrible silence. It probably lasted ten seconds, but it seemed like ten minutes. I kept staring into the keyboard. Finally I couldn't stand it, and I shifted myself around to look at Blake and Jack. And there was Jack with a tear rolling down his cheek, and Blake was misty-eyed. We didn't have to ask them if they liked the song.

In 1962, the song won Johnny and me another Academy Award.

11
Freddie and Bud

From the earliest days of talking pictures, the movie industry has displayed a contradictory attitude toward music. It hires gifted, highly trained composers—people of the stature of Erich Korngold, Franz Waxman, Max Steiner, and Alfred Newman—and then treats some of their music like piles of old clothes. As I've said, the studios, not the composers, own the scores. A movie industry lawyer has gone into court and argued that in commissioning a film score, a studio is like a man ordering a suit from a tailor. Once it is made, he can do anything he likes with it.

Some of the finest American film music has been treated by the studios that own it in ways that can only be called cavalier. Hugo Friedhofer's Academy Award–winning score for *The Best Years of Our Lives* was unavailable for performance or study for thirty years, because the studio had lost it. (It was eventually reconstructed from the sound track by an Australian composer, but the original has never been found.)

All the major movie studios have from the beginning owned large music publishing subsidiaries. The studios automatically get half of the rights to the music, which is called the publishing half. They have ownership of the copyright. The composer who refuses to sign away this half simply doesn't work. The composer retains the writer's half, which means that the money from any later recordings or performances on radio and television is divided between the composer (and lyricist, if there is one) and the publisher, i.e., the movie studio.

Aside from the original fees the composer is paid to write the score in the first place, he derives his income from these royalties. There are three important kinds of royalty. The first, much less important than it was early in the century, is from the sale of sheet music. The other two are known respectively as mechanical royalties and airplay, or performance, royalties. When an album is sold, a mechanical royalty is paid on each song it contains. This money goes to the publisher (the movie company's subsidiary, in the case of film scores), who then pays half of it to the composer (and lyricist). When music is played on the radio or television, an airplay royalty is paid through a performing-rights society, such as ASCAP. This applies to the music in the film when the movie is shown on television.

Copyright ownership and control entail the right to promote the music, to get foreign distribution, and to make subpublishing arrangements in other countries. Since the publisher owns the copyright, he can do anything with it, including selling it to another publisher, who may or may not be to the composer's liking. In recent years there have been so many acquisitions and mergers and sales of publishing interests and movie companies that composers and lyricists frequently don't know who owns their songs and scores.

With the "Peter Gunn" music, I established a precedent that other composers have occasionally been able to follow, though not to the extent I might wish. Indeed, I can't always follow it myself. I was able to do it then only because of Blake Edwards. While "Gunn" was in preproduction, it occurred to me that for the first time I would not be writing for a major studio; Blake's company was an independent. I talked with Blake about it. I said, "Blake, you have no ties to any studio. I would like to own the copyrights to the music from 'Peter Gunn.'" Blake could easily have said that he wanted those rights for his company. He didn't. He said, "Okay, that's fine with me."

And I suddenly found myself in what was possibly an unprecedented situation for a composer, that of owning all the rights to my own music in a hit television series.

But there are responsibilities and duties attached to publishing. Sheet music has to be printed and distributed. Royalties have to be collected and dispersed. The music must be promoted. A considerable amount of clerical work is required. Now that I had all the rights to the "Peter Gunn" music, I had to start a publishing company, a venture I had neither the time nor the skills to run.

In 1955 Universal had hired away from Paramount an experienced, well-known, and highly regarded man named Larry Shayne to run its newly formed Northern Music Publishing Company. Larry was then in his middle forties, a good-looking and pleasant man a little under medium height. I liked and respected Larry and knew he had been thinking about going out on his own. I made an appointment to see him. I said, "I want to make a proposal to you. I'd like you to come in on a publishing company with me, starting with the "Peter Gunn" music, which I own outright. We'll be partners. I'll have my writer's half of the royalties, and we'll be fifty-fifty partners on the publishing."

Larry accepted. We thought the deal was good for both of us. He was able to go into publishing with a solid property that was already earning money. Whereas he was getting half the publishing, I was getting an experienced associate who could do all the work publishing entails. Larry's next question was, "What do you want to call the company?"

Since Ginny and I were living in Northridge and I

couldn't think of anything better, I said, "Let's call it Northridge Music Publishing."

It was successful from the very beginning. We ended up owning several publishing firms, and we opened an office in London, with Terry Oates, a dear friend, in charge. Terry had come up in the music publishing business under Max Dreyfuss, who was the czar of Chappell & Co., Inc., the biggest music publishing company of the time. He was a protégé of the legendary music man Teddy Holmes.

In Northridge's second year, *Music from "Mr. Lucky"* came into the catalog. Aside from mechanical royalties for the albums, the television shows themselves were generating enormous earnings through ASCAP, not to mention the airplay royalties from radio.

Once we had this precedent established, I started to apply this kind of thinking to the movies that I seemed likely to be doing in the next years. I felt I was acquiring the strength to make the demand, and I hoped, furthermore, that the precedent would help other composers get full rights to their music.

I did not, however, get the rights to "Moon River" and "Days of Wine and Roses" because under no circumstances would Paramount and Warner Bros., respectively, give up publishing. I could hardly say to Blake, "I'm not going to work for you, because I want ownership of the copyrights." I couldn't do that to him, in view of all he had done for me, and in any case I desperately wanted to do those scores. They were my break into big pictures. The pictures gave Johnny and me two great standards, even if we did own only half the rights to them, and they earned me three Academy Awards. Larry and I remained partners until 1978, when we had a painful parting that ended up in Los Angeles Superior Court.

Toward the end of 1962, I scored another picture, *Experiment in Terror*, for Blake. This was the kind of picture I loved to do for him. I think Blake's treatment of suspense takes a back seat to no one's, including Hitchcock's. *Experiment in Terror* had dark corners to it; it was done in black and white, and it had great suspense.

We were in the hootenanny period of music, with folk songs, girls wearing long cotton skirts, and boys in short-sleeved shirts. In folk concerts, you would often see someone stroking an autoharp, an instrument on which you can play four kinds of chords by pushing various buttons. The instrument has a great natural decay; the sound seems to last forever. And although the kids were using it to sing about love in America and brotherhood and equality, to me the sound of that instrument was chilling. While experimenting with it I discovered I could get the notes with a guitar pick instead of using the buttons. This was the basis for the music for the opening of *Experiment in Terror*. I used two autoharps, with Bob Bain on one and Jack Marshall on the other, one plucking out the chords and the other playing the melody. It was a very effective device.

The following year, 1963, I did *Soldier in the Rain*, one of the most touching films I have ever seen about the relationship between two men. Jackie Gleason and Steve McQueen played the two soldiers. Blake and Maurice Richlin wrote it, and Ralph Nelson directed. It was very difficult to come by a theme for the love between two men, but when I did find it, it became, along with that of *Two for the Road*, my favorite among my own themes. It was introduced over the opening credits by a haunting trumpet solo by Mannie Klein.

Every once in a while I see the film. There is a scene at the end, after Gleason's character has died. McQueen is all alone in the dayroom, looking at the soft-drink machine, which only Gleason's character could kick just right to get a free soda. This is the only scene in all the films I've scored where the music has an effect on me. It's so touching it brings me near to tears. *Soldier in the Rain* was a slice-of-life

kind of film, with Tuesday Weld and Tony Bill in supporting
roles. It's a lovely, small film.

With all these pictures and the Academy Awards, I was
becoming very much in demand by the studios, and my new
agent, Bobby Helfer of MCA, started making tougher deals
for me. Bobby was a musician, and he had previously been
my contractor—the man who hires and assembles the orchestras used in recording. It is a position required by the
musician's union, but, beyond that, a skilled and perceptive
contractor is invaluable to a composer. Bobby was one of the
best.

Bobby was an intense and complex man of medium
height whom I never saw without a jacket and tie, which is
distinctly unusual in a town where the business style runs to
blue jeans and shirtsleeves. He had been taken into MCA by
Abe Meyer, the guru of film composer agents. Bobby eventually went back to contracting, which was much more
lucrative for him, and remained my contractor until he took
his own life in 1970. It was completely unexpected and
saddened us all. When Bobby went back to contracting, Al
Bart became my agent. Al is a New Yorker. He is not a
musician. His link to the film music business was his good
friend from World War II army days, composer Elmer
Bernstein. Through Elmer, Al went to work with Stanley
Wilson, head of the music department at Revue Studios, the
production wing of MCA. This evolved into a position as
agent for film composers and lyricists on Abe Meyer's staff.
He now heads his own company in partnership with Stan
Milander. Together they represent many of the top film
composers.

But at that time, Bobby was my agent, and when he was
negotiating a picture contract for me, he would try to secure
full ownership of the score for me. In some cases when I
wasn't able to obtain full ownership, I got at least half the
publishing. We worked out a very favorable deal with *The
Pink Panther*, which is a huge copyright, half the publish-

ing. The other half was owned by United Artists. When I
was able to get half the publishing, I owned 75 percent of
the music. And I also had control of those scores and songs.
We were able to make similar deals on *Charade, Soldier in
the Rain, Dear Heart, A Shot in the Dark, Moment to Moment,* and *Two for the Road.* We have continued to make such
deals up to the present, though not with the major studios.

All of this was unheard of at the time. As time went on
and the studios became stronger and stronger, when the
question of publishing came up, they'd come down to
saying, "Look, do you want the picture or don't you?" With
rare exceptions, and only when major studios are not involved, composers have to give up the publishing.

I seemed to myself such an unlikely person for all this to
be happening to. All the major singers were recording my
songs. I was getting the best film assignments. Nearly every
film score I wrote was being issued in album form by RCA.
I had broken out of the anonymity that is the lot of most
film composers—and which I fully expected to last all my
life.

Yet I was so busy writing that I didn't realize the immen-
sity of what was happening. And it was gathering momentum. One day in 1961, I got a call from Jerry Perenchio at
MCA. Jerry was in the concert-booking division, and he was
a stranger to me.

He made a proposal: he wanted me to go out on concert
tours. I turned him down, but he wouldn't give up. He kept
calling me, sometimes when I was right in the middle of
writing or even in the studio while I was recording, and
finally I said, "Okay, what's on your mind? I certainly can't
picture myself with a baton in my hand out doing concerts."

Jerry said, "Johnny Mathis is going to play the Seattle
World's Fair. We're booking him. We thought it would be a
great program if you would go with him. You could do half
the show, Johnny could come out and do his half and then

you could end together doing 'Moon River' and 'Days of Wine and Roses.' "

In the end, I decided to do it. With my whole family—the girls, Chris, and Ginny—I went to Seattle with Johnny. I rehearsed an orchestra, on pins and needles about appearing in public. Of course, I had a certain amount of experience from appearances with Tex Beneke. But I had been a sideman, not the figure in the spotlight. Recording your music is a very different matter from presenting it to a live audience. I didn't really know what I was doing there. I had four hit songs, hardly enough to carry a program, or even half a program. So I went about trying to put together some semblance of a program, one that had pace and would make sense.

We played the Seattle Opera House for a week. On the first night, it was as if I was in a fog; I felt as if I didn't have any legs. I had absolutely no stage presence. That was something I would have to learn, have to build. I went onstage like a sleepwalker and—*zap!*—gave a downbeat. Johnny and I got through the week. The engagement was very successful. By the end of it, I was thinking, Hey, I like this, I like presenting the music directly to people. Obviously I had been bitten by the bug.

Back in California, Jerry began to talk about a series of concerts for me—but on my own. He said, "Let's put together ten or twelve concerts across the country." And that's what he did.

At that time, there was a time lag before things seeped down to the large body of Americans. Although we knew *"Peter Gunn"* and *"Mr. Lucky"* were hits, most of the country hadn't made the connection between my name and the music. And I was a complete novice about concerts. Being so green, I went out all by myself, without a road manager or any key players. I just left home naively with my cases of music and hoped for the best.

The best is not what happened. In fact, that tour was a disaster. I needed forty men for each concert. In their selection I was at the mercy of contractors in the various cities I went to. And the musicians were not the best, which I found out in a hurry at the rehearsals. I needed people who could really play, because I was trying to prepare a two-hour concert with one rehearsal.

Not only did the music sound bad; the box office wasn't good because, hit albums or not, my name meant little to the concertgoing audience. And these were one-nighters, with every concert in a different city. I had to rehearse the orchestras, do the concert once, then move on. After about the fifth city I was really dragging. We had to cancel the last two concerts.

I went back to California in something less than triumph.

About that time, some of the symphony orchestras were starting to take interest in what I was doing. By then I had done a concert album and I was building better programs. For example, I featured a ten-minute showpiece called "Tribute to Victor Young" on one album. So instead of second-string pickup orchestras, I started to think in terms of the nation's major symphony orchestras. I began to get offers from them. Then one came in from the Cleveland Orchestra. Since I was born in Cleveland, I figured if I couldn't make it there I couldn't make it anywhere.

That engagement, in the fall of 1963, was very successful. After that I began to make regular appearances with symphony orchestras, both major ones and local ones like the San Fernando Symphony, in high school auditoriums or even in parking lots. In 1965, I did a concert at the Greek Theater in Hollywood, and in 1968, a program with the Fifth Dimension, the first of many at the Hollywood Bowl.

If I showed any tendency to a swelled head, my father took care of it. I remember that he came to one of the concerts—probably the one at the Greek Theater. The concert was a great thrill for me. I thought I conducted well, and the audience gave me a standing ovation.

After the concert I was walking out through the parking lot with my dad. He gave me one of his I-want-to-say-something-but-I-don't-know-how looks. Finally he said, "You know, Henry, you should take conducting lessons."

Meanwhile, Jerry Perenchio had left MCA and started his own booking company. Working for Jerry was a man named Fred Dale, whom Jerry assigned as my personal contact in the company.

Freddie was a marvelous guy. Born in New York City and originally named de Francesco, Freddie had been a trumpet player. He was the most unlikely-looking agent in the world, short—about five foot six—with a large nose, an Italian with red hair. Freddie was down to earth and funny, and he smoked cigarettes and cigars by the box and carton. He had a postnasal problem of some sort and sniffed constantly while talking. He would prove to be my right arm in the concert field, my companion, and one of the greatest friends of my life.

After we had been doing concerts for some time, we sat down one day for a talk. I said, "Freddie, it's nearly impossible to rehearse almost two hours of music in two and a half hours. There are two kinds of concerts we're doing, the symphony concerts and the college concerts." By now we were performing at most of the universities in the South and Midwest. I said, "I can't continue if I have to rehearse a new band every time." Freddie was a business graduate of Indiana University, where he had booked bands for concerts. He'd also co-led a band with a saxophonist named Al Cobine who he said was still in Indiana, specifically Indianapolis, where he had an organized band. Freddie said, "If we can get Al's band to handle the blowing part of the concerts, and if these key players travel with you, that will take a lot of the pressure off." At that time, we were using a forty-piece band, of which twenty were strings.

Freddie's plan was that Al Cobine would go to Indiana University with his own key players and select the rest of the orchestra from faculty and students. America's music schools contain many students of advanced professional caliber, and the faculties include some quite famous musicians. I.U.'s faculty included cellist Janos Starker, French hornist Phil Farkes, and tubist Bill Bell. The best. Furthermore, Indiana University's music school was one of the most respected in the country. The plan sounded good to me.

And that is what we began to do. We'd fly into Indianapolis and meet Al Cobine, a big-chested man whom everybody called Big Al and a fine arranger in his own right. Then we'd drive to Indiana University in Bloomington, rehearse the band that Al had put together, get on a bus or plane, and play a series of dates throughout the Midwest, with the luxury of using the same band of excellent players who had been adequately rehearsed. By the end of one of these tours, of course, they'd played the music many times and it was taking on a real polish.

I wasn't yet forty, but I felt ancient with all those students in their early twenties who were getting a charge out of going to these concerts. Freddie set all that up for me.

Al Cobine became my permanent contractor for concert tours and later became known as the Pink Panther because he played the tenor saxophone solo with the band. Al has played that theme more times than any man on earth.

Freddie's plan worked so well that I decided to carry a rhythm section and some key players with me to the symphony orchestra concerts. Through Al, I hired Jack Gilfoy on drums, and a bass player, Abe Laboriel. Eventually we decided to add a first trumpet player, and I started using Buddy Brisbois on the road.

Buddy, a highly respected studio player who had been on most of my albums, had one of the highest ranges I had ever

heard. He too became a close friend. Bud was a very handsome fellow, a little stocky, well proportioned but not very
tall. He was the most even-tempered man I ever met, and he
seemed a pillar of stability.

Bud and his first wife were divorced in the mid-1960s.
While we were playing Wichita, he met a woman quite a bit
younger than he was and they were later married. That
marriage didn't turn out well at all, and as the 1960s passed
I could see that he was unhappy.

It must have been in the early seventies that he called and
said, "I'm giving up the trumpet. I can't get anywhere, and
I'm giving up music. I've just had it." If Bud had been
around during the big band era, he undoubtedly would have
had his own band. He was such a spectacular player, and he
had the good looks; he was the matinee idol type. Bud
wanted to make it on his own as a leader, and he'd had
several groups. He'd even tried some rock singing at one
time. It all fell through, and now his second marriage wasn't
working out. He said he was going back to Minneapolis,
where he'd come from.

I didn't hear from Bud for a long while. Then one day I
got a call from him. He said, "I think I'm straightened out,
and I'm practicing my horn again. I want to go back to
playing."

I said, "That's great, Bud," and I was really thrilled. I
said, "As soon as you think you're ready to go, give me a call
and we'll go out on the road." He loved the road. So Bud
was playing again, and I was waiting for him to show up to
go back with Freddie Dale, Al Cobine, and me.

Within a year, I got a call from Bud's sister. She said that
he had driven into the desert near Phoenix, put a gun to his
head, and pulled the trigger.

He was forty-one.

In 1966 I played a concert in Tulsa, Oklahoma. Tulsa has
a particular significance for me. Blake Edwards was born
there. Because of Blake's Indian background, whenever I

play Tulsa I go to curio stores and buy Indian kitsch, T-shirts with teepees on them, mugs with Indian heads on them, and mail this stuff back to Blake. He must have quite a collection by now.

I remember that Freddie Dale and I had just arrived at the airport in Tulsa. Ginny reached me there. She said my father had just died of a heart attack. The feeling was not like the grief of my mother's death. I was just numb. Freddie said, "What do you want to do, cancel the concert?"

"No," I said. "Let's do it."

Jerry Perenchio's company was called Chartwell Artists. He had a great many important and talented clients on his roster, including Andy Williams, then at his peak, selling out in concerts and starring in his own television show. Because of the connection between Andy and me through "Moon River," Jerry said, "You two guys should go out together. I think you'll draw such crowds that theaters won't hold them. We're going to have to play arenas." This was before anybody had ever thought of this. It was a pattern the rock bands would follow. Jerry was just beginning his activities as an entrepreneur, a game at which he later became a master.

He booked the first tour that Andy and I did. We hit all the big cities. It was a tremendous success.

Andy had married Claudine Longet, who sometimes traveled with us. One time she sat out front to watch me rehearse my half of the program. I would do "Moon River" on the piano, and then at the end of the evening Andy and I would reprise it together with the orchestra. When I finished, I went backstage to talk with Andy. Claudine came into the dressing room and said with some indignation and in her inimitable French accent, "Andy, Henry is doing your song!"

In the winter of 1967–68, Andy and I did our first tour of Japan. Then we went to London to play Royal Albert Hall, filling it for three concerts. Jerry Perenchio was the brains behind it all.

Ginny and Claudine went along on our trip to Japan. In the Japanese tradition, we were wined and dined and, at the end of the tour, given gifts.

Our hosts took us to a lavish farewell dinner at one of the big restaurants in Toyko. Ginny traveled with costume jewelry, including a three-strand pearl choker which, she told me later, she had bought for $30 at Bonwit-Teller. It came time to distribute the gifts. A pretty Japanese girl in traditional dress handed one to each person, with a ceremonial bow. The impresario for the tour said, "We wanted to give you some of our finest pearls, Mrs. Mancini, but we noticed that you already have a beautiful set, so we give you these saki cups." The cups were sterling silver. Claudine opened her box. It contained a string of the magnificent Japanese pearls.

Ginny said later, "My heart just sank."

12
Hollywood-on-Thames

The early 1960s was the great period of what came to be known as Hollywood-on-Thames, a time when streams of actors, producers, directors, composers, and technicians were arriving in London to make pictures. There were several reasons for this.

The difference between the value of the dollar and the pound sterling, plus lower labor costs, made it possible for American film companies to produce pictures in Britain for substantially less than they could in America.

In addition, the British government had instituted what it called the Eady Plan, under the terms of which a portion of the proceeds of each cinema ticket was awarded to producers of films provided that, among other things, a certified portion of the production was British, including in many cases the music. For all these reasons, many filmmakers were working in London. Stanley Kubrick made *2001* and *A Clockwork Orange* there.

Stanley Donen was one of the foremost producer/directors taking advantage of the situation in England at that time. Stanley had started as a chorus dancer in the company of *Pal Joey* on Broadway. Later with Gene Kelly he codirected *On the Town* and *Singin' in the Rain*. He then directed *Seven Brides for Seven Brothers* and *Funny Face*. Stanley had had several huge successes at MGM, to which he had been under contract in the forties and fifties.

In 1963, he called me from London, where he had gone to live because he felt he had more freedom there to do what he wanted. Stanley told me he was completing a film with Cary Grant and Audrey Hepburn to be called *Charade*. He thought it was right down my alley, an adventure-romance with a thriller aspect to it. It had a fantastic cast, including Walter Matthau, George Kennedy, and James Coburn, who were just coming into their own. Each of them was at the top of his form and added a great deal to the movie. And with Cary and Audrey as the stars, it was a very appealing project.

I was concerned about the quality of the British musicians, particularly the flute players, especially since I often used alto and bass flutes, unusual instruments. I had no idea whether they would be up to our standards. I was concerned too about where to record. We soon learned about the Cine Tele Sound Studios in Bayswater. *Charade* was one of the first American films to be scored on that stage, which had a unique sound to it—most of John Barry's James Bond scores were done there later.

Stanley wanted me to write the music there, so off I went to London, not knowing what I was facing. It seemed like a big commitment. I had had some success, but I didn't have a real body of work. I was then only thirty-nine. I was set up in a penthouse suite in the Mayfair Hotel, right off Berkeley Square, where I rented a piano and went to work. I stayed for two months to write the score for *Charade*, developing a main-theme melody that I turned over to Johnny Mercer, who wrote yet another of his superb abstract lyrics for it. We were nominated for another Academy Award, though we lost out to "Call Me Irresponsible."

At that point, the Beatles were in the first flush of their success. I was asked to make an appearance on a television special they were shooting in Manchester, to play one of their tunes on the piano. That was all I had to do. I was curious about them, and I went. As I was playing the song

"If I Fell" during rehearsal, I became interested in a little countermelody it had—a kind of thumb l:ne, if you want to call it that. It was very nice. I mentioned it to John Lennon and asked, "Did you come upon that as you were writing, or work it in later? How did that come in?"

He said in his best Liverpool accent, "I don't know, Hank. We leave those things to George." Of course he meant George Martin, their producer and a schooled musician. I guess Paul McCartney and John would play their songs for George, and he would advise them during the polishing process. I don't think this in any way diminishes what the Beatles did. They were, of course, by no means the only rock group to receive this kind of assistance.

I finished the score, and we went into the studio to record. My trepidation about British orchestras vanished at once. I was impressed indeed with the quality of the players, and even now, when I'm there, I recognize faces from those first days of recording in London.

Charade was the first of fifteen pictures I scored in London. This meant at least fifteen trips to England. By then I was doing concerts as well, and all in all I was away from home a great deal of time.

I have always had a lot of admiration for the way Ginny took up the slack during the times when the kids didn't have their father there. My extended absences had a particularly bad effect on Chris as he entered his teen years. Whenever he needed a father to talk with, I was gone. In my own defense, I must say that these were high-earnings years for me, and in my profession you never know how long it's going to last. Nonetheless, the situation created a dilemma, one I did not successfully resolve.

When the kids were young, I tried to interest them in the piano. The girls took to it very well, Chris fairly well, but they weren't really very interested in the instrument, especially Chris. Later all three had very good vocal training with Sally Sweetland, who had sung with the Sauter-Finnegan Orchestra. But Chris, as soon as he could hold one, wanted to play guitar. He resisted any kind of formal training that I wanted to give him. He had a great ear and a great sense of time, but he had a block. And I think I created it. He didn't want to compete with me; he didn't want to do what I did.

I think the fact that I was becoming so well known put additional pressure on Chris. Frequently when he told anyone his name, he would hear the question, "Any relation to . . . ?" People weren't seeing him as a person in and of himself.

The problem was compounded by one of my own problems. Being the son of a father who could not communicate love, I was not always able to communicate it myself. I never made much of birthdays and holidays and other events. Sometimes I think I expressed it all in the music. Chris himself has said I didn't communicate, and I'm afraid he's right.

Bob Dylan was his hero. Chris would go into the poolroom, where there was a record player, put on earphones, and sing along with Bob Dylan. All we could hear was Chris's guitar and voice. Chris was involved in the music he liked, and that music had a lot of emotional baggage.

The deeper we got into the sixties, the busier I got and the longer the tether to the children got, especially the one to Chris. It affected him much more than the girls because they, as twins, had their own complete world, that almost eerie connection that Ginny and I have observed since they were born. Ginny took the full brunt of it. She knew what was going on, but it was my job too to handle it, and I didn't do it.

Ginny and I had a preference for Catholic schools, believing that children were better educated there than in the Los Angeles public school system. Parochial schools were reputed to be more personal, and they were far less crowded than the public schools. But Chris didn't like them and was not doing well in his work. The girls were not enamored of them either, though they both completed their elementary education at Marymount Junior School.

Chris says those schools turned him into a rebel. He says he remembers trying to stay out of trouble, but he just couldn't, and when he got into scrapes, I was never there to advise him, and he resented it. Then we made another mistake. We sent him to St. John's Military Academy. He hated it even more than the other schools. By the time he got to Saint Monica High School in Santa Monica, he'd been to eight schools.

One day in 1969, we got a call from the school telling us to come and pick him up. They were expelling him because of his behavior. Ginny and I were to leave the next week on our second trip to Japan. Of course we weren't happy about his being expelled, but we were getting used to the fact that this was the way life was going to be for a while. We decided to take him with us. On many occasions after that, we took all three kids with us—a concert tour in Israel, a tour of Europe, a charter boat trip through the Italian islands. Whenever I could, I took the whole family. These trips were fun, and Chris was all right at such times. But when he was on his own and at school, he seemed to feel a need to assert himself and do what he felt he wanted to do. Finally we sent him to Judson, a school in Arizona with a ranch style of life.

The girls, being identical twins, had special qualities. They were adorable growing up. We tried not to make too much of their being twins, and Ginny always encouraged them to be individuals; she seldom dressed them alike. Monica was the more extroverted, Felice a little more retiring, although they both make friends easily.

One night when the girls were about thirteen, Ginny was working—on a studio date, as I recall—and the kids and I were having dinner. I had opened a bottle of white wine. For some reason Monica felt pixyish. She dipped her fingers into her water and flicked it into my face. I said, "Monica, cool it." She repeated it, and I said, "Don't do it again." She did. It was a bizarre thing for her to be doing and certainly irreverent, but then I have to keep in mind my own irreverence for authority at an early age and the nickname I had in the Beneke band—Weirdo—for the things I did. She had me in one of those traps kids get parents into, when they're testing you to see how far they can push. I certainly wasn't going to hit her. I could never strike one of the kids, perhaps because of the way I had been treated in my childhood. But if she tested me once again, what could I do? I said, "That's it, Monica. If you do it one more time, this glass of wine is going to go right on your head." She looked at me, trying to make up her mind whether I would really do it. She flicked water in my face again, and I poured the whole glass of wine on her head.

Chris and Felice were choking back laughter. Monica looked as if she didn't know whether to laugh or cry. White wine gets very sticky when it dries, and she went off to wash her hair.

When the girls were little, I had trouble many times telling them apart. Their voices are so much alike that, to this day, when they want to they can deceive me on the telephone. They have slightly different speech rhythms, but they can imitate each other and I'll be taken in every time. The vocal texture, however, is identical, and when they sing together the blend is perfect. Their attachment to and understanding of each other bordered, at times, on the supernatural. They could communicate without speech. One would look at the other, and the other would say, "Okay," and off they would go to the kitchen to get something to eat. They have been in almost daily contact all their lives and could probably get along just fine without the rest of the world. They take great comfort from just being in the same town. Their oneness is still an amazing thing to both Ginny and me.

As there were always the two of them and one of Chris,

who was a tease, they were always running to us with their tales of woe.

During the 1960s there were times that really taxed Ginny's patience and energy. She was getting back into singing and worked with me in the chorus of *Breakfast at Tiffany's*. One of the best session singers in town, she was contracting as well as singing.

When she and her singer friends got together, it was almost like a hen party. You can't keep singers quiet during a session. They have to talk—about the breakfast they just had or whatever—and you nearly have to shout at them to get them to be quiet. Ginny continued to work for several years. Then she walked into a session of mine and discovered we were going to overdub the singers without the orchestra. She said the warmth and sense of camaraderie, the feeling you get from singing along with a big orchestra, was gone. She said that was it, she was no longer interested in the business. At the same time she felt that because there were people in town who needed the money and she no longer did, it was time to bow out.

One thing that helped in raising the children was that Ginny and I held a united front. I can't ever remember speaking an angry word in front of the kids. Chris has said that he has never seen me lose my temper. I don't know if that's good or bad. But Ginny bore the burden of the problems with the kids, and she has come out of it with her sense of humor and our marriage still intact. The credit is all hers.

The kids brought out those curious qualities of personality in my father, who was a frequent visitor. They were well aware of his temper. Yet he used to take Chris to ball games, and Chris had good times with him. But my father would get very nervous when they were just being kids. They bothered him.

Every December we strung up Christmas lights across the rain gutter and across the top of the window of our house in Northridge. One year my dad said, "Let me do it."

He got up on the ladder. The girls, then eight years old, were playing. They ran under the ladder and knocked it down. My dad broke two ribs in the fall. Of course the girls were horrified. The accident only added to his sense of persecution.

We used to have informal dinners, seated on low stools around a large, cut-down, round, antique oak table. That table played an important part in our lives when the children were small. I used to diaper them on it. When bedtime came, they would hop up on the table. I would diaper them and put them to bed.

We often took my father for outings on *The Gunn Boat*. One Sunday afternoon, Ginny and I decided to stay overnight at Newport Beach. He drove the kids back home in his car. When they got home to Northridge, Rebecca, our housekeeper, whom the kids just loved, made them dinner, and served them on that round oak table. The kids started giggling and fooling around. One of them did something, I have no idea what, that infuriated my dad. He put his hands under the table and flipped it over, sending the plates of pasta flying. It terrified the children. When someone does something strange and unexpected, you wonder what they are going to do next. But he did nothing. He'd gotten the anger out of his system, and he never laid a hand on the kids.

That table, it occurs to me, could tell a lot of stories. Ginny purchased it originally from Martha Tilton, who was a singer with several of the top bands. Ginny later donated it to the elementary school of the Church of the Good Shepherd in Beverly Hills. And still today, the nuns sit around it on low stools and grade their pupils' papers.

By 1964, the kids were getting bigger and we were outgrowing the house. I was making the long drive into town to work, sometimes twice a day. Money was no longer a problem. We started to look for a larger place in a more convenient location. Through a real estate broker we found a house in Holmby Hills, one that had once been owned by Art Linkletter and that rests in a pocket bordered by Bev-

erly Hills on one side and Bel Air on the other. The neighborhood had a history. Humphrey Bogart and Lauren Ba-
call had lived across the street. Judy Garland lived on that
street when she was married to Sid Luft. Bing Crosby and
Sammy Cahn both lived there.

The move to Holmby Hills changed our style of life
tremendously. The house, a typical two-story Georgian red
brick, which we eventually painted white, had a big pool in
the back and a pleasant yard. It was set behind a circular
driveway at the top of a small hill. The street, Mapleton
Drive, was just off Sunset Boulevard, and therefore the
traffic was heavier than that we had experienced in Northridge. The kids could no longer leave their bikes out overnight or ride them safely up and down the street. And there
would no longer be their little friends running in and out of
the house, slamming the doors as they went. It must have
been tough on the kids to move to a new place with built-in
restrictions. On the other hand, each of them now had a
separate room and bath.

For Ginny and me, the biggest advantage was that we
didn't have to drive fifty miles a day, or more, to go to work.

We all settled into a new way of life—life in the fast lane.

By 1978, our three children had moved away from home.
Ginny and I started talking about how nice it would be to
build a comfortable house, one that would be exactly what
we wanted, from the ground up. We bought a lot north of
Sunset Boulevard, still in Holmby Hills, from our friends
Stanley and Lynn Beyer. Ginny had definite ideas about the
look and the feel of the house. We hired architect Peter
Choate and designer Laura Mako, and together, with a few
asides from me, they proceeded to design what could be
described as a California, country, French town house.

We escaped none of the pitfalls that beset people who
decide to build. In the end, our nice, cozy, comfortable
California, country, French town house had grown to eleven
thousand square feet. No regrets, however.

13
The Pink Panther

Ginny and I had fallen in love with ocean travel, and when I came back from London in 1963 after finishing *Charade*, we decided to take a trip on the SS *France*, which had just gone into service. I told Blake about our planned voyage. He surprised me by saying that he was booked on the same trip. He and his frequent writing partner Maurice Richlin were starting a script for a film to be called *The Pink Panther*, which Blake was going to direct, mostly in Rome. He said they planned to work on it on the ship. We would have a great time making the Atlantic crossing together.

Most of the script for *The Pink Panther* was written on that voyage. Blake and Maurice would lock themselves in their room all day and write, emerging at night for dinner. Also aboard were our friends Betty and David Rose. The six of us had dinner together every night.

Once he had completed the script, Blake immediately started production. A good deal of the story takes place in Cortina, and there were a number of other Italian locations. Marty Jurow was producing. It was one of the last times Blake directed a picture that he did not also produce.

Peter Ustinov had been cast as Inspector Clouseau. At the last minute, he fell out of the picture. It's a disaster for a filmmaker when something like that happens. The sets have been built, the studios and equipment have been contracted, crews are standing around on salary, the banks are going crazy, and the insurance company is getting very nervous. Then, somehow or other, Blake came up with the idea of Peter Sellers for the part of Clouseau. That was on Thursday. He contacted Sellers, who was interested in the part and flew to Rome from England the next day. Peter started working on the character of Inspector Clouseau on Friday; they were to start shooting the following Monday. Over that weekend, he and Blake came up with the Clouseau character, along with Clouseau's weird and later famous speech patterns. What they accomplished in those three days was quite remarkable.

Because the Pink Panther series became so popular and such a vehicle for Peter, it's easy to forget that Clouseau was not the main figure of the original film. He was just one of many characters in what was essentially an ensemble comedy starring—in addition to Peter—David Niven, Capucine, Robert Wagner, and Claudia Cardinale.

Claudia spoke virtually no English. Blake went ahead and shot all her scenes and then in postproduction had somebody else dub in her dialogue by a process called looping, which is lip-synching dialogue to film already shot.

Italian moviemakers loop almost everything; they just shoot the scenes and put the dialogue in later. When they were making the spaghetti westerns with American stars and Italian supporting players, they didn't care what the Americans—or anybody else—said on camera. They could recite poetry or phone numbers; everything was looped in later anyway. That's why some of those movies are a little weird to watch; nothing quite fits.

One of the roles in the film was played by Fran Jeffries. Blake said there was to be an après-ski scene in a little nightclub at the inn in Cortina. He wanted Fran to do a song with a Latin jet-set feeling. And he wanted it to be in Italian.

By now Ginny and I had flown back to Los Angeles. Blake called to tell me about the song he needed for Fran.

He said he needed me in Rome. I boarded a plane and wrote the basic melody on the back of a menu during that flight.

When I arrived, the next question was what to do about an Italian lyric. This was shortly after Domenico Modugno had a big hit on "Volare"; its lyricist was Franco Migliacci, and I said I'd like him to come in on the job. I played the melody for him, and he came up with the title "Meglio Stasera." Johnny Mercer wrote the English lyric, which was also used in the picture, with the title "It Had Better Be Tonight."

All this time, Fran was in the hospital with a case of flu so severe she could hardly talk. Peter Sellers and I took a taxi there, taking flowers to her. But she learned the song, and when she got out of the hospital we did a prescore session with her singing it.

By now I was getting to know Peter, who was a music lover, a jazz buff, and a great fan of the music from "Peter Gunn" and "Mr. Lucky." Peter loved every kind of music.

None of us really foresaw what was going to happen in the years ahead to the Pink Panther, Blake, Peter, and me. This was, as far as we knew, a one-shot project, which we were very happy about—on a high, really, because the script was so good and the performances excellent. I don't believe there were even the routine problems on the set.

It was during the making of *The Pink Panther* that Ginny and I visited the town where my father was born. When we arrived in Rome, I hired a driver—I had no intention of driving those roads the way they were in those days. We traveled over a rocky, dangerous road through terrible terrain. It looked like a moonscape. I had never seen such rough country—bleak, jagged, and almost devoid of trees.

I kept looking out the window, and I said to Ginny, "My God, how did my dad make this trip? How did he get down to Rome and then to the port at Naples?" When he made that journey, not only were there no cars, there were no roads. I could envision him walking most of the way, perhaps hitching a ride now and then on a horse-drawn cart. The trip took us four hours. It must have taken him two or three weeks. I tried to put myself in his place, making that trip on foot, with very little money, knowing only that he had an appointment with a boat, because he had arranged for a cousin who lived in Detroit (and whose name I do not know) to meet him at Ellis Island. It was mind-boggling to me that a boy could make that trip alone. Why did he do it? Why was he so determined? I couldn't begin to re-create that trip in my mind.

At last we got to Scanno, in Abruzzi. It was a typical mountain town with stone houses and cobbled streets. It probably hadn't changed in a century or more. The women still wore black and carried baskets of bread and various other things on their heads. There was a wedding reception going on in a restaurant near the church. We went to the church, but we couldn't find any records, and as far as I knew I had no relatives there now. Or, if I did, my father had never spoken of them. Scanno had a small country hotel, but there was no reason to stay. Ginny and I looked around, then had the driver take us back to Rome, over those awful roads.

Now a freeway connects Scanno to Rome. There is good snowpack in those mountains, and the terrain is scattered with resorts. The international crowd hasn't discovered it yet; it's where the Italians go to ski.

Blake returned home to edit the picture. He dropped the little piece of information on me that we were going to have a cartoon opening to the picture. He had hired David DePatie and Friz Freleng to do the animation.

By now I was quite familiar with the script and saw the David Niven character, the phantom jewel thief, as an interesting character to score. It was a beautifully written role. He was suave and sophisticated, with a lot of class. The character reminded me of a song called "Jimmy Valentine."

There were a number of scenes in which David would be slinking around on tippy-toes. I started to write a theme for him—one of the few times I wrote a theme before seeing the actual picture. That music was designed as the phantom-thief music, not to be the Pink Panther theme.

I had no idea what DePatie and Freleng were going to come up with, what the little Pink Panther character would look like, until they showed me a cell, one frame, that they had done. Cartoonists are very set in their ways, and among their other quirks, they love to have a piece of music they can animate to.

The scoring date was still far in the future. But they wanted to see what I had. I said, "Well, boys, I don't think I have enough scoring to show you, I don't have a piece big enough for you to animate to. And I don't know how long the titles are going to be. It's ass backward."

I told them that I would give them a tempo they could animate to, so that any time there were striking motions, someone getting hit, I could score to it. I said, "Let me come in after you're finished, and I'll do the music."

They weren't thrilled about this, because from their point of view it was working backward.

They finished the sequence and I looked at it. All the accents in the music were timed to actions on the screen. The brass accents and of course the theme worked in perfectly with the little "dead ant" figure, as it came to be known, in the beginning of the piece. I had a specific saxophone player in mind—Plas Johnson. I nearly always precast my players and write for them and around them, and Plas had the sound and the style I wanted. He is the saxophonist on the original *Pink Panther* film.

I realized that the theme I had written for David Niven's character, the jewel thief, was perfect for the opening credits and the cartoon of the little Pink Panther character. I used it for both.

The picture was released in 1965. It was an immediate and big success. It had a style, as *Breakfast at Tiffany's* did. It was a very "in" picture. Even the people who wouldn't normally go to a romantic comedy went to see it because of Niven and the Clouseau character, which was a personal triumph for Peter.

A few years later I conducted the music for the Academy Awards show. David Niven was on the program. The conductor of the Awards show is responsible for choosing the music for the presenters or the guest stars. Usually the choices are obvious, and I picked the Pink Panther music for David. After we had run the theme down, the production manager told me, "David would like to talk with you. He's in his dressing room."

David said, "Hank, as much as I love *The Pink Panther*, the movie and all the work that I've done with Blake, I don't feel that this theme is 'my song.'"

I said, "David, you're absolutely right. How about 'Around the World in 80 Days'?"

David smiled, and that's what we did.

After we had finished *The Pink Panther* and Peter Sellers had become a sensation as Inspector Clouseau, the Mirisch brothers came to Blake, who had directed several pictures for them, with a play called *A Shot in the Dark*. Blake, with his x-ray eyes, saw that it was a perfect vehicle—with some judicious rewriting—for the Clouseau character. He wrote it with Peter Sellers in mind, further developing the Clouseau-like speech.

Peter was one of the most mercurial characters I have ever met. I kept hearing about clashes between him and Blake, but I witnessed very little of this firsthand. Whenever Ginny and I were out with him socially, Peter was always fun. There were, however, cases where he and Blake really got into it, over the script or a piece of business in a scene. I think two less talented people would have called it a day, but they both realized they were onto something interesting and important, something you can't buy in this business: the welding of two separate talents to create a third historic personality. And I think Clouseau *is* a historic character. But they had heated discussions about the development of that character, and there were many instances when Blake came to me after the day's work or after a screening and I'd say, "How did it go?" and he'd say, "Don't ask."

Somehow they always patched it up and went ahead. The interesting thing is that ninety-nine percent of the actors who have worked with Blake are ecstatic about the experience. He's got a great rapport with the people who work for him. So it was doubly strange that he and Peter Sellers clashed. That clash affected Blake's health. As I said earlier, he has a back problem, and when things grew tense with Peter on the set, he would be in physical pain.

For all of it, Blake had enormous respect for Peter, who could do absolutely anything as an actor. His command of voices was uncanny.

For instance, once during the shooting of *A Shot in the Dark*, Peter and I were riding in an elevator in the Dorchester Hotel in London (he was staying in a penthouse suite). The elevator stopped and two Arabs got in, complete with robes and headdress. They had a conversation as we descended. We all got off on the ground floor. The minute they were out of earshot, out of Peter's mouth came the *exact* voices of these two men talking to each other. Not just the accents—Peter was a genius with accents—but the actual voices. I looked around, thinking the two must have come back, but it was Peter.

Later on, in 1975, Blake and Peter got together again— ten years after *A Shot in the Dark*—to work on *The Return of the Pink Panther*.

Once a year in London, a film is selected for a royal

command performance, the returns from which go to charity. Lew Grade, who had financed the movie, arranged to have the film shown at a command performance that year. The invitation read, "His Royal Highness The Prince Charles requests your presence at a showing of. . . ." The film had already been shown for the foreign press at a big premiere in Gstaad.

The invitations went out. Peter was in between wives at the time, and he was going out with a lady. The invitation was addressed to Peter only. The publicist made it clear that you could not change a royal invitation. Peter was angry. He made a big fuss about his lady friend not being invited and said he would not attend without her. The scandal papers in London picked up the story. Peter didn't go.

After the performance, Ginny, Blake, Julie, and I were talking with Prince Charles. He's a very friendly person, musically inclined, and a real film buff. The conversation got around to the fact that Peter wasn't there. The prince took on his most princely voice, making fun of himself, and said, "The next time, I shall *command* him to be there." And we all laughed.

By this time Blake and I had developed a pretty steady working relationship. It would be hard to imagine three more diverse pictures than *Breakfast at Tiffany's, Experiment in Terror*, and *Days of Wine and Roses*. They covered a wide range of genres. I had delivered well on those, and Blake felt comfortable with me, as I did with him. So as we went along, it was just a matter of his making a phone call and saying what our next picture was going to be. Off we went to England to shoot *A Shot in the Dark*, which was to be the big breakthrough for the inimitably inept Inspector Clouseau.

The Clouseau character is interesting to ponder. The most perceptive piece I have read was published in the October 1987 issue of the film magazine *Premiere*. It was written by Donald Fagen, a New York musician and composer who cofounded the group Steely Dan. He wrote:

> During the '50s there had been a number of TV shows that exploited the combination of film noir and jazz-based music, but the 1958 *Gunn* series was the iciest to date. Edwards's update of the Hammett-Chandler detective story, with its tense visual style, demanded a suitably chilled-out soundtrack, and Mancini, who scored Orson Welles's *Touch of Evil* that same year, seemed to understand what this show was all about: style, and nothing much else in particular. "The *Miami Vice* of its time," a friend of mine remarked. Craig Stevens as Gunn would cruise around a narcotized and vulgarly luxurious L.A. like Cary Grant on Miltown, doing his job of detection and occasionally alighting at Mother's, a nightclub where his main squeeze, Edie, worked as a jazz singer. . . . Every so often he'd check in with his pal, Lieutenant Jacoby, the good cop. But Gunn may as well have been drifting through a landscape of boomerangs and parallelograms, so little did the plot matter. What counted was the sense that these people had been around the block a few times, had found a way to live amid the stultifying chaos of the modern world, keeping their emotions under control except for occasional spasms of sex and violence.

America, and the world, were going through great changes, as Fagen notes. "The language of hip was changing," Fagen said:

> In his own way Blake Edwards was sensitive to this shift in consciousness. Supersuave Peter Gunn had evolved into Inspector Clouseau, who tries to stay cool but finds the world just too opposed to the notion. The luxurious environment is still there, but the alienation is played for laughs. The expensive objects (custom pool cues, cigarette lighters, etc.) attack Clouseau. When Edwards began to sabotage his own hero, it should have been a tip-off to what was coming.

Egos were cracking. Self-image and sexual identity got hazy around the edges. When Clouseau runs across a cool jazz combo in *A Shot in the Dark,* it's in a nudist colony, and they're playing in their birthday suits. The old hipster identity has been literally stripped naked. As for the music in the early *Panther* films, it has become an extravagant parody of coolness—funny because it's too spooky, too cool to be believed.

Very perceptive indeed. Possibly people liked Clouseau because, in an increasingly complicated world, they couldn't cope either, and they liked him for his effort to keep face in spite of his pratfalls. Whatever the reason, Blake had another hit on his hands.

Immediately following *A Shot in the Dark,* Blake made another call to me. He said we were going to do a picture called *The Great Race.* Now this was a biggy: a big film with a big budget, and for Warner Bros. Blake had had it on his mind for a long time, a period piece about an automobile race from New York to Paris. It was something I had looked forward to. The pictures we had done before were stories that stayed pretty much in one locale. They were about people, not about great expanses, the big sweep.

Blake's script was marvelous. Partly, I think, because he has family roots going back to the era of the silents, Blake has an enormous knowledge of the great comedians of that era, early comics like Buster Keaton, Chaplin, and Laurel and Hardy, and the classic slapstick director Mack Sennett. He had absorbed their work and now in his script had been able to create something of his own with roots and style in the early days of film. Blake is, I think, the most successful of the directors influenced by early film, and *The Great Race* was to be done as an homage to those people. It was like keeping something precious alive. In physical comedy he has few peers.

We had several set pieces in that picture, such as the big pie fight, for which I wrote "The Pie in the Face Polka." There were all kinds of delightful little bits along the way. We had Jack Lemmon as Professor Fate, the villain with a sidekick, Max, played by Peter Falk. Then there were the shiny-toothed hero and the feminist, played by Tony Curtis and Natalie Wood.

Johnny Mercer and I wrote two songs for that picture. One of them was for a production number for Dorothy Provine. We wrote "He Shouldn't-a, Hadn't-a, Oughtn't-a Swang on Me," a classic example of Mercer playing word games with the vernacular. Toward the end of the picture, after the pie fight, just before the finale, you see Tony Curtis and Natalie Wood after they have escaped the villain and are on their way to Paris to see who will be the first to reach the Eiffel Tower and win the race. They are on a riverbank. Tony Curtis is shaving and Natalie Wood is playing the guitar. It's a very soft scene. Blake said, "I think we need a song here." Natalie was supposed to sing it, because the feminist has loosened up and is starting to dig The Great Leslie, as Tony's character was called. Johnny and I wrote the song in about two days. Natalie didn't sing, so we had to hire someone to come in to dub the voice for her. The sequence was shot the next day. The song was "The Sweetheart Tree."

Just to show you how John's mind worked, he came in with two lyrics. The first of them began, "There are ninety-nine cars on the freight train." It was a weird lyric, which I'm sure Ginger still has somewhere among his papers. He sang the whole thing for me, and I said, "Whoa, John. What else do you have?"

Then he sang me the second version, that touching lyric that begins, "They say there's a tree in the forest, a tree that will give you a sign. Come along with me to the sweetheart tree, let me carve your name next to mine."

Working on the picture took me all over the world musically, and I loved every minute of it. I still encounter people who feel *The Great Race* was one of the better comedies. Yet it was not a great success, certainly not compared to the Clouseau pictures.

By around 1960, Ginny and I had started going to Hawaii for Christmas, which we did for five years. Then we decided to change and go to Sun Valley with Andy Williams and Claudine Longet. We stayed at the Sun Valley Lodge.

One of the regulars there was Bobby Kennedy, along with his wife, Ethel, his kids, and his whole crew, including Pierre Salinger. Andy was friendly with Bobby and Ethel, and we soon found we were attending events with Andy and the Kennedys. Ted and Jackie were there at times, during that period before she married Aristotle Onassis.

In those days you heard conflicting stories about Bobby Kennedy's personality. I found him to be pleasant, a congenial fellow to be around. Of course, if you mind your own business and don't bug people, I guess everyone is pleasant to be around.

It was during the Sun Valley visits that I learned to ski. Chris and the twins took to it immediately, but Ginny and I were already in our early forties, and it took us a couple of years to get the hang of it. Once I did get over to the big mountain to watch Ethel and Bobby and their kids go down that slope. They were very serious about skiing, as they were about all sports. They were all very good skiers, and gutsy ones.

The more I saw of the Kennedys, the more I liked them, and, with Andy, I began to be involved, in a peripheral way, with Bobby's campaign for the Democratic presidential nomination. Andy and I performed for Bobby at the Los Angeles Sports Arena during the campaign, a big benefit concert for an audience of at least twenty thousand. His was a point-of-view-of-the-people campaign, a populist campaign, a real grass-roots operation. He was not a great speaker, but he had found something the people really accepted. Bobby looked like a sure thing to take the nomination and then win the election. I felt very good about it, very enthusiastic about Bobby and country. Ginny and I were registered Democrats and felt that his campaign was going to move the country forward.

I was performing at the Sahara in Lake Tahoe for two weeks. I opened the show with an orchestra, then the Young Americans came on. While I was back in my dressing room during their segment of the show, I happened to have the television on. An announcer broke in with the news that Bobby Kennedy had been shot. I waited in shock in my dressing room till it came time to go back onstage. Nobody in the audience knew about the shooting, and I did not announce the news.

After the show, I tried to reach Ethel. I left a message to try to tell her how we felt.

In the next day or so, we were invited to travel with the family on the train from New York to Washington with the casket. I had a commitment I could not get out of. Andy made the trip. He told me later that Ethel was a brick. She handled herself beautifully. Andy said she kept walking through the train trying to keep everyone's spirits up, when she was the one who had lost the most.

14
The Crazy Italians

Right around the time of *The Pink Panther*, I did a film for Warner Bros. whose original title was *The Out-of-Towners*, with Geraldine Fitzgerald and Glenn Ford—a pleasant picture about a lady who goes to a convention, taking along her own linen, pillow, and light bulbs so that her room will feel like home. It was a sweet story. We decided that there should be a song. Mercer wasn't available, so I called in Jay Livingston and Ray Evans to write the lyric. Jay and Ray are fine lyricists who are always happy to tell people that they got their break in motion pictures when Mercer got too busy for a job and recommended them for it. They read the script, looked at her character, and came up with the title "Dear Heart."

It was a charming song, a waltz right straight down Middle America, with a bow toward the South. Everyone liked it, including Jack Warner, who said, "Let's call the picture *Dear Heart*, it's a better title than *The Out-of-Towners*."

In those days, when you wrote a song for a picture, it was not a matter of someone coming out with *the* version on one label. It was always a fight to see how many cover records you could get on a given song. We had a great many covers on "Charade," "Days of Wine and Roses," and "Moon River." We started to get a lot of records on "Dear Heart," including one by Jack Jones. The song was starting to happen. This was around September of 1965, just before the Academy Award nominations were announced.

Warner Bros. was undecided about when to release the picture. Larry Shayne and I had half the publishing on the song, and we retained administrative control. We asked Jack Warner if there was any chance of having the picture released in time to qualify the song for the Academy Awards. Warner thought a minute and said, "Yes, I'll release it—if you'll pay for the advertising." He referred only to local advertising. By the rules of the Academy, a picture had only to be released in Los Angeles and play for one week for anything in it to qualify for nomination. Warner said $10,000 would cover the ads. Larry and I concluded it was worth that to try for a nomination on a song that was already showing up on the charts.

We paid for the advertising in Los Angeles, and the song did get a nomination, which helped establish it. For the money involved, it was well worth it.

Today you couldn't do that. You have so many committees to go through, the marketing plans are now computerized and planned far in advance. You cannot have that one-on-one relationship with a studio head; there is no one person you can go to who can say, "Yes, release it."

That's the good side of what the industry was like then. Here's a bit of the bad side.

I have been a friend of Quincy Jones since 1959 or 1960. At that time he was a recording artist, an outstanding jazz composer and arranger. He was also head of Artists and Repertoire at Mercury Records, and he was responsible for an album of my music on that label, as well as a Sarah Vaughan album of my songs. As I made more and more albums, I tried to return the favor, recording such things of his as the "Ironside" theme and "Stockholm Sweetnin'."

Quincy broke into pictures with a score for *The Pawn-*

broker, which Sidney Lumet directed, and he had done an excellent job. He got the fever and wanted to be a film composer.

About 1965, I got a call from someone at Universal, where Quincy was up for a film. I was trying to figure out what the point of the conversation was, and then gradually I realized I was being felt out, in a roundabout way. Finally it came: Did I think a black man could handle a dramatic picture?

Almost gritting my teeth to control my anger, I said, "He's fine, you couldn't do any better than that. What's the problem?"

Quincy was not the first black musician in the film studios. That distinction went to Will Voudry, who started orchestrating Broadway shows with the Ziegfeld Follies of 1913, became a much sought-after orchestrator of musicals, and worked as an arranger on *Show Boat* for Jerome Kern. After that he moved to Hollywood, where he was an arranger and musical director at Fox Films. Benny Carter had been writing for film since the 1940s, although he encountered discrimination in the nature of the assignments. Along with Quincy, J. J. Johnson, Benny Golson, and Oliver Nelson became accepted as film and TV composers.

All these years after Will Voudry, I found the question about Quincy almost unbelievable. But it happened and it wasn't that long ago. And while we are on the subject, I am still saddened by how few black musicians there are in our symphony orchestras. But that's another story.

In 1966 I scored another film for Blake, an excellent comedy with Dick Shawn and Carroll O'Connor titled *What Did You Do in the War, Daddy?*, which did not experience the success it deserved, and another Stanley Donen film, *Arabesque*, with Gregory Peck and Sophia Loren. Again I went back to London to work on it—away from home and exacerbating the problems these absences caused.

That was the second picture for Stanley in what I call my Stanley Donen trilogy, first *Charade* and then *Arabesque*. The following year, 1967, I got a call from Audrey Hepburn in the south of France. She and Albert Finney were shooting *Two for the Road* with Stanley. My secretary put the call through and I heard that unmistakable voice.

"Hank—" she has a way of saying my name that sings— "we would love it if you would do our film. I spoke with Stanley and he wanted me to call you personally to ask you to do it."

I said, "Audrey, I don't think there's any problem. Of course I'll do it."

It was the only time the star of a picture ever called me about doing a score.

Two for the Road was a unique picture, far ahead of its time. The style, the way of telling the story, was very unusual for 1967. I read the script by Fred Raphael. The story kept going back and forth in time. I said, "Stanley, I can't make head or tail of this."

Stanley said, "When you see it on the screen, it will be much more obvious—the change of clothes, the change of cars. It'll be much clearer."

I'm afraid the picture was a little too imaginative for its time. It received excellent reviews, but it was just not a box-office hit.

Usually you can tell if a picture has legs by how often it shows up on cable television. Some pictures never show up. Certain pictures with certain stars, or with a certain mystique that makes them interesting, continue to show up, and that picture does.

If I regret that Audrey Hepburn didn't sing "Moon River" on the album of the *Breakfast at Tiffany's* music, I made another error on *Two for the Road* that makes me want to kick myself. I was searching for a sound for that picture. I wrote one melody as a theme, but Stanley wasn't taken by it. He said, "It's very nice, but I don't get anything from it. It doesn't move." It didn't have many notes to it (although neither did "Moon River"). But I sat down and came up with another theme, which had a moving figure in the counterline.

I wanted to get something touching. I had always been a fan of the French jazz violinist Stéphane Grappelli. I found some recordings of his ballads and told Stanley I wanted that sound in the picture. Stanley said, "Great, see if we can get him." Stéphane was in Paris. We contacted him and arranged for him to come over to London to record.

The orchestra was assembled. A door opened at the back of the studio. It was wintertime, and Stéphane entered in a hat and coat with his fiddle under his arm. The orchestra was facing the door. All the string players began tapping their bows on their violins the moment they saw who it was, their accolade for a great artist.

Here again, I took the whole score back to Los Angeles and re-recorded. I probably shouldn't have done it, but I was trapped in a monster of my own making. The real sadness is that I didn't have Stéphane on the recording. He is, however, the violinist in the film.

I did two pictures with Audrey that year. The other was *Wait Until Dark*. Because of the sinister characters in the story, I thought it needed something a little unsettling. I went over to Warner Bros., where they had matched twin Baldwin pianos. I thought it would be very effective to use two pianos, one tuned at 440, the other tuned a quarter-tone flat. If you played a chord on one piano and the same chord on the other, the difference in pitch would be very disturbing. It was an experimental device, but I got proof even before we were very far into the first recording session that it was effective indeed.

My pianists on that picture were Pearl Kaufman and Jimmy Rowles, both excellent artists. After we had made three or four takes on the main title, Pearl looked up and said, "Hank, can we please take a break? This is making me ill!"

She made my day. The device was working.

By 1968 and 1969, a great deal was happening in concerts. I was playing a lot of them with Al Cobine's band out of Indiana University. I was also becoming more and more involved with symphony orchestra pops concerts. I had been to Cleveland several times, as well as Minneapolis, Philadelphia, and Dallas.

In 1971, I got a call from Alfred Hitchcock's office. He wanted me to do the score for *Frenzy*. It was the only score I've ever had rejected. In 1979, Tony Thomas published a book called *Film Score*, containing chapters on various film composers. Memory was fresher then, and I can do no better than to quote—with Tony's permission—what I told him then:

> One of the advantages of having arrived at the position I am in now is that I do have considerable choice of what assignments I'm going to take. I try to take them with directors or producers with whom I can communicate. However—and this is a very big however—no matter how good you think you are at your job, or how famous you think you may be, you can still fail at the assignment if the chemistry isn't right. Many of the best composers in this business have had scores rejected and tossed out. It happened to me when I worked on *Frenzy*.
>
> We scored *Frenzy* in London, and Hitchcock was there throughout the recording session, which I found disconcerting. It was not so much a matter of his being there as that he didn't say much when we were doing it. He sat through every piece and nodded approval, and finally, when he was alone in the dubbing room, he decided that it didn't work. His reason for thinking so, I was told, was that the score was macabre, which puzzled me because it was a film with many

macabre things in it. It wasn't an easy decision to accept, and it was crushing when it happened, but I thereupon joined a very exclusive club, the composers-with-scores-dumped club. If I were doing the score again, I really don't know what I would do differently. It turned out that Hitchcock wanted a lighter score, which also confused me, because he and I discussed the musical requirements beforehand, and seemed to be in agreement. He afterwards hired Ron Goodwin, who is a friend of mine and with whom I later discussed the situation. Ron read me a detailed analysis of what Hitchcock had in mind after he decided he wanted another score. It was interesting because I wish I had been given something like that to go by. It might have been a different story. But it was quite an experience. Apart from the film, I found Mr. Hitchcock to be a gracious and generous man. During lunch one day, we got into a discussion about a mutual interest we had, wine. The next day, a case of Chateau Haut Brion— magnums—was delivered to me. Come to think of it, I guess the whole adventure was not a total loss after all. I still think what I did on *Frenzy* was good—a score complete without themes, because it seemed to me the film didn't require any.

During this same period when I was performing in concert and scoring films, my recording career was also in full swing. I was doing a pretty good juggling act keeping the three balls in the air at once. I had become a member of the impressive RCA roster that included Perry Como, Harry Belafonte, Ed Ames, Elvis Presley, Peter Nero, and Jack Jones, among others. Unlike the groups of today, who are lucky to get an album made every two years, our contracts stipulated that we must make a minimum of three albums a year. Since I did all my own arranging on these albums, the work load was heavy. My producer during most of this time was Joe Reisman, a portly Texan and a fine arranger and conductor in his own right. In fact, he had been the arranger of many of Perry Como's hits. To have a musician of Joe's experience sitting in the control booth, keeping track of and listening to everything, was a great help to me. We had a fine working relationship, and Joe became a dear friend.

Through the first half of the 1970s, things were changing rapidly in the recording business. I am reminded of a line from James Michener's novel, *Hawaii*, wherein the native chief muses that it's difficult to be king when the gods are changing. The RCA label was making a shift away from the so-called middle-of-the-road music that I represented. The big bucks spent on promotion were now going to build up the rock groups who were more in touch with the youth market. The promotion men were getting younger and younger. I knew my days were numbered when one of them met me upon my arrival at the airport in Dallas and called me Mr. Mancini.

I had recorded sixty albums in my twenty years with RCA. To go on at that pace without the full support of the record company seemed pointless to me. In 1978, in mid-contract, I had a meeting with Bob Sommer, who was then head of the record division, and told him I was leaving. There were no tears on either side.

It has not escaped my notice that RCA has reissued on compact disc a great many of the albums I made for the company. Apparently the powers that be have concluded that somebody out there still likes me and enjoys my music.

In 1984 I made a return visit to my alma mater. Jimmy Galway and I recorded an album, *In the Pink*, in London. I had met him for the first time the year before, at the Grammy Awards ceremony at the Shrine Auditorium in Los Angeles. The performers had dressing rooms on the second floor behind the stage. As I walked down the hall to my dressing room, I heard someone playing *The Pink Panther* theme on the flute. My curiosity piqued, I knocked on the door. It opened, and there stood James Galway. We had a long conversation, by the end of which we had agreed to meet at some future date to record an album of my music, which we did the following year.

This Irishman is one of the most open, honest, and loving people I have ever met. His only fault is that he's not Italian. He and his wife, Jeannie, have become our good friends.

In 1968, I scored another picture with Blake and Peter Sellers, *The Party*, which was not a big success. It's an interesting picture, too, in that it is part of a particular body of Blake's work, a series of films satirizing the Hollywood movie industry itself. Peter plays a would-be actor from India who, working as an extra in one of those Khyber Pass kind of movies that had a vogue in the late 1930s and early 1940s, disastrously fouls up the shooting of a major scene. Later he is invited to a big Hollywood party, where his antics continue to create disaster. Blake would continue to expose the flaws and the follies of Hollywood until he did what most people would consider his major work in this area, *S.O.B.* But *The Party*, for all that it was only a modest success, is still worth seeing. Peter was brilliant in it, as usual.

That year I also scored a picture, *Gaily, Gaily*, for another director, Norman Jewison. Norman and I are good friends. Ginny and I have often visited Norman and his wife, Dixie, on their farm north of Toronto. The relationship started before *Gaily, Gaily*. Norman and Marty Ransohoff had wanted me for *The Cincinnati Kid*, but I was not free at the time. Lalo Schifrin did that score. Then I got a call to do another Norman Jewison picture, *The Thomas Crown Affair* with Steve McQueen, and I couldn't do that either. Michel Legrand wrote that score. Then I got a call for *Gaily, Gaily*. I was available. It starred Melina Mercouri.

Alan and Marilyn Bergman and I wrote two songs for the picture, one of which Melina was supposed to sing. She was not a singer and had reservations about doing it, although she had sung in *Never on Sunday*. Alan, Marilyn, and I would go up to her house in the Hollywood Hills to discuss the song with her. Invariably, before she ever mentioned it, she would sit us down to a home-cooked Greek meal, which sometimes lasted several hours. We were the best-fed song-writers in Hollywood at that time. As an afterthought, she would talk about the song. It was called "There's Enough to Go Around."

But the picture was not a roaring success. And Norman Jewison is not accustomed to not having roaring successes. Most of his pictures have done very well. And so every once in a while, when we're going up a ski lift or going down the slopes, he sticks the needle in, saying, "You know, you did one of my few failures."

And I always say, "Thanks a lot, Norman."

In 1970, I went to Brazil as a judge at their international song festival. I got a call in Rio de Janeiro from Paramount, asking if I'd be interested in doing a picture called *The Molly Maguires*. I said, "I thought that was scored already."

I was told that it was but they didn't like the music.

I looked at it when I returned. It was an interesting picture, and I wrote the music. But here again, someone else had had a score rejected. I enjoyed that film because it permitted me to write purely dramatic music rather than a song score.

That year Joseph Levine produced a picture called *Sunflower*, which was shot throughout Italy and the Soviet Union with Marcello Mastroianni and Sophia Loren. It had great scope. The studio insisted on using dubbed voices for the American release, which threw the whole film out of kilter, and it was not a success here.

Still, that picture was fun for me, for many reasons. The producer was Carlo Ponti and the director Vittorio De Sica. One of the special reasons I wanted to do this movie was De Sica. Not only was he one of the truly great directors, but there was never an actor I enjoyed more on the screen. To me he was the quintessential Italian, and I wanted to get to know him better.

One day I went to visit Sophia Loren and her husband,

Carlo Ponti, at their home in the country, a huge estate near
the Pope's summer residence. Wandering throughout the
grounds were exotic animals in pairs, like Noah's ark. The
Pontis were very gracious to me, charming people. And
what man can meet Sophia without being slightly shaken by
the experience? She is much taller than you expect her to
be, and even more beautiful offscreen than on.

The only problem I had was the conflict between Ponti
and De Sica, which nobody had warned me about. I went
into a spotting session with the two of them, both of whom
spoke English fairly well, fortunately. We began to discuss
the music, and I suddenly realized I was caught in the
middle of an argument that had been going on since the
picture had started. They obviously had been having at each
other, for various artistic and procedural reasons, fighting
the good Italian fight. There was no shouting, but the
gestures were sarcastic and very eloquent. I soon got the
point. I was trying to find the appropriate dramatic places
for music, and they were going at each other with me as the
battleground. Ponti would make eye contact with me as he
talked about the film, wanting my undivided attention. He
would say, "Now this is a very dramatic scene, and the music
should be. . . ."

I would glance over at De Sica, and he would be giving
me that famous forefinger dragging the corner of the eye
down, meaning, "Don't pay any attention to this fool."

This continued, De Sica making fun of Ponti. Then it
would reverse. I would be talking with Vittorio, and Carlo
would be making gestures seeming to tell me to pay no
attention to *this* damn fool. Whatever one said, the other
would be ridiculing him behind his back with that incredible vocabulary of insulting gestures the Italians have. It was
hilarious, but I controlled myself. Indeed I didn't dare
laugh; that would have betrayed the trust. You couldn't tell
one gentleman the other was mocking him, especially when
they were both Italian.

I wrote the score for that film in L.A. and recorded it in Rome with a large orchestra. It was my first recording experience there, and it came as somewhat of a shock.

There's a lack of discipline among the musicians in Rome, and we're just not ready for it. For example, if one of the musicians feels nature's call, he just gets up and leaves—even in the middle of recording—and you're left standing there on the podium with one of your players missing. There's nothing you can do about it; you have to wait until he comes back.

I found too that I had to be very, very careful how I spoke to the musicians. The Italians have fierce pride, and they just don't behave the way our musicians do. Many times when you're running down the music for a scene for the first time, you'll encounter wrong notes, which may be errors of the copyist or even the composer. In correcting wrong notes, I had to be very tactful. Though my Italian is limited, numbers and notes I can handle. There was an error in the part of one of the French horns. I looked at the first horn player and said, not sharply or critically, "In bar thirteen, the first note is a B-natural." The guy stood up, indignant, tapped his finger on the music, and said, "I played what it says on the paper! It says B-flat, and I played B-flat!"

"Okay, okay," I said, backing down quickly. I didn't want a horn player walking out of the session.

He took it as a personal affront that I would correct a note he had played. Recording in Rome can be very interesting.

Curiously enough, although *Sunflower* did not do well in this country, it was a big hit in Japan. The theme from the picture is my biggest success there. The Japanese love sentimental waltzes. "Moon River" and *Charade* are also big hits in Japan.

Another insight into the Japanese:

Right after we won the award for "Moon River," and it was a big success all over the world, Ginny and I went into

La Scala for dinner one night. A friend of mine was sitting with a Japanese lady. I said, "Hello."

He said to her, "I would like you to meet my friend Henry Mancini. Henry wrote 'Moon River.'" She became very flustered. The Japanese have a way of cupping the hand and putting it over the mouth when they are embarrassed, as if to hide emotion. She made that gesture, blushing, and then she couldn't contain herself, and she blurted out, "Happy New Year!"

One of the most unusual projects I did overseas was a film produced by David Wolper and Stan Margulies called *Visions of Eight*. It was a documentary, filmed during the 1972 Munich Olympics, directed by eight different directors from different countries. Each had picked his subject and imposed his vision on it. The French director Claude Lelouch, for example, had taken the subject of losers; John Schlesinger had done his segment on the long-distance runners; Juri Ozerov of the Soviet Union, Milos Forman from Czechoslovakia, Kon Ichikawa from Japan, Mai Zetterling from Sweden, Michael Pfleghar from Germany, and Arthur Penn from the United States had each done a segment. It was a very ambitious project.

I went to Paris to meet with the various directors. Milos Forman decided to shoot his section to the "Ode to Joy" movement of the Beethoven *Ninth Symphony*, so he was taken care of. Kon Ichikawa provided his own music—one of the early electronic scores. Mai Zetterling decided music would not help her section, as did Arthur Penn. I had meetings with Schlesinger, Claude Lelouch, and Juri Ozerov about their segments.

I came to admire Stan Margulies greatly. The picture was supposed to be roughly two hours and a few minutes long. Juri Ozerov came in with an opening segment that ran about an hour on its own. He adamantly maintained that this was his cut and he would not hear of anyone editing it down.

We were doing the work in Claude Lelouch's cutting room in Paris. He has a big complex of small theaters and technical facilities. Stan had a meeting with Ozerov that lasted at least three hours. I had no idea what was going on. When Stan came out and told me he had the segment cut down to length, I said, "You are the Henry Kissinger of movie producers." In 1983 I again had the pleasure of working with Stan, this time on *The Thorn Birds*.

I played some themes for Lelouch and Schlesinger. Schlesinger threw me a curve in that he had used a temp track for the big final race. This is a fairly common practice, using an already existing piece of music as a temporary score. He had used Prokofiev's *Lieutenant Kije*. I was slightly intimidated by that, as I am many times when temporary scores are put in so that the movie is more easily watched by those who are going to sell it.

I returned home to write the score, then sent it to Munich, where we were to record. I flew over, and in the Bavaria studios we set up the orchestra and started to record.

My experience with the German musicians was almost the diametrical opposite of the one I'd had in Rome. The Germans were disciplined, all right—perhaps too much so. Some parts of the score were in a "legitimate" classical style, but others were in a popular idiom, with some jazz and rock inflections. There were problems in phrasing these sections correctly. But the music came out all right; it was released as an album.

In 1974, a picture came along that I enjoyed a great deal. I was hired to do the compilation and all the needle-and-thread work for *That's Entertainment!*, a film produced by Jack Haley, Jr., that covered the history of the MGM musicals. All the music in the picture, from the earliest days up to and including my music, was recorded on the same stage. Because of this, when we'd come out of a number with Fred Astaire or Gene Kelly, and I would pick it up to underscore the next narration scene, there would be no difference in the sound, even though these segments of score had been recorded many years apart. At that time they had changed nothing on the stage. I liked working on that picture because I enjoy getting back to just arranging.

Another picture that year was *The White Dawn*, about three Boston whalers stranded around Baffin Bay early in this century. These three sailors, lost on an ice floe, are found by Eskimos. The story raises questions of who is actually civilized.

I was concerned about what to do with Eskimo music. I found that about all they had in the way of music was the human voice (which is, of course, the first instrument) and some strange drums made of hoops stretched with walrus or seal bladders. Phil Kaufman, who directed the picture, had recorded an old Eskimo woman singing a chant. Surprisingly, she was right on pitch with our European tempered scale, so much so that I could take the woman's voice and put orchestra behind it. She was perfectly in tune with our system and with herself.

The White Dawn was a film composer's dream because there were so many open sequences, with no sound but the wind. There was little dialogue, no cars crashing or people slamming doors to get in the way of the music. So the score ran an hour and twenty minutes in a two-hour picture. Producer Martin Ransohoff and I finally succeeded in getting together on this film. He is a true producer in the best sense of the word, and I enjoy working with him. So far the relationship has produced, among others, *Silver Streak* and *Nightwing*, directed by Arthur Hiller, and *Welcome Home*, directed by Franklin Schaffner.

The next year, Blake filmed *The Return of the Pink Panther* with Peter Sellers. On this film I met Tony Adams. Blake brought him in as associate producer. He is a bright, young Irishman who entered the film business under the wing of director John Boorman. He has been associated with Blake on all his films since then. It was filmed in England, as were all the subsequent Pink Panther pictures, including in 1976 *The Pink Panther Strikes Again* and in 1978 *The Revenge of the Pink Panther*. Peter died in July 1980; thus the last two were without his participation. *The Trail of the Pink Panther* was a compilation of previously unused footage of Peter interspersed with some new scenes. In the last one, *The Curse of the Pink Panther*, Blake tried to cast someone new who would carry on the Clouseau tradition, but it didn't really work, so that was the end of it. It was obvious that Sellers was one of a kind and couldn't be replaced, and finally the Pink Panther film series was laid to rest.

I wrote the scores for David Niven's last two pictures. I first began to notice something wrong in 1982, when I worked on *Whose Little Girl Are You?*, which was shot in the south of France with David and Art Carney. David was having trouble articulating. His words were sometimes garbled and slurred. You could see in many scenes he was struggling. His image to the public, and in real life, was that of a highly articulate and precise speaker, and he was trying to maintain it. None of us realized we were seeing early symptoms of Lou Gehrig's disease.

Using various means, he got through the picture. In the postproduction phase, he went in and did a lot of looping. Looping, as I mentioned earlier, is a process in which the film is projected on a screen and the actor re-records dialogue lines, lip-synching to the picture. It is done for various reasons. Sometimes extraneous noise gets into the sound track—a jet passing overhead, a car horn in the distance—or a word or two will not come through clearly in an otherwise good take. But in this case it was because David's speech was deteriorating.

By the next picture, which was to be the last of the Pink Panther films, the problem had grown much worse. Blake assembled some of the original cast of the first Panther film, including Robert Wagner, Capucine, and David, for *The Curse of the Pink Panther*.

By now it was hard to understand David's lines. If you look at the picture you can see his deterioration. When Blake went into postproduction, it was obvious that entire scenes were a problem, and David was no longer capable of looping his lines. As he so often had done in the past, Blake came up with a solution. He brought in Rich Little to loop the lines in an absolutely remarkable imitation of David's voice. Few people who see the picture ever guess that they're not hearing Niven.

David and I had become good friends. He was a professional Englishman, in the best sense: polished, witty, and articulate. Lou Gehrig's disease is one of the tragedies of our time, and for this man, to whom words meant so much, to lose his power of speech was particularly ironic.

15
Blake and Julie

For some time, Blake had been wanting to make a picture called *Darling Lili*. In 1969, Paramount gave him the go-ahead. Johnny Mercer and I wrote the songs for it. It was an appealing project, since the songs were to be performed in the story, not simply used in underscore, and we had a great singing star in Julie Andrews. It was a colorful period piece, set in World War I, with Julie as a German spy who infiltrates the Allies and then falls in love with an American pilot, played by Rock Hudson. But the picture was to prove traumatic, for both Blake and me.

Julie and Blake were married in November of 1969, while the picture was in production. All of us among his friends had long since overcome our initial shock at their relationship, which seemed like a classic mismatch. Their courtship had been fairly long. He would bring her to screenings and other events. They weren't much for parties, though if there was a party at Blake's house, she would be there. Like many people, Ginny and I found ourselves saying, "No, this can't be. What in the world is Blake *thinking* of?"

But this was because none of us really knew Julie, who is one of the most remarkable women I've ever met. She was trying—she's *still* trying!—to shed her Mary Poppins image, which is not her at all. She is funny, she can be delightfully bawdy, and she tells a joke with gusto and great humor.

She goes right down to the roots of life. But we didn't know that about her. We smile at the way some members of the public identify an actor with a role, even going so far as to write to someone who plays a doctor to seek medical advice. But even those of us in the industry tend to be deceived by roles people play, and we all thought Julie *was* Mary Poppins. The more we got to know her, the more we realized that she and Blake had a great deal in common. They were extremely compatible, they understood each other, and she appreciated that gallows humor of his, the dark source of the world in his movies in which everything always goes wrong.

Professionally, Julie is marvelous. She has superb ears. She hears everything in the orchestra. Sometimes an orchestrator writes things that might not be right for the lyrics of a song, even one of his own; or he gets far too involved in the arrangement itself, thinking purely musically, to the detriment of the words. A few times during the making of *Darling Lili* she made very astute judgments and corrections on parts of my arrangements that weren't giving her and the songs the best possible support. And instantly, when she drew my attention to these things, I'd say, "You're right."

I have never seen Julie flustered, either in personal life or in professional situations. Since then, I have conducted for her in concerts, and she is always the consummate professional. She will not sail uncharted waters and will hold back on a decision until she knows exactly what she is going to do. Some people try to wing it, but she won't, and working with her on *Darling Lili* was a delight.

It became apparent during the making of *Darling Lili* that Blake and the studio were at odds. There was one problem after another over finance and other matters, and the tension kept rising. It was turning out to be a lovely picture, but the studio was down on it. It was a very depressing time for Blake.

During filming I got the strangest visits from studio emissaries, asking my opinion on what a particular song should be, if it should be in this scene or that. Being somewhat naive by nature, I didn't see what they were up to, so I would talk with them. Then they used whatever I said as a weapon against Blake. They would decide on a certain attack and then approach me because I was so close to him and supposedly had influence. Then they went to Blake, saying they had talked to me and that I agreed with them about the scene. When at last I discovered how I had been used, I resented it deeply.

It almost destroyed my friendship with Blake. But "almost" is a big word, and in the end the professional and personal relationship was too strong to be destroyed by such methods of manipulation.

Ginny and I had rented a house at Malibu; Blake had one nearby. One day around midday, I was on the porch, and Blake walked by on the beach. We exchanged the amenities. He didn't want to talk about the situation, but I did. So I got into it with him and told him what had happened. I told him that I had been misquoted and used by the people from the head office. The last thing in the world I would do to Blake—or any director—is to second-guess him or go behind his back. It is not good professionally or morally.

Blake and I straightened things out that day. In 1988, our professional association became thirty years old. We had done twenty-five films together.

Darling Lili put a strain on Blake's relationships with a lot of people around town, and particularly with people who had any connection with that picture. It came to seem that anybody who had anything to do with it had a curse hanging over them. It was because of Paramount and the experience with *Darling Lili* that Blake concluded that Hollywood—at least for that period of his life—was not where he wanted to live and work, and shortly after our talk on the beach he and Julie moved to London and then on to a residence in Gstaad, Switzerland.

In 1979, I worked for Blake on *"10,"* which dealt with a

man's crisis upon reaching age forty. He had written it some years earlier for Jack Lemmon. Finally he had the approval to do it for Orion Pictures. At first George Segal was to play the lead, but at the last minute he bowed out, leaving Blake in a spot, as he had been when Peter Ustinov withdrew from *The Pink Panther*. Blake came up with Dudley Moore, who contributed greatly to the rousing success *"10"* was to enjoy.

Every time I read something that Blake writes, if I set my mind in the right direction and look carefully, I find something autobiographical in it. I think Blake went through the same change at age forty, though not as a songwriter, that the protagonist of *"10"* is going through. Later on, he dealt with the crisis of age sixty in *That's Life* and this time Jack Lemmon did play the part.

Blake's control of the medium is enormous. He seems to know exactly what to do. There's a scene near the end of *"10,"* when Dudley Moore follows Bo Derek down to Los Hades in Mexico, and he finally gets her into bed. The music behind that scene is Ravel's *Bolero*. Everybody gives me credit for a brilliant touch in using it, but I don't deserve it; Blake had written it into the script. *Bolero* is the great cliché in music, supposedly the perfect background music for making love, from the quiet beginning to the climax. During the course of the production, someone from Orion who had been watching, looking out for Orion's interests, came up with the idea of doing it in a disco version. Disco was really hot at the time. Overlooked was the fact that the purely classical rendition of the piece was what made the scene funny. Blake refused, and we did it as written.

Blake is not a creature of the system, and the criticism that started with the sabotage of *Darling Lili* continued. His antistudio stance raised a lot of hackles, and by 1981 he had been saddled with a completely undeserved reputation as an extravagant filmmaker.

It is not surprising, then, if Blake harbored great resentment of the movie establishment. It festered and finally came to a head in 1981, in *S.O.B.* It was right on target, a devastating satire, one of those pictures where you can almost guess the real identities played by the characters—including that of the studio head, played by Robert Vaughan. Blake took everything he ever felt needed to be told about the industry and packed it into that picture. It was a picture with a lot of controlled venom; it was on the mark. Hollywood has been exposed in many films, among them *Sunset Boulevard, The Big Knife,* and *The Bad and the Beautiful,* but it was never done from a more personal point of view than in *S.O.B.*, which stands for *Standard Operating Bullshit.*

I then worked with Blake and Julie on a film I thought was one of the most perfect pictures I'd ever done. *Victor/Victoria* encompassed everything I'd been trained to do. It had to do with songwriting, it had to do with scoring, it had to do with visual music on the screen. Leslie Bricusse and I wrote the song score, which won the Oscar that year, 1982.

I first met Leslie early in 1963 while in London writing the score for *Charade.* I was staying at the Mayfair Hotel, off Berkeley Square. One afternoon while I was working at the piano, the phone rang. It was Sammy Davis, Jr., who was staying in a bizarre *Arabian Nights* type of suite down the hall from me. In bidding for the posh trade, the hotel had redone a number of their suites; good taste was not the goal of the decorators.

Sammy asked if he could bring a songwriter friend over to my suite to use the piano. He had a song he wanted Sammy to hear. Sammy arrived at my door and introduced me to Leslie Bricusse. Since I was right in the middle of writing, I asked if I could sit off to the side and listen. The pianist, Ian Fraser, started, and Leslie sang "If I Ruled the World." His performance was not exactly in the Sinatra class, but his heartfelt rendition made up for that. From this meeting I struck up a friendship with Leslie. After many social encounters at which the phrase "Let's write something together" was prominent, Leslie and I finally did a few years later: Leslie wrote the words for *Two for the Road*.

Leslie is the consummate Brit and a graduate of Cambridge University. His first love was, and I think still is, musical theater. He and Anthony Newley wrote the musicals *Stop the World—I Want to Get Off* and *The Roar of the Greasepaint, the Smell of the Crowd*.

Leslie has an encyclopedic memory for things theater, going back, it seems, to the Greek tragedies. Sometimes I just like to sit back and watch his mind work. It worked a great deal on *Victor/Victoria*.

Every scene in that picture followed logically from the one before it; everything was perfectly choreographed. The script was brilliant, Julie's performance was one of her best, and Robert Preston and James Garner were excellent. The picture was shot at Pinewood Studios outside London. They knocked out a wall between two major stages and built the exteriors, the interiors, everything on this huge combined set. There wasn't a foot of that film shot anywhere else, and this gave Blake perfect control over the look of the picture.

This was the second time Bob Preston had played a gay role for Blake. The previous year he'd played the Dr. Feelgood character in *S.O.B.*, and in *Victor/Victoria* he played the old song-and-dance man. He did it well, making the character very warm and sympathetic.

The picture was very successful for everyone.

There are very few pictures I've done that I have the patience to sit down and watch. It's not a question of whether they're good or not; I just don't like to do it, once they're finished. But *Victor/Victoria* is one that I *can* watch again. There is something about that picture that gives me pleasure to this day.

With Paul McCartney and John Lennon during a rehearsal for a
television special in Manchester, England, 1964. ♪

With favorite leading lady Audrey Hepburn on the set of her film
Wait Until Dark at Warner Bros. studios in Burbank, California,
1967.

♪ ♪
Trumpeter Buddy
Brisbois was a favorite
musician, traveling
companion, and close
friend.

With Johnny Mercer in 1970.

Drummer Shelly Manne, who is heard on many Mancini albums and film scores, with Hank and friend at Lion Country Safari, California, 1972. The occasion was the taping of one of the shows in the Mancini Generation series.

Chris and Henry Mancini share a laugh in Los Angeles, 1972. ♪♪

1974 marked Henry's fiftieth birthday. At the party held at the Beverly Hills Hotel, he is seen with A. C. Lyles, James Cagney, and Helen Hayes.

Henry and Ginny with close friends Betty and David Rose, Beverly Hills Hotel, 1975. Fellow composer Rose helped Hank break into writing for radio before the film days.

At the premiere of *The Return of the Pink Panther*, Gstaad, Switzerland, 1975, with Blake Edwards (center) and Peter Sellers.

H.R.H. Prince Charles, Prince of Wales, at the Royal London premiere of *The Return of the Pink Panther*, 1975.

With Anthony Newley, Sammy Davis, Jr., and Leslie Bricusse at the Shubert Theater opening night party for *Stop the World—I Want to Get Off*, Los Angeles, 1978.

Longtime musical associates: drummer Jack Gilfoy; saxophonist Don Menza; trumpeter Cecil Welch; guitarist Royce Campbell; bassist Jim Johnson, with Henry at Caesars Palace, Las Vegas, December 1979.

Holding the Father of the Year Award, Henry is flanked by twin daughters Felice on the left and Monica on the right at the Biltmore Hotel, Los Angeles, 1982. ♪

Ginny with her irrepresible mother, Jo, in Holmby Hills, California, 1985.

Henry and Luciano Pavarotti at a recording session for the bestselling *Mamma* album in Geneva, Switzerland, 1984.

Two flutists: James Galway and Henry at the Barbican Centre, London, 1984.

(Photo by Doug McKenzie of P.P.S.)

H.M. Queen Elizabeth, the Queen Mother, shaking hands with Henry at the Royal Command Performance, London, 1984. James Galway is to Henry's left.

Ralph Musengo with his wife, Helen, in Cleveland, 1985. Helen is the cousin Hank thinks of as a sister.

Composer Morton Gould, president of ASCAP, and Blake
Edwards, Henry, Julie Andrews, and Quincy Jones, when Henry
received the ASCAP Golden Soundtrack Award. The ceremony
was at the Century Plaza Hotel in April 1988.

Henry with his grandson, Luca Nicola Mancini, Los Angeles, 1988.

(Photo by Alex Berliner)

Grandson Christopher with his 46-pound Nile perch, caught in Lake Victoria, Kenya, during an unforgettable African trip, August 1988.

(Photo by Penny Wolin, Los Angeles, 1989)

The Mancini family. At left, Felice Mancini Erenberg, Douglas Erenberg. Holding her son, Luca, is Analei Mancini. Chris stands behind Henry and Ginny. Next is Monica, and in front of her is Christopher. Leila, Analei's daughter, is in the foreground.

West Aliquippa, November 1988. The house on Beaver Avenue that Henry Mancini grew up in during the 1930s. The evening after this photo was taken, he conducted the Pittsburgh Symphony Orchestra.

Paul Newman is a good friend, and, as with Blake and me, I'll go months at a time without even speaking to him on the phone. Working with Paul is completely different from working with Blake.

I had known Paul for several years when, in 1971, I got a call from Harry Garfield, head of the music department at Universal, who said there was a picture coming in called *Sometimes a Great Notion*, based on the Ken Kesey book. Paul was the star, and he had directed.

I went in to the studio to see it and thought it was a very good film. We discussed the music.

While shooting *Sometimes a Great Notion* in the timber country of Oregon, Paul had found that there was a lot of country and western music on the radio and the jukeboxes, so that was the kind of score I wrote—a good deal of Cajun music and country guitars. It worked out well. I used the country feeling against the larger orchestral dramatic material.

Later on I scored *The Shadow Box*, a two-hour TV movie he directed, and then *Harry and Son*. In 1987, he asked me to write the music for *The Glass Menagerie*, which starred Joanne Woodward, his wife, and which Paul directed.

His "shorthand" was something I had to get used to. We'd be talking about a scene and he'd say, "Bassoon."

I'd say, "What do you mean, Paul? A bassoon with what? Or just a bassoon?"

He'd say, "Yeah."

And I had to figure that out. I'd keep talking until I deciphered his meaning. I love to talk with Paul, because he is always so deeply involved in whatever he's doing. He might say, "Oboe," and I'd have to go through the same thing again. I came to understand that what he was actually saying was that there were certain qualities of a given instrument that he wanted in the scene in question. He did not mean that he literally wanted bassoon or oboe in the score at that point, but something that made the kind of sound he wanted. Usually bassoons are used as comedy instruments, but they can be very touching. Oboes are melancholy. I learned to understand what he meant. As we talked I found that Paul does indeed have a deep appreciation and knowledge of many kinds of music.

Blake seldom even went to spotting sessions with me. As I've said, he'd give me the picture, and I'd decide what had to be done. I might discuss it with him briefly, and I might in some cases let him hear the theme I was going to use. He sometimes didn't hear the score until recording was finished.

With Paul it was totally different, and yet just as comfortable. Paul was involved with the music from the spotting session to the final recording. When I went in to spot, Paul always came with me. We'd sit in front of a machine called a Kem, which has a ground-glass viewing screen. Reels of film are mounted on wheels flat on the table, and the sound track is synched up to the picture, which is seen on the Kem's screen, about a foot and a half wide. We'd spend hours at the Kem discussing a scene, getting the start right, getting the end right. I would constantly question him.

I learned that when it came to scoring a film, he had an aversion to strings. It started in *Sometimes a Great Notion.* When we got to *The Shadow Box* and *Harry and Son* and especially *The Glass Menagerie*, he said, "No damn violins."

I said, "That's a pretty strong statement, Paul."

He said, "No. I don't want any violins."

What he meant is that he did not want syrupy, soaring, swooping, melancholy Muzak sounds. But I needed some what I call glue for the score. I didn't want to get into synthesizers, which are very good for making glue. I had woodwinds—flutes, bassoons, oboes, clarinets, in pairs— one keyboard, and harp. But I needed something for glue.

Joanne Woodward had done *The Glass Menagerie* on the stage. That version had incidental music by Paul Bowles. Joanne particularly liked the theme Bowles had written for her character. So did I. Paul—Newman, that is—told me, "It's up to you. If you want to use it, go ahead." I kept it. And that theme was for solo violin, so I knew I could get away with one violin. But I still needed my glue. I wrote for a double string quartet. This has a particular sound of its own. You write exactly as you would for string quartet, but you've got two instruments on each part. The instruments would play harmony notes, mostly in the vicinity of the center of the keyboard, not going too high or too low.

We recorded in New York—the first time, curiously enough, I had ever recorded there. The musicians were already assembled when I walked into the studio with Paul. He looked down and asked darkly, "What are *they*?"

I said, "Well, Paul, they're violins, violas, and cellos."

He said, "I know what they are. And I don't want strings."

I said, "Paul, you won't know they're there. I guarantee you won't know they're there."

He took on that mock gruffness of his and said, "All right, we'll give it a try." And as it worked out, he liked the music. The score was very intimate, as was the picture.

Paul and I often went for walks between sessions, usually to restaurants. He likes to walk, and he won't take cabs just to avoid people. It was winter. He'd put his cap and heavy jacket on, and we'd walk down Broadway and other places. People who recognized him would simply say, "Hi." They wouldn't bother him. He'd tip his hat and say, "Good morning."

Once we were looking for a restaurant in Midtown. He wasn't certain of the address. After a while it was obvious that we weren't making any headway. He said, "Wait a minute, I'd better look it up."

We crossed the street to a shop that sold tapes, records, cameras, and audio equipment. The windows were covered with bars, and you had to press a buzzer by the door for admittance. Through the glass and with Paul wearing a cap, the people inside couldn't see who it was. We went into the shop, where two teenage girls and a guy were working. Paul said, "Have you got a phone book?"

The two girls saw those blue eyes of his and that gray hair under the cap and couldn't believe it: Paul Newman coming into their shop. Their eyes widened. But they didn't make a big deal of it, and neither did he. I'm sure they told all their friends about it that evening.

I've been around when people did make a big deal of it and his privacy was violated. I have, I realize, a certain amount of public visibility, but it isn't remotely like what Paul has. His is one of the best-known faces on this planet. Paul doesn't like intrusions on his privacy and won't allow them. And this toughness in no way contradicts his sensitivity and decency in dealing with people in his work.

I think Paul is an actor first, a director second, and he sees things through an actor's eyes. When he is rehearsing and one of his actors suggests a reading, he'll let him try it his way. He has great respect for actors, though he retains control within the parameters of the project. And he adores his wife, both as a woman and as an actress. He is impressed by her. In *The Shadow Box* and in *The Glass Menagerie*, in a spotting session, we might be talking about some detail of the music while viewing one of her scenes. He'd sit back in the chair and his eyes would go kind of glassy and he'd say, "Isn't she something?"

There is one especially touching scene in *The Glass Menagerie*. I was in the studio conducting, and Paul was in the booth, behind the glass; my back was to him. In that scene Joanne is talking about the gentleman callers and how things used to be in the South with the jonquils in a softer time. It's very poignant, one of the best scenes Tennessee Williams wrote in the play. The music at this point was very sensitive, ending with just solo cello and piano, fading off into infinity. It was so quiet. No one said a word. I turned around and looked at Paul. It was the first time he had seen the scene scored, and he was sitting there like a little kid with tears coming from his eyes.

I haven't done anywhere near the number of scores for Paul that I have for Blake, but both relationships have been happy ones for me.

Paul stayed to the very end of *The Glass Menagerie* recording sessions. I think it was one of my best scores. And he didn't complain once about those damn strings.

A footnote to this matter of intrusions on your privacy when you're trying to have dinner.

Some time after *The Pink Panther* came out on record, a man came up to me in a restaurant, insisted on shaking my hand, and proceeded to tell me how much he loved my music. He really went on at length in that vein as my dinner grew cool on the plate. Then he said, "You know side two, track three on that album?"

"Yeah, I know it," I said. The track is "Cortina," which is quite sensual and romantic.

"Well," he said, "you know, my wife and I . . ."—and he gave me a salacious wink to make sure I knew what he was talking about—"we really like that track," he said, "and we . . . well, you know what I mean."

And old Weirdo from the Tex Beneke Band just couldn't resist. I said, "She can't be very happy. That track is only one minute and fifty-two seconds long."

16
The Process

"What do you do? Do you see a rough cut of the film? Do you read the script first? Exactly what do you do?"

I have been asked these questions hundreds of times over the past years, as has every film composer.

It all starts, of course, with someone somewhere saying, "Let's get Mancini for the score."

Sometimes I get the call directly, but most of the time the producer or director calls my agent, Al Bart, to check on my availability. This call can come at any phase of the production of the picture. Sometimes it is in an early stage of the writing of the script, sometimes after the entire film has been shot. If the script is available, I'll read it, and if there is a cut of the picture, I'll see it. If I decide to accept the assignment, Al Bart will start his negotiations. The "negotiations" go through the same legalese that everything else does in Hollywood. Most of the time, I sign my contract for the film long after it has been released.

Sometimes there is a humorous side to this ritual. Recently, the ABC-TV network bought "Peter Gunn" to be presented as a two-hour Movie of the Week. Al proceeded to make my deal with the production company. When the subject of ownership of the copyright of the "Peter Gunn" theme came up, Al told them that I was the sole owner of that copyright, and therefore they would not share in it. The attorney, who was on the sunny side of thirty, inquired with a straight face, "Would Mr. Mancini write a new 'Peter Gunn' theme?"

Now the process starts. Before a single note is written, a meeting of all those involved takes place. The number of people in the room gives an indication of how many people will have something to say later on. Specifics of the music are not really discussed at this time. The main purpose is to reach a sort of agreement on the overall approach to the score—what themes, if any, are needed, and how they should be applied.

What comes next is, for me, the most difficult hurdle: the composition of the thematic material. This can be agonizing, not to mention time-consuming. In the heat of developing themes, sometimes one is guilty of petty theft—a little pinch here and there of other people's thoughts, plus outright stealing from yourself, which is worse. I prevent this by the use of my second set of ears, Ginny's. Every theme or song that I write must first pass her scrutiny. More than a few times she has saved me from embarrassment down the line.

My old boss, Joe Gershenson, once gave me a sage bit of advice, "Take partners," meaning: let the other people in on what you intend to do. Following Joe's advice, I take the next step: letting the front office hear what I have written, with a simple tape of the material played on the piano, as in the old days, or a more elaborate demonstration using synthesizers. I have a basic four-track recording setup in my studio at home, which includes synthesizers, drum machine, and an echo unit. A good demo can only enhance the music to the ears of nonmusicians.

Once everyone agrees to go with what I've written, we wait until the final edit of the film, then proceed to the next step, which is called spotting. This is the process of deciding where the music will be placed and the exact beginning and ending of each piece of music. (The "pieces" are called cues in film parlance.) It is here that we discuss the fine points and nuances. By now a few more people have joined the team. The film editor is usually there and, sometimes, the sound effects editor. Some scenes may be carried by sound effects alone, and at this point such matters are decided. Now another person enters the story, who is invaluable to the composer—the music editor. His job is to provide all the technical information I will need to get the music onto the sound track of the film. He will provide timing sheets that show, down to one-tenth of a second, exactly where I am at each point in a cue. To aid me later, when I am conducting and recording the music, he will prepare each sequence with both visual and sound references that I will need to keep the music in perfect synchronization with the film. I work mostly with two music editors: John Hammell, an alumnus of Paramount Studios, whose experience and credits go back to the days of Cecil B. De Mille; and Steve Hope, who came up through television and is up-to-the-minute with the synthesizers and other toys and gadgets that have become necessary in the electronic age.

When the spotting session is completed, the work begins. The film editor gives me a VHS cassette of the picture, and the music editor starts to feed me the timing sheets. It helps me to look at the film straight through several times before starting to write. Film composing is a problem-solving process, and each time I see the picture I find that more problems are resolved.

Usually I try to score the film in sequence, starting at the beginning and going right through to the end. If I am having difficulty with a certain sequence, I will put it aside and turn to another, knowing, however, that I will fret over the uncompleted sequence until it is finished.

For purposes of identification, each cue is given a numerical identity such as 1-M-1, which indicates that it is the first music cue in the first reel of film, and so forth. It is also given an actual title for purposes of copyright. Ever since film composing began, composers have been vying to see who could make the worst pun on the title of a cue. The entries are legion. However, one sticks in my mind, although I'm sure the author intended no pun. A prominent Viennese composer who spoke English perfectly, except for a slight accent, was scoring a western. He was quite a proper fellow, not taken to much joviality. On the first day of scoring the very first cue, he mounted the podium, tapped his baton, and announced, "Gentlemen, . . . Hoof Hearted."

A film, from spotting to recording, takes me about four weeks. When writing music for dramatic purposes, you start to take on in your mind the pace of what is happening in the film. One's own emotional reaction is dictated by what's up there on the screen. Pace and tempo are critical. Four different conductors performing Beethoven's Fifth Symphony will come up with four different timings for the first movement, sometimes minutes off from each other. Unless grossly exaggerated, each of them will be artistically valid. A film composer has no such leeway, as he is boxed in by precise timings that must be adhered to. That perfect tempo to your music, the one that is neither too slow nor too fast, is sometimes elusive. To me, tempo is of prime importance. It could be a deciding factor in whether a scene works or not. It gives me great pleasure to hear one of my friends' scores and be touched by it. I know what he's gone through.

The orchestration of my sketches comes next. Some of my colleagues prefer to do their own orchestration, but in most cases the time crunch does not permit me to do this. Jack Hayes has been my orchestrator since the early days of *Breakfast at Tiffany's*. Jack wrote with a partner, Leo Shuken, for many years, until Leo died. Jack is a consummate musician. More than a few times in the past, he has been called on to ghostwrite film scores for people who have been assigned to them but can't write a note. These "composers" are known among musicians as "hummers," for obvious reasons.

Upon completing his orchestration, Jack turns the music over to the copyist. My copyist is my old friend from the Tex Beneke days, Jimmy Priddy. When it comes time to record, Jack sits in the control booth, monitoring the music. Because the engineer is hearing it for the first time, Jack is a big help to him.

Even as I wallow in the muse while writing, another part of me has to remain aware of the logistics of recording the score. The best studio musicians are, of course, constantly in demand, and the top players are often booked two or three months in advance. Therefore I must decide very early in the process what the exact instrumentation is going to be.

Now another person comes into the picture: my orchestral contractor. For many years my contractor was Marion Klein, wife of the master trumpeter Mannie Klein, but Marion retired recently and now their son, Gus, has taken over. I give Gus the instrumentation, most times accompanied by a list of specific musicians I want. Gus then puts out the call and hires the musicians for me.

At this point the decision must be made as to where to record and who will be the music mixer. In contrast to earlier days when studio soundstages were aging and inadequate, they have been refurbished and are now state-of-the-art. Over the years I have mainly used three engineers: John Richards, whom I first met at CTS in London and who is now at Evergreen Studios in Los Angeles; Dan Wallin, who at present is at MGM; and Bobby Fernandez, who has been with The Burbank Studios for several years. Discussions between the composer and engineer are necessary to achieve the intended sound of the orchestra.

Now that the music has been composed and copied, the orchestra assembles in the studio in a small forest of music stands and microphones. There is the usual banter and joking among the musicians. I stand on a podium, facing the orchestra, my back to the double-paned glass window to the control booth, through which the engineer and any interested observers—the producer, the director, sometimes even some of the cast—can watch us. This is my favorite time. Now I will find out how close the sounds in my head are to the sounds I am about to hear. I give the first downbeat and run the musicians through whatever cue is to be recorded first, checking for mistakes—either my own or those of the orchestrator or copyist. It is difficult indeed for three men to write all those thousands of notes by hand without an occasional error creeping in. If I hear a wrong note from one of the instruments, I tell the player about it and he corrects it.

These first run-throughs are made without viewing the picture. Now it is time to hear the music in conjunction with seeing the scene it was written for. I ask for it to be projected on the screen, without dialogue or sound effects. The screen is behind the orchestra, so that I can see both— orchestra and picture. We play the music as the scene goes by. This is the moment I have looked forward to most. I can tell now whether or not I have accomplished my job. If the music works, it's pure heaven. If it doesn't, I fix it, and then we start going for a final take, one that is both musically satisfying and perfectly synchronized to the film.

Musicians are hired for three-hour sessions. Thirty minutes of those three hours are taken up by rest periods, in accordance with union regulations. I have found that, under normal financial pressures and taking into account the difficulty of the music, I can record up to ten minutes of music in that time. Television scoring demands up to fifteen minutes of music in the same time. Incidentally, the only real differences I find between feature film composing and television composing is that television pays less and you have less time to complete the job. The average film contains thirty to forty-five minutes of music. The epics, of course, can have wall-to-wall music.

In the old days, the music was recorded in mono, but nowadays it is recorded on thirty-two or more tracks. After the final recording session, it is ready for the mix-down process. I spend many hours with my engineer, going through each musical sequence in the film, condensing and balancing all the tracks into the final mix, which is on three tracks. This is to make the music more manageable for the next phase, which is called re-recording or dubbing.

At this point real life takes over. The euphoria of the scoring stage playback, with its large speakers, is history. The music will now become part of the overall sound of the film. Of the three sound elements in a picture—dialogue, music, and sound effects—dialogue is the prime concern. A great deal of care is expended to ensure that every word is clearly audible. The music and sound effects must take their proper place, subordinate to the dialogue.

The dubbing room is actually a small theater containing a full-size screen on one wall and a large mixing panel facing it. Usually there is a three-man crew at the panel, one of whom handles the music tracks. All the sound tracks—dialogue, music, sound effects—are fed into the mixing panel from machines in an adjoining room. The film is mixed one reel (one thousand feet) at a time. In earlier years, you had to complete an entire reel to achieve a "take." If a cue was missed at, say, 750 feet, you had to start over again from the beginning. Today, by means of a system called "rock and roll," you need only replay the miscue and insert the correction. The system, among other advantages, permits you to run the film forward or backward at high speed. Electronics has entered the field. This whole procedure can be accomplished by means of videotape. Indeed most television shows are either shot on tape, or shot on film and transferred to tape for editing and dubbing.

Many a composer's heart is broken in the dubbing room. Sometimes music is severely subdued, or cut out entirely. Sometimes it is used under scenes it was not intended for. Cries of "How can they do this to my music?" have been heard. "They" can and "they" do.

The film is now ready for the first screening. Changes may be made—scenes tightened or even omitted, for example—but essentially the process is now completed.

I feel that the old adage, "A good score is one that you're not aware of," is only half true. To be sure, this is so of scenes with important dialogue. But if the viewer is unaware of the music during a three-minute main title—as the part of the film giving the opening credits is called—the composer isn't saying much. The importance of music at this point in a picture is attested to by the "Moon River" title sequence in *Breakfast at Tiffany's*, by Bill Conti's music for the opening of *Rocky*, and by John Williams's music for *Star Wars*, among many examples I could cite.

With the new technology that keeps entering the media, film composers are constantly being placed in new learning situations. Acknowledging this and realizing that one must keep up, I maintain, nonetheless, that the real creative power is in the mind and heart of the composer.

17
The Perks

The ultimate perquisite of a composer's life is being able to make a living doing what you truly love to do: create music. And there is an enormous satisfaction in hearing your music in unexpected places. You get used to hearing it in elevators and supermarkets, even to having one of your tunes played while you're on an endless hold trying to get a telephone call through to one of the airlines. But there's a special lift that comes when it turns up in unlikely contexts.

One evening Ginny and I were watching television reports of John F. Kennedy and Jackie's arrival in Berlin, where he was about to make his famous "Ich Bin ein Berliner" speech. We saw the presidential party descend from *Air Force One*, amid pomp and ceremony. He began his inspection of the German honor guard, walking up and down between rows of soldiers at attention. And the band was playing "Moon River"! I found out later from Andy Williams that it was one of the president's favorite tunes, and he had specifically requested that it be played during the inspection.

Ginny and I were watching television the night of Jimmy Carter's inauguration. At the inaugural ball, he and Rosalynn began to dance their first waltz. The Lester Lanin Orchestra went into an introduction and, sure enough, again it was "Moon River."

Richard Nixon invited Ginny and me to dine on June 19, 1969, at the White House. It was the year my record of Nino Rota's "Love Theme from *Romeo and Juliet*" became number 1 on all the charts. It was rare for a tune like that to break through the solid wall of rock and roll in the radio industry. It earned a NARAS nomination as Record of the Year and won a Grammy for Best Instrumental Arrangement. The dinner was in honor of the *Apollo 11* astronauts, Tom Stafford, John Young, and Eugene Cernan, who were there with their wives.

It turned out that the record was a favorite of Nixon's daughter, Julie, who had just been married to David Eisenhower. I was asked to play the piano, which I did for about fifteen minutes after dinner. I asked the president if he listened to music. He said, "Come on upstairs, I'll show you." Opposite the sleeping quarters was a little room where, he said, he did all his reading. It contained a high-backed easy chair, shelves of books and records, and a hi-fi system—not state-of-the-art gear but enough to hear the records. I asked, "What's your favorite album, Mr. President?"

He pulled one from the shelf and handed it to me. It was the Richard Rodgers music for the television series "Victory at Sea." He said, "I sit in here by the hour and listen to that album." He had several Lawrence Welk albums, some Mantovani, and *The Sound of Music*, along with some Tchaikovsky.

Like so many people who dined at the White House during the Nixon administration, we noticed on this June day the president's peculiar practice of keeping a roaring fire in the fireplace and the air-conditioning going full blast.

Nixon seemed to me quite social. He was talkative, and carried conversation easily. Ginny found him most gracious. His wife, Pat, was very quiet, saying little if anything at all when he was present. The president showed us through the living quarters, and you couldn't help but feel strong emotion about the place, musing on the great, and some not-so-great, men who had walked these corridors and lived in these rooms, the speeches written here, and the enormous decisions made here by people who were, after all, only human.

Given that weight of history, it was all the more surprising that the piano I had to play was terrible. It was pretty to look at, mind you, but the action was bad, its innards dilapidated, and it was just barely in tune. I couldn't let its condition pass unremarked—after all, this was the seat of our government; Abraham Lincoln and Franklin D. Roosevelt had lived here. I said, "Mr. President, for this piano to be in the White House is unseemly. Surely the White House deserves a better instrument. After all, artists such as Arthur Rubinstein and Vladimir Horowitz play it."

The second time we went to the White House (also during the Nixon administration) was for a visit by the premier of Italy, and it seemed that almost every prominent Italian in America was there. I was at a table with Joe Garagiola. Phil Rizzuto was at another table. There were many figures from both the sports and business worlds.

The music was provided by a group of strolling players, an accordionist and some string players. As I was having dinner, these strings passed behind me and started playing "Moon River." I felt a kick under the bottom of my chair. I ignored it. Then I felt another bump, this one more insistent. I looked around. There stood a fiddle player from Indiana University who had been out on the road with Freddie Dale, Al Cobine, and me many times before he was drafted into service and assigned to the Marine band. He gave me a big wink and went on playing "Moon River."

The third White House visit came during Jimmy Carter's presidency. The occasion was a gala dinner and presentation by the American Film Institute. I was asked to perform at the Kennedy Center, and prior to the dinner the president held a reception at the White House.

The fourth visit to the White House came in 1987. Johnny Mathis and I had been invited by the Reagans to perform. The same piano was still there, but, I was pleased to find, the innards had been fixed, possibly even replaced. I did not find out who was responsible for its restoration, whether it was done on Nixon's order after I drew his attention to it or under Jimmy Carter or Ronald Reagan; but it was in very good shape.

The event was a dinner given for the prime minister of Japan, Yasuhiro Nakasone. Johnny was seated with Mrs. Reagan. I was seated at the president's table, two chairs to his left. Between us was Edie Wasserman, the wife of Lew Wasserman, the head of MCA. The president had known Lew since his own MCA days. On the president's right was Mrs. Nakasone, the prime minister's wife.

The president had a reputation for telling a good joke, which he liked to do. But he ran into a bit of a problem: Mrs. Nakasone didn't understand a word of English.

The president started out to entertain everyone, as was his way. Mrs. Nakasone's interpreter was sitting between her and the president and slightly to their rear. The president would start a story. He'd get the first line out then have to wait until the interpreter translated it for the prime minister's wife. Now the president's sense of timing on a joke was known to be good, but these pauses for translation were messing it up. He'd deliver a line, wait for the translation, then do the next line. If the joke was more than six or eight lines, he'd have to endure six or eight long heavy pauses, and by the time he got to the punch line, the wind had gone out of the sails of the joke, totally deflating it for those of us who understood English. When the interpreter translated the punch line to Mrs. Nakasone, she had no reaction at all. Nothing. Blank. He tried about three jokes, but it was all very awkward, and you could see him getting desperate and exasperated, until finally he gave up with a wink to Edie Wasserman and me.

He was a gracious and charming host who made all the guests feel at home, which was also true of Nancy.

We went into the East Room after dinner to perform. I opened.

In addition to being the official guards of the White House, the Marine Corps is responsible for providing it with musicians from a huge pool of excellent players, including strings. That evening we used a small orchestra drawn from that pool, about twenty-five musicians including ten strings. The East Room, where we played, was not very large, and Nancy was very sensitive about loud music. In accordance with her wishes, the band was always instructed to "cool it." It was a very quiet performance.

I performed "Baby Elephant Walk" with the orchestra, with myself on piccolo. When I'm in a spot and feel the need to do something more than just stand there waving my arms, I pick up a flute or a piccolo and play along. The *Pink Panther* theme followed, after which I was to introduce Johnny. I had started to thank the president and the prime minister for this memorable evening when I had a complete blackout on the prime minister's name. I thought for a minute and said, "I blew it!" It was very embarrassing for me.

Inevitably when I have been at the White House I have found myself thinking, at least for a few moments, about West Aliquippa and my beginnings. I thought, What am I doing here? How did I get here? I don't think I'd ever refuse to play there, no matter who occupies it. The irony is that, Democrat though I am, of the four times I've been to the White House, three of the visits were under Republicans. But the institution transcends politics. I like Dizzy Gillespie's response when he was taken to task for playing the White House under Reagan. He said, "It's my White House too!"

In addition to the four White House visits, I have been invited three times to take part in command performances for members of the British royal family at the Palladium in London—including the one Peter Sellers refused to attend.

These command performances are not what most Americans think. They are not a collective obeisance to the Royals, as they are called in Britain. They are charitable events, and the members of the royal family are there for the same reason the artists are, to raise money for some good causes. No one is paid. The artists contribute their services, and the proceeds go to these causes.

Command performances are always hectic, frantic affairs, because the producers crowd in as many acts as they can find to attract the crowd. They are gigantic shows, and backstage chorus girls are everywhere. Essentially they are what the British call variety or music hall—vaudeville to us—with everything from tumblers to singers to dancers to stand-up comics. Many major American performers have taken part in them, and it is an honor. It can also be fun.

The first one I did was for the Queen Mother. She is a well-loved woman and a joy. She sat in her box and laughed at everything. On the next two occasions, Prince Charles was present, the second time with Princess Diana. I presented the same pieces each time: they want the hits, they don't want to hear your latest dramatic score of which you're so proud. Afterward you stand in line to meet members of the royal family. You are told not to offer your hand until they do, and what to say and how to say it. It must be a burden for them to keep conversations alive, but it's their job and they're good at it.

One of the nicest perquisites of my career is the friendship Ginny and I share with John and Annie Glenn, whom we came to know through the Kennedys while skiing at Sun Valley. Whenever I play Washington, D.C., John and Annie turn out for the concert.

John and I were both born in Ohio. I have played in various places to help his political campaigns. I respect him enormously. He is one of our hardest-working and best-informed senators. We've been going to Vail together for ten years. It's stimulating to hear some of the real insights into what's going on in the world from John as we're going up on a ski lift. Presidents and premiers, White House visits and command performances. All very well and a great honor, but of the associations I value most that my career has brought me is our friendship with the Glenns.

Over the years we've been known to throw some pretty good parties. One of the best of them was on my fiftieth birthday in 1974. Ginny felt that a good blowout would soften the shock for my journey down the other side of the hill. As usual, she was the guiding hand behind the whole thing. She didn't tell me exactly what she was up to, only that the event would be held at the Crystal Room of the Beverly Hills Hotel. She managed to keep all the details from me until the night of the party.

The guest list was impressive, headed by Jimmy Cagney and his wife Bill, and Helen Hayes. Ginny managed to round up just about anybody who'd had anything to do with just about every aspect of my life. During cocktails I saw people I hadn't seen in years. There were many teary reunions. The lights were flashed announcing dinner, and when the drapes were pulled back from the entrance to the Crystal Room, there were Tex Beneke and the whole band, including many of our friends who had been there when Ginny and I were with them; they had all come back to play the party. Tex started in with "Moonlight Serenade," and for the first time that evening, I dissolved into Jell-O.

For what happened next, I would like to turn to a piece written by Charles Champlin, entertainment editor of the *Los Angeles Times*:

Ginny Mancini had first sung with Mel Tormé's inventive and influential Mel-Tones, and he and she and other voices reunited to do Tormé's famous tight-harmonied version of

"What Is This Thing Called Love?" Beneke, the hostess, and some modernized Modernaires did the early Miller hit "Kalamazoo." Jo Stafford sang "Embraceable You," and later as Darlene Edwards with husband Paul Weston at the piano, she did a gloriously off-key version of Mancini's "Days of Wine and Roses."

Writer Earl Brown and the team of Ray Evans and Jay Livingston created special material for the night, including a joshing tribute to their father from son Chris and twins Felice and Monica Mancini; ribald cheers from his fellow composers Bronislaw Kaper, John Green, Pete Rugolo and Quincy Jones and balladeering by Tony Martin, Tormé and Andy Williams, who did a deft parody called "Mooncini," to the tune of the maestro's first and greatest song success.

However, the thing that turned the Jell-O to water followed. Ginny got up and sang "What Are You Doing the Rest of Your Life?" It was one of the warmest and most touching moments we've ever shared.

She did it again for our fortieth wedding anniversary party in 1987, but this time she stretched the horizons. The party was given in Paris at the St. James's Club. The entire family flew over, and friends came from all over the world. Michel Legrand had the shortest trip of all, coming from just outside Paris. As a gift to us he played and sang "How Do You Keep the Music Playing?"

It turned into a three-day celebration. The sixty invited guests were wined and dined to a fare-thee-well. As we enjoyed the final dinner with everyone gathered, my mind flashed back to the greasy bag that contained my salami sandwich back in West Aliquippa. Things had changed.

The last day, five couples, including ourselves, took off for two weeks of barging on the Burgundy canals. We were a crazily compatible group: Danny and Donna Arnold, Jack and Bobbi Elliott, Polly (Bergen) and Jeff Enderveldt, and, to keep an eye on us should the food and drink take ill

effect, our friend Dr. Gary Sugarman, and his wife Barbara.
This is the stuff that good times are made of.

There are of course disadvantages to being well known.
They certainly don't outweigh the advantages, but they're
there.

In 1975, while driving in Los Angeles, I heard a news
broadcast saying that Such-and-Such Mancini was picked
up for some heavy felony, a dope charge I think. Of course
the name caught my attention. The last thing the newscaster
said was, "He is Henry Mancini's brother." Needless to say,
this startled me.

I called the public relations office I employed at the time.
I suggested they get on this before the story was picked up
by the wire services, which they did, and it died right there.

But this business of my supposed brothers and sisters and
assorted other relatives keeps haunting me. I am simply not
eligible for the ranks of brother or uncle, and the only
person I know who can legitimately call me cousin is Helen
Musengo in Cleveland. (There may be some cousins in Italy,
but if so I don't know who they are.) The name Mancini is
not uncommon, even in America. There are quite a few
people with that name, particularly in the East, and it is very
common in Italy.

When I'm out on the road, I frequently hear from people
coming backstage, "Your brother says hello." Or it might be
a sister or nephew who sends this greeting. I've become
used to it. So I simply say, "I'm an only child," and let them
stand there and figure it out.

While I was doing *Charade* in England, Pat Campbell,
the promotion man for RCA Records, and I became great
buddies. We used to go to the Arsenal soccer games on
weekends, and I became an Arsenal fan. Soccer is a great
spectator sport.

About ten years later, I noticed the Arsenal team had
acquired a player named Terry Mancini, nicknamed Moon

River. This of course aroused my interest, and I asked about it.

It was explained to me that he was a very flamboyant player who was prone to getting into hassles with the fans, yelling back and shaking his fist at them. During one game, he got so angry that he pulled down his pants in the middle of the stadium, bent over to expose his backside, and mooned the crowd. From then on, the press had it: Moon River Mancini. It stuck with him for the rest of his career.

Not all the people who like your music, of course, are princes and presidents. Back in the days when Freddie Dale and Bud Brisbois were on the road with me, we played Chicago. The impresario who presented us was Italian, and, naturally, since Freddie and I were Italian, he took it upon himself to take us to some of the better Italian restaurants, where we were always treated royally. And Chicago having the history it does, it quickly became obvious who owned and who patronized some of those places.

At one of them, I was told someone wanted to meet me. So I went to the back of the restaurant, where a man was sitting with his back to the wall, keeping an eye on the door.

Our impresario said, "Hank, Mr. Giancana would like to meet you," and introduced us.

I shook hands with him. Did he say anything interesting, revealing, startling? No. Sam Giancana came out with a great cliché: "It's good to see a nice Italian boy making it."

The next restaurant the impresario took us to had the same kind of ownership and, presumably, clientele. It's important to this story that you understand that many Italian-Americans think I wrote absolutely everything from the *William Tell* overture up to and including the music for the Lord's Prayer.

We had a great meal, and then the owner brought out a huge cake with a sugar replica of the Oscar statuette on top. Written on the cake in colored icing was "Born Free." I didn't write the *Born Free* score; John Barry did. He'd received the Academy Award for it the previous year.

I looked at Bud Brisbois, who was about to explode with laughter, and then at Freddie Dale who, being Italian, found the situation even funnier than Bud did.

Through gritted teeth and *sotto voce* I said to both of them, "Shut up!"

That was another of the perquisites, knowing Freddie Dale.

Freddie was booking me all over the world at that time. I'd been to Japan three times, Australia twice, and played both Albert Hall and Festival Hall in London.

Then in 1972, he was instrumental in setting up my own half-hour television show, "The Mancini Generation," directed by Stan Harris and syndicated throughout the country and seen on more than 150 stations. I had already done three specials for Monsanto. This was unusual for a film composer. "The Mancini Generation" shows were good and were well received. I had a superb band with a large string section. Many of my regulars were in that band. However, I had two brilliant new players in the sax section, Don Menza and Ray Pizzi. Both are dyed-in-the-wool Italian-Americans. Don is a rare breed, a red-headed Sicilian. We call him The Red Baron. He plays great straight-ahead, no-nonsense jazz, in addition to being a first-class arranger. Ray is a short firecracker of a fellow, originally from Boston. In addition to the saxophones, Ray has become a master of the jazz bassoon. In 1981, I wrote "Piece for Jazz Bassoon and Orchestra" for him. It was first performed at the Dorothy Chandler Pavilion of the Music Center in Los Angeles with Jack Elliott's New American Orchestra. Another of the Sons of Italy, Chuck Domanico, joined us on bass.

We taped twenty-eight shows, shot on location at places such as Disneyland and Lion Country Safari. When, as happened on occasion, the budget precluded strings, we used the big band. I went through every big band arrangement I had in my library. In a way, those shows heralded MTV. I gave scholarships to film schools throughout the country. Students would pick a recording of mine and shoot film to it, then submit it, and the winning entry each week would be presented on the show.

One of the great joys of my career has been to walk into a recording session, a film scoring session, or an orchestra rehearsal, and be among the musicians without whom I would be nothing but a lot of pencil marks on score pages. This applies to those whom I have conducted throughout the world. The majority of my work, of course, has been performed by Los Angeles players. If a film sequence or a recording arrangement I have written is not working, it's usually not the musicians' fault. I can always count on them, especially the soloists, to add that certain something that gives the music life.

I can also count on them at times for outrageous humor and behavior. To wit:

I was recording the album *Hollywood Musicals* with Johnny Mathis. A good-sized orchestra had been called. My drummer was Steve Schaeffer. Aside from being a brilliant player, he was of a younger generation and favored the more current modes of dress. We had scheduled three days of recording. On the first day Steve came to the session, everyone noticed that he was wearing a small golden earring in his right ear. This was common, of course, for rock and roll people but not exactly the norm in day-to-day Hollywood session work. Snide remarks questioning his masculinity were thrown about during the session. That was the end of it, or so I thought.

The next day, just before the morning session, Steve was seated behind his drums, the earring still in place. A few minutes before the downbeat the four French horn players, led by Vincent De Rosa, walked in. They had their horns in one hand, the other hand on their hips in their best "come hither" manner. Overnight they had raided their wives' jewelry cases and had come up with the most outrageous earrings they could find hanging from each earlobe. They paraded past Steve, who was convulsed with laughter, and took their places in the orchestra. It took ten minutes to calm everyone down enough so that we could start the session.

Erno Neufeld, my concertmaster, who held that position with the Universal contract orchestra, remained with me until he retired recently. Erno was a superb violinist and a warm and kind man. We both smoked cigars around that time, and at every session I would take one of my Monte Cristos over to Erno and give it to him before the music got under way. One day he declined the cigar and sheepishly said he gave up smoking about three months before and "just couldn't waste these great cigars."

Shelly Manne was my drummer until he passed away in September 1984. Shelly and his wife, Flip, lived near us on a miniranch in Northridge, where they trained Tennessee walking horses. Flip is a first-class rider. Shelly had a great sense of humor, which I think is true of most jazz musicians. His humor lay in a pocket somewhere between gallows and black. Sessions could not officially start until Shelly told the most recent jokes off the street.

Shelly Manne's playing needs no praise from me, but I will praise the way he tenaciously kept his jazz club in Hollywood, the famous Shelly's Manne Hole, going in spite of adversities. Shelly would pay the performers first and then take what was left after expenses, which usually was not much. He constantly recharged his batteries by leaving the studio scene to play at jazz festivals throughout the world.

During recording sessions, there was always a stream of

quips between various musicians and me. None were funnier than Shelly's. I remember one in particular. I had written a period jazz piece for a film score, and I wanted to get from Shelly the rhythmic feeling of that era. Just before giving the downbeat at the rehearsal, I looked over at Shelly and said, "Give me 1926." Without missing a beat, Shelly inquired, "What month?"

Knowing people like Shelly and Freddie Dale comes high on my list of the perks of my profession.

Although he was a big-time agent and first-rate executive, in reality Freddie remained a second trumpet player. He never forgot that. For all the companies he founded and directed, for all his brilliance as an executive, Freddie liked nothing as much as hanging out with the musicians. My music is transported in black fiberboard cases, six cases that hold about forty pounds each for the symphony concerts, and four cases for the forty-piece band. Freddie was always concerned after a concert that all the music was put back into the boxes, and he'd stay around, a funny, determined little guy with his red hair, big nose, and a cigarette or cigar in his mouth, to do it himself.

I'd say, "Freddie, they've got people to do that."

He'd say, "No, no, somebody will screw it up. I have to take care of it."

In 1974, the smokes caught up with him. He contracted lung cancer and in 1975 he passed away, in his forties.

I still miss him.

In 1974, just before his death, Freddie formed Regency Artists. His partner was a bright, energetic attorney named Richard Rosenberg. Richard captured Freddie's personal touch immediately. I feel that Freddie's spirit lives on in Richard.

Let me preface the next little story by a truth I have learned the hard way many times. That is, when you are becoming a bit full of yourself and a bit above the fray, something will occur to bring you down with a crunch.

Every Christmas for the past ten years we have gone to our place in Vail to ski. George and Jolene Schlatter have been there at the same time. George was the producer of "Laugh-In" and has produced and directed countless comedy and music specials. He is my skiing buddy, and we go out on the slopes every day.

George and I had decided to take a mid-morning break. We went down to Vail village and entered a tiny shop. We ordered hot chocolates and were standing at the counter drinking them when I felt a tap on my shoulder. I turned around and saw a young, good-looking couple.

The man asked, "Are you Henry Mancini?"

And I, giving my best "ah, shucks" crooked smile, replied, "Well, yes, I am."

He said, "You dropped your credit card."

18
Changes

In January 1976, my son Chris, then twenty-six, informed us that he and the young woman he had been seeing, Julie Shapiro, the adopted daughter of a Chicago physician, were expecting a baby. Christopher Michael Mancini was born at Cedars Sinai Hospital in Los Angeles on August 18 of that year.

Chris had met Julie while they were both at the Judson School in Arizona. They didn't see each other for several years, but then Julie came to Los Angeles and they became reacquainted. Neither she nor Chris had established a career, and during the first year of young Christopher's life it became apparent to Ginny and me that they did not have the means to take on raising a child. Ginny and I felt that it would be better for everyone if he came to live with us, which, when he was one year old, he did. This left Chris and Julie free to work out their lives, and at the same time it assured the boy stability and comfort.

But it changed our lives radically. Because Chris and the girls had their own apartments, Ginny and I were now more or less free, and we enjoyed the situation. But now the house was scattered with toys. Its routine changed to accommodate young Chris's presence. We redid Felice's bedroom as a nursery and hired a nanny. Suddenly, at the age of fifty-two, Ginny and I found ourselves parents again. It was not easy.

We also found ourselves attached to Christopher, a blond and beautiful little boy. For all purposes, he was another of our children. We took him with us almost everywhere we went, and by the age of ten he had visited more cities and countries than I had at forty. He was as at home in the Inn on the Park in London as he was in our backyard, and he was familiar with New York. I remember taking him to a concert I did in Mexico City. From the time he was three, his Christmases were spent in Vail, where he started skiing when he was four; he has developed into an excellent skier.

In June of 1987, I was to record an album called *Volare* with Luciano Pavarotti. It was our second album together. Three years before that, I had recorded with him in Geneva, Switzerland, an album called *Mamma*, which was a worldwide success. I met Luciano at the Academy Awards ceremony of 1981. I was the conductor that year, and he sang. Later, he sang at a Lifetime Achievement tribute that UCLA held for me at the Pauley Pavilion, and in due course we decided to record together.

For the second album, which was to be done in Bologna, Italy, I took Ginny and Christopher with me. For one thing, I wanted him to see something of Italy, which is part of his heritage.

It was a delightful trip. One weekend while we were working on the project, Luciano invited us to Pesaro, where he has his seaside country home, a lovely and simple farmhouse overlooking the Adriatic. As always, Luciano was a gracious host. He and Christopher became immediate friends. As part of his fitness regimen, Luciano rode his bicycle outside around the house. He had an extra bicycle, and Christopher would accompany him. I have a vision of the two of them, riding around and around the house. It was one of those vivid little incidents you don't forget.

Christopher has always had an intense love for animals, especially dogs and cats. We found on this trip that birds too were among his loves. He found a baby bird that had fallen out of the nest, picked it up, and built a little nest for it in a small box. He fed the bird with an eyedropper, and for the next two days his sole purpose in life was to keep that bird alive. It was a losing struggle, and the bird died. Heartbroken, the boy got a glass jar from Luciano and put the bird in it. He wrote a note and put that in the jar too. Then he went out behind the house to a patch of woods and buried the bird in a place only he knew. Luciano was very taken by this incident.

We went to Venice for three lovely days, on to London for several more days, and then back to California.

For some years Ginny had been talking with me about going to Africa. I was not particularly interested, despite the great interest our friend William Holden had in Africa or the similar interest he had inspired in Stefanie Powers, with whom he had been involved for several years. After Bill died, in 1981, Stefanie took up Bill's cause of the preservation of wildlife. She built a home in Kenya and became a guiding force in the wildlife movement there. We also talked to our writer friend Tom Mankiewicz, who had a home there near Stefanie's. Jimmy and Gloria Stewart had been going there for years. Bill Holden had started the Safari Club in Kenya in the early 1970s. Upon his death, Stefanie stepped in and took over his work.

In the summer of 1988, Ginny, Christopher, and I left by way of New York and London for Nairobi and a two-week safari. I was still reluctant, but when we got there and I started to see this new world, it all began to be very exciting to me. Kenya has prohibited hunting for many years now, and the purpose of most safaris is photography.

We hired a guide, a marvelous Kenyan of Scandinavian descent named Tor Allen, a sandy-haired, tall, handsome man in his forties. He and his wife, Sue, operate a safari company that has been in business for a number of years. Tor was totally at home in the bush and took excellent care of us.

He met us upon our arrival on July 13. We stayed in the heart of Nairobi at the Norfolk Hotel, a quaint place typical of the British colonial period. We started out at Lewa Downs in Meru National Park. Six or seven Masai tribesmen worked with Tor, and within hours they had set up our little village. Ginny and I had our own tent, complete with a shower. Christopher and Tor each had his own tent. In addition, there was a dining tent and a cooking tent.

Stefanie had offered us her beautiful, newly built home, in which we spent several days, although she was not there at the time.

Along the way we had started to encounter the animals. We would get up about six in the morning, have a little tea, and be out in the bush by six-thirty, because it was the best time to observe the wildlife. Christopher and I had cameras and Ginny had brought a video recorder. I said, "If you want to take a video camera, you've got it, you are the cameraman." She spent a great deal of time reading the instruction booklet, but finally she got the hang of it and took some great videos.

Christopher was keeping a list of animals he had observed, which eventually came to fifty-three. He was thrilled.

We went through the Shaba Game Reserve. Christopher likes to fish. So do I, though I rarely get the chance. We flew up to a fishing camp on the southeast shore of Lake Victoria, which is enormous, a great freshwater inland sea that touches three countries. We went out on a boat for a day, having heard that there was a fish indigenous to the area called Nile perch, which weighs up to two hundred pounds.

Christopher got the first strike of the day, but the fish,

which was quite large, got away. In the meantime, I had caught three thirty-five-pound Nile perch. As the day wore on and Chris kept trolling, he saw me reeling in more fish. It began to bother him. The Nile perch makes wonderful eating, but how many of them can you eat? We began throwing them back. I began to think, "This kid had better get a fish today or we're not going to be able to live with him."

About mid-afternoon, when it was almost time to go back, he got a strike. At that time, he was thin-boned, lanky, seventy pounds or so. When this thing hit his line, his eyes lit up and he began fighting to bring this fish in. Our guide had to help. They finally got the fish in, and it was the biggest of the day, at forty-six pounds. When we weighed it on a scale hanging from the trees, the fish was almost as tall as Christopher. He'll remember that fish for the rest of his life.

During the trip, I carried a tape recorder with me. At various times, the native help would come in, I would turn on the tape recorder, and they would sing their songs for me. In the bush, we were always guarded at night by two tall Masai warriors in their tribal garb each holding a long staff, since hyenas and other animals were prone to coming in to steal food. I asked them if they would sing something. They said they'd return the next night and bring some friends.

The next night after dinner, these two men and two friends who had joined them sat down and proceeded to do some of their tribal songs in a way that would have turned the Manhattan Transfer green with envy. The songs were performed in a rough but beautiful way. The music was pentatonic, truly tonal, involving a drone that was handled first by one man and then transferred to another. It was well structured, and no doubt centuries had gone into perfecting it. Christopher was very much taken with it.

Throughout the trip, but especially when I was going through the Masai Mari Game Reserve, I couldn't help remembering the picture *Hatari!* When we were out scouting one day, I asked, "Tor, where did they shoot that picture?"

He said, "You won't believe it, but you're there now. We're driving over where they shot the film."

It was something of a shock to visit, twenty-five years later, the area where the rhino hunt and the baby elephant sequence of *Hatari!* had been made. Some of the local Masai people I met had worked on the picture.

While at Lewa Downs, we were taken to a little factory where women sat all day making wonderful native rugs. I wanted to hear some of their work songs. Tor, who spoke the local language, talked them into singing for us. They started off tentatively, shyly. After they got into it, the place started roaring. Finally they got up and went outside and started to dance and sing. I was taping the music and Ginny was videotaping their dancing.

Tor came up with the idea that they should listen to some of my music. He had a tape in the four-wheel-drive land rover that he played. The first thing on it was *"Peter Gunn."* They heard the beat, started to sway and smile, and applauded at the end. Then came "Baby Elephant Walk." Spontaneously, they began to dance to it. One of the men got up and did a dance far more sophisticated than anything you'd see in a disco. After that came "Days of Wine and Roses," which starts out with Vince De Rosa's French horn solo. He plays only the melody, soulfully and plaintively. There was a hush, and those who were smiling became very somber and still. They didn't move a muscle. The chorus came in with Johnny Mercer's lyric. They couldn't figure it out, but it held them. I watched with fascination. In the middle of Kenya these people—who had no radios and no television—were hearing a sound that obviously had an extraordinary effect on them. Their reaction in turn certainly had an effect on me.

We went back to Nairobi and then to the Inn on the Park in London. I flew back to Los Angeles, because I had concerts to do, but Ginny and Christopher stayed on in London for a few days, then returned home in early August.

Ginny and I felt closer to Christopher than we ever had before. It was not a matter of two grandparents taking a boy on a trip; we were just three people on a journey to a fascinating land.

In 1983, my son Chris recorded an album of his own rock songs for Atlantic. The album was very well done, but it just didn't catch on. I felt I had to do something for him.

I went to Billy Meshel, then president of the Arista Music Publishing group, and asked him to give Chris a chance in the publishing area. In 1984 Chris started working for Arista. His musicality was unquestioned. He has a great ear and a sense for songs off the street. It was a great change for Chris, since he had never had to be anywhere at a given time and do what anyone told him to do. There was an adjustment, at first, in getting used to a structured existence. But once he took hold and established a rapport with Billy, his life began to take shape. He was able to put his street smarts to good use. And he had a knowledge of publishing.

The biggest change came when he began to feel that he could make a difference in his own life, and he was well on his way. He had a stable income. He began seeing a charming young lady named Analei London. They seemed to be very much in tune. She had a daughter from a previous marriage named Leila. He and Analei were married April 4, 1987. Within a short time, they told us that Analei was going to have a baby. On March 3, 1988, in Santa Monica Hospital, a boy was born whom they named Luca Nicola Mancini. (Nicola is my middle name.) Ginny and I got a chuckle out of this—that's about as Italian as you can get.

Chris is doing well. He has had a hand in placing some songs with some good recording artists. He's starting to get recognition in the profession.

Both girls have been married and divorced. Felice has remarried. In 1988 in Venice, Italy, she married Douglas Erenberg, whom she had known since she was ten years old. Both Monica and Felice have lovely voices and have been on a number of my records. Monica has also done a number of song demos for me. She was somewhat more ambitious in this area than Felice. Monica has always had an artistic gift, and we sent her to art school She and a friend now have an active interior decoration business. She started by doing our beach house in Malibu, and she showed such great taste that other people began to notice. She has since then done work for Rob Reiner, Billy Crystal, and Michael Keaton. In the meantime, she continues to sing. She has sung at several functions honoring me, and she has put a lump in my throat quite a few times with "Days of Wine and Roses" and "Two for the Road."

Felice has always had an interest in writing. In 1970, she was attending the University of Denver. At Christmastime she wrote a poem to us as a gift. It was touching. I decided to set it to music and called it "Sometimes." I knew that the Carpenters were looking for material for their next album on A&M records. I made a simple demo, just me on piano with singer Sally Stevens. Sally is the most in-demand of the session singers in Hollywood. I sent it over to Richard and Karen Carpenter, and within an hour Richard called to say that they loved the song and would record it, not with orchestra but just as we had done it—piano and voice. It was on the album *Carpenters*, which sold well beyond the platinum status. I was so happy for Felice. It is rare when something done with such love pays off like a Las Vegas jackpot.

Sometimes
not often enough
we reflect upon
the good things
and those thoughts
usually center
around those
we love
and I think about
two people
who mean so much
to me
and for so many years
have made me so
very happy
and I count
the times
I have forgotten
to say
"thank you"
and just how
much
I love
them

Felice

We lost Ginny's mother, Josephine, at the start of 1987. Jo, as everyone called her, was a marvelous woman. She married Ginny's father, John O'Connor, in the early 1920s. Ginny was the only child of that marriage. Johnny was a pretty good boozer, and they were divorced.

Jo was born in Chihuahua, Mexico. Jo's mother and grandmother had a big influence on Ginny as she was growing up. Although she was Spanish-speaking, as Ginny is, she had no accent. Jo played piano, things like "Twelfth Street Rag" and "In a Shanty in Old Shanty Town." At a party, someone would call out, "Okay, Jo. 'Shanty in Old Shanty Town.'" And she'd sit down and play.

She was very close to Ginny, and the kids loved her. She was always active, always doing something. As I mentioned, she had not been enthralled with the idea of Ginny marrying a musician. When Ginny was running around with the Hollywood crowd, I think Jo thought her little girl was going to marry somebody successful. But Jo and I got along. She was my biggest booster.

Jo had been widowed for some time and lived alone. She refused to live with us; she always wanted to be on her own. We bought her a mobile home in a park at Point Dume, at the upper part of Malibu, on the coast. It was a pleasant two-bedroom home. Many retired people lived near her, and she knew everybody. She loved it there.

But she was now in her early eighties and her health had started to go. It was not helped by a couple of automobile accidents. She started to suffer the common ailments of aging, and by 1986 she was bedridden and had to have help, at first part-time and then full-time. She hated it. She became cantankerous, which she had never been before.

In 1986, the whole family was in Vail for the Christmas holidays—the twins, Chris, and little Chris. On Christmas Eve we got a call from Ginny's half sister Maureen—Jo's daughter by Jim Byrne. Maureen said she had been called by the police to get out to Point Dume. There had been a fire. Jo's electric blanket had caught fire somehow. The lady who was living with her managed to get her out of the bedroom and out of the home and had saved her life. The fire fighters were able to put out the blaze fairly quickly, but Jo was seriously burned over a great part of her body. She was taken to a burn center in Culver City.

We all flew back to California. Jo was in intensive care in very poor condition. Her weight had dropped to about eighty pounds. Her condition was such that the doctors couldn't give her painkillers. We were there constantly. She was kept under antiseptic conditions because of the danger of infection; we had to wear special shoes and sterilized robes. She was sinking. Ginny had several heated talks with the doctors about their refusal to give Jo painkillers. They said that if they gave them to her she would lose functions that were keeping her alive.

We went to the hospital New Year's Eve, taking some caviar and a bottle of champagne in a bucket—not knowing, of course, whether she would be able to have them. But we were desperate to cheer her up. The moment we entered the room it was obvious that she was failing. Ginny leaned over her and said, "How are you feeling? Can you hear me?" She just nodded. Ginny and I went off to talk. She said, "She doesn't feel that she can go on. She is in such pain." Ginny made the difficult decision, which I fully supported, that Jo should be taken off the life-support system. The decision had to be made, and Ginny made it. Jo slipped away on New Year's Day.

Ginny had discussed her wishes with her. In accordance with what she wanted, she was cremated. We made arrangements with the Neptune Society and took the urn containing Jo's ashes out from San Pedro Harbor. A couple of miles offshore, Ginny and I, along with her sister Maureen and Maureen's husband, Tom Moore, scattered the ashes upon the ocean.

19
Mr. Lucky

O ne night a couple of years ago, Ginny and I came home
from a symphony concert. I have a habit, at the end of
a day, of emptying my pockets of whatever coins have
accumulated, putting them on a tray in the bedroom. On
this particular evening, as we prepared for bed, I happened
to have a lot of pennies. I dropped them into the tray as
usual.

Ginny told me later that she suddenly fixed on them. She
stared at them, thinking how much they would have meant
to her as a little girl, trying to save up enough of them to go
to a Saturday matinee and escape the dreariness of her life.
Ginny simply never forgets her origins, which is why, I
think, she has such compassion for people and gets herself
involved to the point of chronic overwork in various charities. I have trouble understanding people who *do* forget their
origins. When life has been good to you, I think you owe
something in return.

As far back as the 1960s, I was faced with the fact that I
would rather make donations to charities than give it all to
the government. Sometimes I found myself near the 90
percent income tax bracket. Everyone who was making any
amount of money was getting into tax shelters, investments,
and write-offs to keep some of the money they were making,
particularly people in uncertain professions like mine where

you might suddenly find yourself out of fashion and out of work.

For the first time, I retained a law firm, Rosenfeld, Meyer & Susman, an excellent and prestigious firm involved in entertainment law. I found I needed such a company on retainer, if only because so many contracts were coming in daily. Many of them were for assignments overseas, and these entailed the tax laws of other countries as well as our own.

One of the firm's partners, Larry Kartiganer, is my contact in the company. Don Rosenfeld was the tax brain of the firm. He had handled Jules Stein and the MCA account for a long time. Don had gone through intricate maneuvers when MCA switched over from being a talent agency to becoming a production company, acquiring in the process my old alma mater, Universal Pictures. It took a great deal of knowledge to make that transition, and Don was one of the people entrusted to do it.

Don had been thinking about how I could keep more of the money I was making. One of the things we invested in was the Phoenix Suns, formed when a Phoenix NBA basketball franchise became available for that city. I held onto those shares until 1983.

Don came up with a way to take advantage of the charitable contribution clauses in the tax law. I was recording three albums a year. He noted that, because of the sales of my previous albums, the masters of my new albums were worth a certain amount of money in the eyes of the tax department, and could be donated to a school or charitable organization.

At the same time that I retained Rosenfeld, Meyer & Susman, I also retained the accounting firm now known as Freedman, Kinzelberg and Broder. I had had two unfortunate experiences with previous business managers and now felt I needed a first-class organization to get my financial affairs in order.

Remembering how insecure and uncertain my life was when I went to New York and enrolled at Juilliard, I began to set up scholarships. I established two at UCLA—the first a film music scholarship, which would give a student $2,500 a year and, in tandem with that, a fund that a student composer could draw on to record a score for a student film. I funded a composition scholarship at Juilliard and an endowment at the University of Southern California to buy the necessities for running a music department—band instruments, music stands, lighting—and set up a scholarship for the American Federation of Musicians Congress of Strings, which nurtures young string players from all over the country. I also became involved with SHARE Inc., which is made up mostly of show business wives and is devoted to helping the mentally retarded. Ginny has been involved with it since the earliest days of our marriage. She is a past president.

I have contributed a lot of time to SHARE. Every May to raise money the ladies stage a western shindig called the Boomtown Party. The first one was at Ciro's, but the show then was on a small scale. It has grown to the point where they have had to hold it in the Santa Monica Civic Auditorium or the Pauley Pavilion at UCLA.

Miriam Nelson and various dance directors (including Nick Castle until the time of his death) would create big production numbers for these ladies, most of whom are nonprofessionals. They start doing their situps and their jogging around January to get in shape for the rehearsals. Arrangers such as Paul Weston, Pete Rugolo, Dick Hazard, Bill Byers, and I would contribute our writing, and in various years I conducted the show. Everybody would be called upon, and although the American Federation of Musicians would not waive fees for the musicians, the people I worked with a lot—the best in town—were willing to play the job; and the orchestra of about thirty musicians was invariably excellent.

Some of the best studio singers in town, including Monica and Felice, contributed their time, and we usually had a vocal group of eight in the pit.

Al Mello, one of the best rehearsal pianists ever, would get the ladies ready in the rehearsal halls donated by Paramount and the other studios. Al would run the numbers down, make sure all the accents were in the right places, and do all the liaison work from the piano to the orchestration. It was a kick for me to walk into rehearsal and see some of these ladies, housewives called upon to don tights, look their best, and shape up fast. After a big number, they spent the next ten minutes coughing and gasping and trying to get their breath back.

It has always been done in a wonderful spirit, with goodwill and laughter. It was great fun for a great cause. The organization has grown quite large and has done a great deal not only for retarded children but in recent years for other causes as well.

After "Peter Gunn" and the big pictures of the early 1960s, it occurred to me that when I was growing up there were very few books that could help someone learn to arrange and that I was simply very lucky to have met Max Adkins, who had developed a system for teaching it. There was, as I said earlier, the Frank Skinner book, which was excellent but already dated even when I was studying it. Russ Garcia wrote a good book on commercial arranging in the 1950s. And there were the classical orchestration texts, but they showed nothing about dance band arranging and of course didn't even mention the rhythm section. There was no book at all that had actual examples of the way various combinations of instruments sound, music you could read and listen to at the same time. I realized that if I used my RCA recordings as the basis of a book, it might fill a great need. The music was available and well known.

My next thought was to put it in a form such that people

who wanted to sit down at the piano and play the examples
didn't have to go through the transposition of instruments.
This is a rather technical point for the layman, but it's
important. Many of the instruments of the orchestra are
what are called transposing instruments. A score is written
in different keys for those instruments, though they do not
sound in different keys; they sound in what is called concert
pitch. And a score in which the parts are not transposed is
said to be "in concert." So, whereas my scores are all
written in transposition, I decided to reassemble them in
concert to make it easier for someone not yet skilled in
transposition to study them.

I published the book, *Sounds and Scores: A Practical
Guide to Professional Orchestration,* in 1961 through Northridge Music, with five-inch records of the examples—in
later editions with cassettes. It is now in its fifth edition and
has sold close to one hundred thousand copies. It is enormously gratifying to me that there now is a generation of
young arrangers, some of them very well known, who
started with that book. I run into people all over the world
who tell me that the book was the beginning of their writing
careers. It's been used as a reference book in various universities and colleges, and it did everything I wanted it to do.

As it turned out, it also capped off the big band era in
writing. It took the arranger right up to the end of that
period, before rock started, summarizing what had come
before.

For all the good fortune I have had, I nonetheless still
have to sit myself down and give myself a lecture from time
to time.

The situation in film music has changed with the arrival
on the scene of a number of excellent younger composers.
The clock goes around. I find myself thinking, "Some of
these new fellows are really good. I can feel the heat." And

I'll go on that tack for a while and get myself depressed. Then I'll say, "Well, wait a minute, look at this. If I never worked again, the family wouldn't have to worry. Everything is taken care of for after I go." And then, to counteract the depression, I do a litany of what I've achieved. It's a constant discussion within my own head, an ongoing internal conflict.

I try to take a long look at it. I realize that since 1958, I have been averaging about three pictures a year, and for lack of time I have had to turn down two or three more. I conduct at least fifty concerts a year. The calls keep coming, which is gratifying. I look back on my recording library. Since 1958, I have recorded more than ninety albums, all of them my arrangements. That's a lot of notes to put on paper. I have three rooms stacked to the ceiling with the music I've written over the years. I examine what I've done, and it seems to be a considerable body of work.

When I turned forty, even when I turned fifty, I didn't think about any of this very much. But when I turned sixty, something happened, an alarm went off. I started to say, "I'm going down the other side of the hill now." I remembered the friends and colleagues who are gone, like Max Adkins, Freddie Dale, Bud Brisbois, Peter Sellers, Nick Castle, Joe Gershenson, and Johnny Mercer. I started to reflect, "Well, you'd better start thinking about what you're going to do with the rest of the time that you're allotted. Who knows how much it's going to be?" I look back and examine everything I've done, and I feel that I am doing what I set out to do, heat or no heat.

I remain a staunch supporter of ASCAP, of which I have been a member since Nick Castle and I wrote our "Soft-Shoe Boogie" for Arthur Duncan's act.

I still get paid through ASCAP for music I wrote at Universal, countless hours of it for the Kettles, Francis the

Talking Mule, Abbott and Costello, and various rubber-suit
monsters. All this music was logged on cue sheets—timing
sheets made up by the producer and sent to the performing
rights societies both here and abroad. Joe Gershenson and
his staff were scrupulously careful and honest about seeing
to it that Herman Stein and the rest of us received accurate
credit for every note we wrote. And when those films are
shown on television (and in Europe and everywhere else but
the United States, in theaters), the composers, or their
families, are paid according to those cue sheets. My name
was plastered all over those cue sheets. And those movies,
those strange pictures I worked on like *Creature from the
Black Lagoon* and *It Came from Outer Space*, have proved to
be the solid rock on which my ASCAP earnings are
founded. In some country, somewhere, at this moment, in
some little tent theater or on some little television station,
those pictures are being shown. It's a huge base, all those
terrible movies.

I always worry about ASCAP. Although ASCAP is em-
bedded in constitutional law, the broadcasters have made it
clear, from the earliest days of the radio industry, that it is
their unrelenting intent to destroy ASCAP and stop paying
any money whatsoever for the use of music. ASCAP is not
to be taken for granted, because the broadcasters have gone
to court repeatedly to reduce payment of royalties, and there
is no question that their long-range goal is to stop it entirely.
If the price of liberty is eternal vigilance, it's also the price
composers and lyricists must pay to continue earning a
living from their work. The broadcasters have lawyers who
stay awake nights trying to figure out how to deprive composers of their living. In the long term it's stupid, because it
would stop the composition of music and leave the United
States a kind of cultural leper, separated from the rest of the
civilized world. The public doesn't understand this and
probably thinks it is a pretty abstract issue. It isn't. It has
been a battle to keep ASCAP going. Some of the new

fellows do take it for granted, thinking, "Well, this is the way it is." Well, it's not the way it is. It is only as long as we're willing to fight the broadcasters for our rights.

I'm thankful for the concept of ASCAP, started by Victor Herbert and his colleagues in 1914 at Luchow's restaurant in New York. I was on the board of ASCAP from 1964 to 1968.

ASCAP is the financial pillar of my life. It's going to be around for Ginny, the kids, and the grandchildren. In that way, I feel very lucky. I am high in the financial hierarchy of ASCAP, and I am proud to see my name surrounded by legendary names. At such moments, I can feel sure I've accomplished something.

I suggested earlier that group singers are a breed apart. They love to gab and gossip. And interestingly, they have a kind of loyalty to each other. It's a nice thing to see. Ginny still retains her friendships with all the singers she knew in the big band days, the members of the vocal groups like the Mello-Larks, the Modernaires, the Pied Pipers, the Crew Chiefs, the Andrews Sisters, the King Sisters, the Clark Sisters. They all know each other and they all stay in touch.

And they all became aware of some horror stories. Ella Mae Morse, whose records made millions for Capitol in the 1940s, was working in customer service at a Sears store in Torrance, California.

The situation for former bandsingers was even worse than it was for the solo stars, who at least at one time had been paid mechanical royalties for sales of their records. People like the Eberle brothers, whose records had all been made when they were employees in bands, were paid a flat fee (about $35 in those days) for each record, and no royalty at all. The bandleader alone got royalties.

Bob Eberle was dying of cancer in a charity ward in a New York hospital until Frank Sinatra (who, surprisingly, had never met him) heard about it and booked him a private room, picked up his medical expenses, and helped make his passing a little easier. In Atlanta his brother, Ray, suffering a heart condition, was simply put out of a hospital because his medical insurance ran out. He died two days later.

Ginny and her friends knew something had to be done. Too many people who had given America and the world so much pleasure were suffering as they grew older and faced health problems. They formed what they called the Society of Singers, SOS, to build up a fund and take whatever other actions they thought appropriate to help these people. And they elected—*drafted* might be a better word—Ginny as their first president, knowing that whatever she goes into gets the full measure of her incredible energy and her very considerable organizational talent. Bea Wain was named treasurer. Frank Sinatra became honorary chairman.

On September 8, 1986, Ginny gave a party at our home to announce the organization and its goals to the press. Caterina Valente flew in from Europe to perform. The guests began to show up. I never saw so many singers in one place in my life. I didn't know there were that many singers in the world. They included Sue Brown, Peggy Clark of the Clark Sisters, Rosemary Clooney, Jeanne Hazard, Kitty Kallen, Tony Martin, Sue Raney, Roberta Sherwood, Al Martino, Giselle McKenzie, Rose Marie, Nancy Sinatra, Joannie Sommers, Kay Starr, Kay St. Germaine, April Stevens, Art Lund, Gilda Maiken, and Ella Mae Morse.

And then, wouldn't you know it, they started to sing! All of these trained group singers, who can hear harmony parts and improvise them on the spot. In my living room there was this massed choir of gifted people from whose mouths was coming this incredible sound as they sang Johnny Mercer's "Dream."

I turned to a friend and said, "Do you know what it would *cost* to get a blend and a sound like that on a record date?" And they were doing it *for fun*.

Since then, Ginny has devoted an enormous amount of time to the SOS, and they have made great progress, quietly helping people who need it and deserve it. It occurs to me that with my scholarships I am trying to help some of the young talent coming up, and with the SOS Ginny is helping some of the older talent that is getting on.

Sometimes I have to stop and think about the people who helped put Ginny and me in that position. We've worked hard, but it wouldn't have happened except for certain special people. What would have happened to me had I not met Glenn Miller that day? What would have happened if Shorty Rogers hadn't insisted that I make the *Peter Gunn* album? If Jerry Perenchio hadn't come up with that idea about my doing concerts?

If I hadn't needed a haircut that day and bumped into Blake Edwards? I've thought a lot about that haircut.

And, above all, if I hadn't met Max Adkins? One of the regrets of my life is that Max didn't live to see it happen. Because I certainly owe the good fortune I've had first, foremost, and always to Max Adkins.

I've been back a few times to Aliquippa. One of those occasions was a two-day celebration the town held in my name on the Fourth of July weekend in 1961. There were banquets, one of them in the Sons of Italy Hall near our old house on Beaver Avenue, another in the hall of the Eagles Fraternal Order. The town built an outdoor bandstand, covered with patriotic bunting, especially for me so that I could conduct the latest edition of the Aliquippa High School band, of which I had once been a member, performing a concert of my music. My dad was there, proud and beaming and on this occasion not once mentioning my lack of a college degree. So were Ginny and Chris who, as young as he was at the time, still remembers it. There was a "Welcome Home" banner strung across the street and a parade with a motorcade. The Italians, the Serbs, the Czechs, the Croatians, and the Poles all came together for this occasion. It was quite an event.

It couldn't happen again. With the collapse of the steel industry in those western Pennsylvania towns, their economies caved in. When I headed back in November of 1987 to conduct four concerts with the Pittsburgh Symphony, one of the great orchestras of the world, I couldn't imagine what Aliquippa must look like now.

I thought about the old Loew's Penn, where I saw *The Crusades*, and the Stanley, where I studied with Max. Both, I had been told, were gone now.

As the plane approached Pittsburgh, the events of my youth seemed very long ago, a different state of mind, far away in another time and another place.

And they were.

Afterword
by Gene Lees

November 13, 1987.

The audience devoured the concert. Afterward there was a reception given by the Rotary Club in a large room in the basement of Heinz Hall. From the head of the staircase you could see them sipping from wineglasses, talking, laughing. As Hank descended the broad stairs, ladies pressed programs upon him for autographs, all the faces in the room turned suddenly upward to watch him. One person and then another would say some variant on, "Henry, do you remember me? I used to. . . ." And he always did remember. It was amazing. He stayed for a time, signing autographs, chatting with strangers and old acquaintances alike, and then, with a conspiratorial smile and a lift of the eyebrows, suggested it was time we left. It was obvious that when he is traveling, the company he prefers is that of his "guys," and some of them were waiting.

Al Cobine said the symphony musicians sometimes ask, puzzled, "Why does he do this? Obviously he doesn't have to, he doesn't need the money."

"Because he likes it," Cobine tells them. He always tells his guys to live well on the road, sup well, sleep well. As we left with one or two of them, laughing about something or other, I suddenly realized what Henry Mancini, in his heart of hearts, really is.

Henry Mancini is an old road musician.

November 14, 1987.

About noon the Musengos arrived—Helen, the cousin Hank had said was like a sister, and Ralph, the one-time CIC officer with whom Hank had spent those three days at a villa at the end of the war. They drove down from Cleveland, perhaps a hundred miles on the freeway. When Quinto Mancini made the same trip in 1929 to apply for work at Jones and Laughlin, the roads were bad, and though it is not recorded how long the journey took, it was probably an ordeal. Henry was five then. The family waited eight years to move to a company house.

Ralph Musengo described Ann Pece Mancini as "a really nice woman. She and Helen's father came from a family of contentment and joy."

Quinto Mancini's grandfather, according to Ralph, was a farmer who owned a house. So he was a man of some property, not a sharecropper.

Quinto, Ralph said, disliked his cousins, and with cause. When Quinto's grandfather died, the property was deeded to Quinto's father and his brother. The uncle cheated Quinto's father out of the property in some Machiavellian maneuver that is the dark side of the Italian character. "That sort of thing was common in Italy," Ralph said. Quinto and his siblings were thrown off the land.

"I think Quinto was a sentimental man," Helen said. "He cried when Ralph and I got married and when our first child was born. Quint always talked about Henry and the great pride that both he and Annie had in him."

Quinto was making fifteen dollars a week, Helen said. She remembered that Anna once forswore a winter coat so that Henry could have his arranging lessons.

I said, "Hank told me that he doesn't remember his father ever showing one sign of affection to either him or his mother."

Helen said, "I think it was the era. Parents of that generation were not as outgoing as they are today. I think Ralph will agree with me. We thought Quint was very loving toward Henry. A very sentimental person, I always thought."

Ralph said, "Especially away from his immediate family. It was more noticeable then. In front of friends, relatives, there would be less reason to show emotion, unless there was a drastic occasion, such as a death. Or a marriage."

Helen said, "I don't remember that my parents were real huggy, or kissin' all the time. There was no question that Henry was just everything to Quint and Anna, they were both very supportive, and did everything they could for him."

Ralph said, "Henry looks like his father. And so does his son Chris and even little Chris. They all look like Quint."

Helen said, "Little Chris looks exactly like Henry did as a child. Henry was blond. He had the banana curl when he was a baby. Annie was madly in love with Quint. I was just a little kid, about four years old, when they were married. She had other opportunities to marry, but she was mad about Quint.

"As far as I know, Annie was about two years old when they came over from Italy—the mother, the father, Annie, and my father. These were people who were landowners in their little town."

Ralph said, "In about '41 or '42, we made a trip to visit Annie and Quint in West Aliquippa. It was a very meager home, meager surroundings. You could tell that there wasn't much money in the family."

Helen said, "But she was happy, made the best of everything."

Ralph said, "She was always happy. It shows how much she loved Quint. And I'm sure it was reciprocated."

Helen said, "My cousin Ada always used to say Annie really loved that man, and she would have known because she was the same age, they were buddy-buddy and used to share secrets. Annie used to have a little garden behind the house, she used to grow Swiss chard, tomatoes, the usual kind of stuff. I still remember the soot that used to fall on the produce. Annie was a great cook, she was always cooking.

"When Annie and Quint and Henry would come to Cleveland for the holiday meals, it was her job to fry the rice croquettes and the fritters in the morning.

"We used to serve ravioli with a mixture of ricotta and eggs in them with a tiny bit of cinnamon and a bit of sugar— we were the only ones in the area, I think, that made them that way. Henry used to call them cheese boxes."

Ralph said, "You know, I remember the two Italian boys that came to the villa near Nice with Hank just at the end of the war. We had a hell of a lot of fun. One of those boys said, 'Someday this guy's gonna be a big star. You wanna put some money on it.' As much as we knew of him at that time, it was very premature for us to even think of it. Helen's father died in January of 1945. He would have appreciated Hank's success more than anybody, being musically inclined."

Helen said, "I remember about 1950, on radio, Hank did a piece of music for something. And at the end of this program they said, 'Music was composed and conducted by Henry Mancini,' and we all cried. You know, Quint always felt so bad that Max Adkins never lived to see Henry's success. He always used to mention that."

Before the concert that evening there was another glorious Italian dinner at another restaurant, with Hank in an elated mood and ordering the wines with the grand satisfaction of some great *signore* entertaining his friends. "This is what life on the road is all about, man," he said.

The Musengos attended the concert. Backstage at intermission Hank's face was full of affection for them.

November 15, 1987.

The next morning in a rented Lincoln we drove out along the Allegheny River, with its countless bridges, into the point of land where the Monongahela meets it, creating that prow point of downtown Pittsburgh called the Golden Triangle. We crossed a bridge heading north and found ourselves in a tangle of small streets in an area of small industries. "Hey, I remembered!" Hank said triumphantly as he made a turn into one of the streets.

"What, are you afraid senility is setting in?" I chided.

"No, man," he said, "it's just that it's been so long." We picked up a street on the northeast bank of the Ohio called, logically enough, Ohio River Boulevard. The day was clear, and exceptionally warm for November. The road ran along the shoulder of the high riverbank. Bare trees stood like black lace on slopes made brown by fallen leaves. The car glided smoothly along to Ambridge, a community whose name is contracted from that of the American Bridge Company. We crossed the river on a long bridge, then swung north. We were now, Hank told me, in Aliquippa. Aliquippa at this point consisted of a treed slope above us on the left and a long—very long—expanse of dead factory on the right. I had heard about this, read about it, seen it on television, but all of it together had not prepared me for the vision of a dead industry. What had been the Jones and Laughlin Steel Company, stretched for miles northward along the riverbank, was a deserted dead thing, with smoke-stacks like the fingers of supplicant hands against the sky. All the prayers in the world wouldn't help; the massive mismanagement of the economy had done its work, and American capital had fueled the steel mills of Korea, among other countries, whose newer equipment and advanced management had destroyed the livelihoods of hundreds of thousands of American workers. American banks had lent the savings of the people who had worked in these places to deadbeat nations around the world whose leaders had said the magic words, that they were standing up to Communism. Even now, as we drove, they were reneging on their loans, and the banks that made them were quaking.

We passed long stretches of chain-link fence protecting properties whose furnaces would never be warm again. And a few miles to the south, in West Virginia, towns such as Davy were dying because Pittsburgh no longer bought their coal. In a strange bleak way, this vista of ruined industry was impressive. One thinks of America as young, and growing, and vital, not depleted and moribund. Yet Carbondale, Illinois, died when the coal was exhausted; and before that Nevada towns died when the silver gave out. But such cities died of the exhaustion of resources. The United States is a land of capable, willing, and skilled workers, a great people blended of all the nationalities of the world, and these Pennsylvania communities were dying not of the depletion of resources but the misuse and mismanagement of the economy. The terrible reality we were seeing was heartbreaking. And awesome.

I said, "Hank, do you remember a song Gordon McRae did called 'River of Smoke'? It was about a worker who sees these rivers of smoke on the sky as wonderful, because they enable him to make the money to marry his girl."

"Yeah, I remember it," Hank said.

At last he turned off the highway. "Well, this is it," he said. "West Aliquippa."

It was the worst of all. Hank swung the Lincoln into shabby streets of a tiny town. They were paved with brick cobbles; the town had never even got to asphalt. Grass grew between the bricks. "Now at one time we lived . . . ," Hank said, turning a corner. "It's gone!" We looked at an empty lot between two crumbling and deserted frame houses. "Wait a minute," he said. He seemed completely disoriented. He drove on. Nobody lived in these houses. This town wasn't dying, it was dead. "Now, this is one of the places we lived," he said. "This is 401 Beaver Avenue." We got out of the car and looked around. Hank walked up the short sidewalk to the house. The house was painted a hideous green, and it was in an advanced state of decay. I turned 360 degrees, surveying the decay of the community. Perhaps because I once was a construction worker, I have a reverence for buildings, and I felt an overwhelming urge to restore these places, yet realized even as I detected the emotion that such an attempt would be futile. I thought about the condition that the wiring of these places must be in, the crumbling foundations, the dry rot and wet rot of the wood, all the ravages of neglect. There was nothing you could do for this town but let nature reclaim this devastated terrain.

I tried to imagine the boy Hank had been, playing stickball in the streets. I listened for the cries and laughter of children. I heard nothing, not even wind. It was a still day. I turned and looked at 401 Beaver Avenue. Hank was sitting on the steps to its porch. He was wearing an exquisite black windbreaker of thin glove leather and a black Greek sailor's cap, purchased perhaps in Athens. Then, just for a second, I almost saw the boy who used to practice flute in this house.

We got back in the Lincoln. Ahead of us a cat crossed the cobbled street. We drove around the town a bit; it comprises no more than ten square blocks. Hog and Crow islands, where Hank's mother tended her vegetable plot, were gone; landfill had joined them to the shore, and on it stood a large steel plant. It appeared to be fairly new, but it was deserted.

We passed a building whose windows and doors had been bricked in. Why? Why preserve it? It would never be used again. "That was the Sons of Italy Hall," Hank said. One house we passed had a well-tended little vegetable plot in the backyard. An old man was standing looking at it. Somebody still lived here. I wondered what he thought of the

Lincoln passing by. "We lived here for a while, upstairs," Hank said. It was a two-story building of flats. "There was a fire, and I remember my father carrying me down the steps." But the steps were gone, and the sagging balcony would fall in a year or two. "Over here was the Serbian hall, and that empty lot, that's where the bandstand was, where we played in the Sons of Italy Band."

We left West Aliquippa, and not far away turned into the main street of Aliquippa proper. Hank said it was named for an ancient Indian queen. Its main street lies in the length of a wooded ravine cut eons ago by some feeder of the Ohio. It was a much larger community, not yet as dead as West Aliquippa. A few people were to be seen on the street, though they seemed to be going nowhere in particular. Storefronts were boarded up, there was trash and broken glass in the gutters and on sidewalks, and weeds grew in cracks in the cement. "How do you feel, seeing this?" I said.

"Empty. Hollow," Hank said. "Just hollow."

He headed the car up a slope of the riverbluff. "This was my high school," he said. It was an extensive brick plant on the brow of the hill. We got out. "I want to see if I can find the band room," Hank said. We entered a door and looked around. Hank walked ahead of me. A small stern woman in her sixties emerged from an office and said to me severely, "Can I help you gentlemen?" Hank was too far ahead of me to hear her.

"My friend," I said, "used to go to this school, and he wanted to look around."

"And who is your friend?" she said, with no loss of suspicion. Maybe she thought we were dope pushers. Who knows nowadays?

"Henry Mancini," I said.

"Henry!" she cried, her face lighting. "I graduated with you!"

And she rushed toward him. I thought she was going to

embrace him. She told him about her family, and Hank remembered them. Hank said he was looking for the band room. She led the way, and they talked about old friends.

We climbed a flight of stairs, and in a dusty cluttered office the woman introduced us to the band director. This is how the world has changed: the band director's name was Victoria Eppinger, and she told us she had graduated from the University of Illinois. She was in her late twenties or early thirties. "What's your instrument?" I asked her. "Trombone," she said.

"I've found a lot of clippings about you," she told Hank, and dug them out. "I've only been here this year, and I'm still going through old files." She showed us the newspaper clippings, most of them about his occasional returns to Beaver County, to play benefits for one cause or another. "Henry Mancini Returns to Help," one headline proclaimed.

She even had his high school yearbook. The entry on Hank said that he wanted to be an arranger and hoped some day to have his own band.

We went into the band room. Two boys were sitting on folding chairs, looking at music stands. "Hey, that's the same piano!" Hank said, looking at a scarred old brown spinet standing against the wall by a blackboard. The keyboard cover was secured by a padlock. "I think that's the same damn padlock! I used to play this piano!"

We went to the school's main office. The lady who had greeted us so severely introduced Hank to two women on the staff. One of them asked Hank if he remembered So-and-So, her cousin. He did. At last we left. We were standing in front of the school's pillared portico when a black man in his forties with a compact, neat, muscular body came up to us and said, "Aren't you Henry Mancini?"

"Yes," Hank said.

"You went to this school."

"Yeah," Hank said.

"I work here," the man said. He had a bright, warm, accepting smile, which Hank reciprocated. In photos Hank has a rather stiff smile, not unlike the uncomfortable smile of Glenn Miller, but in person it is ready and easy. "Man, what a pleasure to meet you," the man said, pumping Hank's hand.

In 1946, Pittsburgh instituted a grand reclamation project. Blighted areas were razed and laws were put in place requiring the steel and coke industries to put scrubbers on their stacks and cease their pollution of the air. Today the rivers of smoke are gone and Pittsburgh is one of the cleanest cities in America. Further, its dead industries are being replaced by computer and communications companies and it is becoming a major medical and educational community. It is a great city, rated by surveys and studies as probably the best in America in which to live. And that orchestra is superb.

I had become curious about the two theaters that had played such an important role in Hank's youth—the Stanley and Loew's Penn. He'd told me as we were en route to Pittsburgh that they were both gone now, victims of progress. But since our arrival, he'd learned that the Stanley hadn't been torn down. On the contrary, it had been refurbished at a cost of millions and now was named the Benedum Center. Hank has endowed a theater seat in Max Adkins's honor. Its stage had been enlarged and now it was a home for opera and musical theater. *I Pagliacci* had just closed; *Cats* was coming in next week. And Hank had arranged to go through it when we got back from Aliquippa.

We stood in the wing stage left, watching a crew break the set of *I Pagliacci*. "I used to stand here and watch the bands," Hank said. "You know that mist they use on movie sets for effect? Well, they didn't need that: the air looked like that on this stage in those days. You could always smell the coke ovens. I remember watching the Ellington band here. You see that first balcony out there? Well, in the 1937 flood, the water was right up to there."

Hank asked someone on the Benedum staff about the basement of the place, where he'd studied with Max Adkins. But the whole basement had been restructured and that office was gone. Hank asked when the old Loew's Penn had been torn down. He was told that it had never been torn down; on the contrary, it had been restored on a grant from the H. J. Heinz people, and it was now Heinz Hall, home of the Pittsburgh Symphony.

It hit us both at the same time. I said, "That's where you're standing to conduct. Just in front of the proscenium! Right where the screen was on which you saw *The Crusades*."

November 17, 1987.

Hank is one of those fortunate souls who can sleep on airplanes. As we flew back to California, I envied him this ability. After a while he awakened.

I felt I had come to understand something about the Peces and Mancinis. Most of the immigrants to America came from deep poverty, from a desperate peasantry. The Pece family had money. And so, until his father was cheated of the house and the lands around it, did the Mancinis. Possibly—we'll never know now—this was the reason for Quinto Mancini's silence, a bitterness that he, he of that family in Abruzzi, had to work in a steel mill. There was probably a knot of anger in his stomach. James Joyce's short story "Counterparts" describes a man's frustrations during his working day which, at its end, he takes out on his kid. Maybe that's what Quinto Mancini did. But he made sure Henry had his music lessons, and Henry never went to the steel mills. Who wrote, "We are all the victims of the victim"? I told Hank what Ralph Musengo had recalled of the family history, the theft of the house.

"I never knew that," Hank said, and fell silent.

"Helen," I said, "gave me an impression of a warm and affectionate man."

"Yeah," Hank said. "Well, that's what he showed to the world. It's not what he showed me."

He sat quietly for a moment. Then he said, "But I loved him."

Appendix
Awards, Accomplishments, Discography

GRAMMY AWARDS

Henry Mancini has received seventy Grammy nominations from the National Academy of Recording Arts & Sciences—more than any other musician has received since the inception of the awards in 1958—and won the following twenty Grammy Awards.

1970	Best Contemporary Instrumental Performance
	Theme from Z and Other Film Music
	RCA Records
	Best Instrumental Arrangement
	"Theme from Z"
	Theme from Z and Other Film Music
	RCA Records
1969	Best Instrumental Arrangement
	"Love Theme from *Romeo & Juliet*"
	A Warm Shade of Ivory
	RCA Records
1964	Best Instrumental Composition (Other Than Jazz)
	"The Pink Panther Theme"
	The Pink Panther
	RCA Records
	Best Instrumental Performance (Non-Jazz)
	The Pink Panther
	RCA Records
	Best Instrumental Arrangement
	The Pink Panther
	RCA Records
1963	Record of the Year
	Days of Wine and Roses
	RCA Records
	Song of the Year
	"Days of Wine and Roses"
	Our Man in Hollywood
	RCA Records
	Best Background Arrangement
	"Days of Wine and Roses"
	Our Man in Hollywood
	RCA Records

Best Instrumental Arrangement
"Baby Elephant Walk"
Hatari!
RCA Records

1961   Record of the Year
"Moon River"
Breakfast at Tiffany's
RCA Records

Song of the Year
"Moon River"
Breakfast at Tiffany's
RCA Records

Best Performance by an Orchestra Other Than for Dancing
Breakfast at Tiffany's
RCA Records

Best Arrangement
"Moon River"
Breakfast at Tiffany's
RCA Records

Best Sound Track Album or Recording of Score from a
Motion Picture or Television Show
Breakfast at Tiffany's
RCA Records

1960   Best Arrangement
"Mr. Lucky"
Music from "Mr. Lucky"
RCA Records

Best Performance by an Orchestra Other Than for Dancing
"Mr. Lucky"
Music from "Mr. Lucky"
RCA Records

Best Jazz Performance (Large Group)
The Blues and the Beat
RCA Records

1958   Album of the Year
The Music from "Peter Gunn"
RCA Records

Best Arrangement
The Music from "Peter Gunn"
RCA Records

ACADEMY AWARDS

Henry Mancini has been nominated by the Academy of Motion Picture
Arts and Sciences for the following Academy Awards. The four Oscars he
won are indicated with an asterisk.

1986   Best Song
"Life in a Looking Glass"
That's Life

1982 *Best Original Song Score
   Victor/Victoria
1979 Best Song
   "It's Easy to Say"
   "10"
   Best Original Score
   "10"
1976 Best Song
   "Come to Me"
   The Pink Panther Strikes Again
1971 Best Song
   "All His Children"
   Sometimes a Great Notion
1970 Best Song
   "Whistling Away the Dark"
   Darling Lili
   Best Original Song Score
   Darling Lili
   Best Original Score
   Sunflower
1965 Best Song
   "The Sweetheart Tree"
   The Great Race
1964 Best Song
   "Dear Heart"
   Dear Heart
   Best Scoring (Substantially Original)
   The Pink Panther
1963 Best Song
   "Charade"
   Charade
1962 *Best Song
   "Days of Wine and Roses"
   Days of Wine and Roses
1961 *Best Song
   "Moon River"
   Breakfast at Tiffany's
   Best Song
   "Bachelor in Paradise"
   Bachelor in Paradise
   *Best Musical Score for a Dramatic or Comedy Picture
   Breakfast at Tiffany's
1954 Best Score for a Musical Picture
   The Glenn Miller Story

ADDITIONAL AWARDS

1989 Golden Score Award: American Society of Music Arrangers
   for outstanding achievement in the fields of arranging and
   composing

Golden Plate Award: American Academy of Achievement—
honoring America's outstanding leaders
1988   Golden Soundtrack Award: ASCAP Life Achievement
Award for outstanding contribution to film music
1987   Lifetime Achievement Award: National Italian American
Foundation
1983   Aggie Award: American Guild of Authors & Composers
Honary Doctorate: California Institute of the Arts, Valencia
1981   Honorary Doctorate: Washington & Jefferson College,
Pennsylvania
1980   Honorary Doctorate: Mount Saint Mary's College, Maryland
1976   Honorary Doctorate: Duquesne University, Pittsburgh,
Pennsylvania
1971   Golden Globe Award: Hollywood Foreign Press Assn. Best
Original Song for a Motion Picture for "Whistling Away the
Dark," from *Darling Lili*

COMPLETE MUSICAL SCORES

Motion Pictures

1989   *Welcome Home*
1988   *Sunset*
        Without a Clue
        Physical Evidence
1987   *Blind Date*
        The Glass Menagerie
1986   *The Great Mouse Detective*
        A Fine Mess
        That's Life
1985   *Santa Claus—The Movie*
        Lifeforce
        That's Dancin' (arrangements)
1983   *Harry and Son*
        The Man Who Loved Women
        The Curse of the Pink Panther
1982   *Victor/Victoria*
        Trail of the Pink Panther
        Second Thoughts
        Whose Little Girl Are You?
1981   *S.O.B.*
        Mommie Dearest
        Condorman
        Back Roads
1980   *Change of Seasons*
        Little Miss Marker
1979   *Nightwing*
        The Prisoner of Zenda
        "10"

1978   *Revenge of the Pink Panther*
           Who Is Killing the Great Chefs of Europe?
1977   *Silver Streak*
           Alex and the Gypsy
           Angela
           House Calls
1976   *W. C. Fields and Me*
           The Pink Panther Strikes Again
1975   *The Great Waldo Pepper*
           The Return of the Pink Panther
           Once Is Not Enough
1974   *The White Dawn*
           99 & 44/100% Dead
           The Girl from Petrovka
           That's Entertainment! (arrangements)
1973   *Oklahoma Crude*
           Visions of Eight
1972   *The Thief Who Came to Dinner*
1971   *The Night Visitor*
           Sometimes a Great Notion
1970   *Darling Lili*
           The Hawaiians
           The Molly Maguires
           Sunflower
1969   *Me, Natalie*
           Gaily, Gaily
1968   *The Party*
1967   *Two for the Road*
           Gunn
           Wait Until Dark
1966   *Arabesque*
           What Did You Do in the War, Daddy?
1965   *Moment to Moment*
           The Great Race
1964   *A Shot in the Dark*
           The Pink Panther
           Dear Heart
1963   *Charade*
           Man's Favorite Sport
           Soldier in the Rain
1962   *Experiment in Terror*
           Days of Wine and Roses
           Hatari!
           Mr. Hobbs Takes a Vacation
1961   *Breakfast at Tiffany's*
           Bachelor in Paradise
1960   *High Time*
           The Great Imposter
1959   *Never Steal Anything Small* (arrangements)
1958   *Touch of Evil*
           Voice in the Mirror

1957   *Damn Citizen*
        Man Afraid
1956   *Rock, Pretty Baby*
1955   *The Benny Goodman Story* (arrangements)
        Ain't Misbehavin' (arrangements)
        The Second Greatest Sex (arrangements)
1954   *So This Is Paris* (arrangements)
        The Glenn Miller Story (arrangements)
1953   *Walking My Baby Back Home* (arrangements)

Television Films

1989   *Peter Gunn*
1983   *The Thorn Birds*
1981   *The Shadow Box*
1979   *The Best Place to Be*
1977   *The Money Changers*
1976   *A Family Upside Down*

Television Themes

"Peter Gunn"
"Mr. Lucky"
"Mystery Movie"
"NBC News Election Coverage"
"What's Happening?"
"Mancini Generation"
"Cade's County"
"The Blue Knight"
"Sanford Arms"
"Curiosity Shop"
"Newhart"
"Remington Steele"
"Ripley's Believe It or Not"
"Hotel"
"Late Night with David Letterman"—Viewer Mail

DISCOGRAPHY

RCA Records

In The Pink (with James Galway)
The Best of Henry Mancini, Vol. III
The Theme Scene
Just You and Me Together, Love
Mancini's Angels
Henry Mancini—The Cop Show Themes
Henry Mancini Conducts the London Symphony Orchestra
Symphonic Soul
The Return of the Pink Panther

Henry Mancini: A Legendary Performer
Hangin' Out with Henry Mancini
Country Gentleman
Oklahoma Crude
Visions of Eight
Brass, Ivory and Strings
Mancini Salutes Sousa
The Mancini Generation, Vol. II
Brass on Ivory
Mancini Concert
Mancini Plays the Theme from Love Story
This Is Henry Mancini
Darling Lili
Theme from Z and Other Film Music
Six Hours Past Sunset
Debut! Henry Mancini Conducting the Philadelphia Orchestra Pops
A Warm Shade of Ivory
The Big Latin Band of Henry Mancini
The Party
Encore
Gunn
Two for the Road
The Best of Mancini, Vol. II
Mancini '67
Music of Hawaii
A Merry Mancini Christmas
What Did You Do in the War, Daddy?
Arabesque
Henry Mancini Presents the Academy Award Songs
The Great Race
The Latin Sound of Henry Mancini
Dear Heart and Other Songs About Love
The Concert Sound of Henry Mancini
The Best of Mancini
The Pink Panther
Charade
Big Screen, Little Screen
Uniquely Mancini
Our Man in Hollywood
Hatari!
Experiment in Terror
Combo!
Breakfast at Tiffany's
Mr. Lucky Goes Latin
Music from "High Time"
The Blues and the Beat
Music from "Mr. Lucky"
Mancini Touch
More Music from "Peter Gunn"
Music from "Peter Gunn"

Columbia Records

Me, Natalie
The Hollywood Musicals with Johnny Mathis

United Artists Records

Revenge of the Pink Panther
The Pink Panther Strikes Again
Gaily, Gaily
The Hawaiians
Trail of the Pink Panther

Paramount Records

The Molly Maguires

Avco Embassy Records

Sunflower

MCA Records

The Great Waldo Pepper
Sometimes a Great Notion
The Glass Menagerie

Warner Bros./Epic Records

"10"
Who Is Killing the Great Chefs of Europe?
The Thief Who Came to Dinner

Polygram Records

Victor/Victoria

London Records

Mamma (with Luciano Pavarotti)
Volare (with Luciano Pavarotti)

EMI Records

That's Dancin'
Santa Claus—The Movie

Varese/Sarabande

Lifeforce

Motown

A Fine Mess

Reader's Digest

Moon River: The Many Moods of Henry Mancini
Henry Mancini Plays Your All Time Favorites

Denon Records

Premier Pops (with the Royal Philharmonic Pops Orchestra)
Mancini Rocks the Pops (with the Royal Philharmonic Pops Orchestra)

Index